# THE GLORY GAME

Also by Frank Gifford

**The Whole Ten Yards**

# THE
# GLORY GAME

## HOW THE 1958 NFL CHAMPIONSHIP
## CHANGED FOOTBALL FOREVER

# FRANK GIFFORD

### WITH PETER RICHMOND

HARPER

*An Imprint of* HarperCollins*Publishers*
www.harpercollins.com

HarperCollins books may be purchased for educational, business, or sales promotional use. For information, please write: Special Markets Department, HarperCollins Publishers, 10 East 53rd Street, New York, NY 10022.

Permission to use poetry of Kyle Rote granted by Nina Rote.

FIRST EDITION

*Designed by William Ruoto*

Library of Congress Cataloging-in-Publication Data is available upon request.

ISBN: 978-0-06-154255-8

08 09 10 11 12   OV/RRD   10 9 8 7 6 5 4 3 2 1

To my family, to my teammates, and especially to Wellington Mara, who made all of this possible

# CONTENTS

# PREFACE

In the early years of my twenty-seven-year stint on *Monday Night Football*, whenever we called a game on the West Coast, I'd always take a red-eye back East, sitting in the smoking section of a 707. I could never sleep. I'd look down through the window and see those lights, 35,000 feet below, all the way across the country. As we flew south of Vegas, or over Reno, then across the Plains, then maybe over St. Louis, or Indianapolis, I'd follow those clusters of lights across the country: big cities, small towns, like the ones I grew up in, in Texas and California, the son of an oil field worker.

And whether that night's game had been a good game or bad, I'd always find myself thinking the same thing: about all the people in all of those cities and towns so far below. I'd look down, and I'd think, *Did they watch the game? Did I say the right thing? Do the right thing?*

And then I'd move on to thinking about all the guys I played with in my career as a New York Giant in the fifties and sixties. Were they down in one of those towns? What were they doing? Did they watch the game in a bar? What did they think about the broadcast? I'd look down and think, *Did Dick Modzelewski watch?*

*Did he point to me on TV and say to his kids, "That's Frank—I played with him"?*

Since retiring in 1964, I'd been in touch with some of my ex-teammates through the years, but not many. It was not always an intimate contact. Maybe someone wanted an autographed picture of some player; maybe I'd see someone at an appearance somewhere. But I'd think about them, all the time. As the years went on, and the plane changed—to a 747, to a 757—I'd still find myself looking down and wondering, *Where have they gone? What have they done with their lives?*

Now, as I've spent the last year writing this book, I've talked to each and every teammate who played in the 1958 NFL Championship—at least, those who are still with us. When I began this book, there were eighteen of them alive. When I finished it, there were seventeen. Time takes its toll. The memories, thankfully, stand strong.

As I visited with each of my old teammates, they told me their tales, and I told them mine. My original reason for seeking them out was to tap their memories. But the funny thing is, we spent just as much time talking about each other. Our conversations drifted from our memories of the game into the stories of our lives, and then into conversations about our friends: What are they doing? How are they doing? Unexpectedly, I had become a messenger, relaying the news—the good, the bad, the joyous, the mundane—from one teammate to another. It was a pleasure and a privilege. It was sometimes painful. It was always a joy.

I talked to every Colt who had played in that game, too: nineteen at the start of the process, eighteen when I finished. And I discovered something else: that we're all teammates now. At reunions, at dinners, at golf tournaments, at games I was broadcasting, I had come to know some of the Colts over the years, but not too many.

Now I feel as close to them as I do my own teammates. I know now that on December 28, 1958, a cold and distant winter afternoon, we shared something that was extraordinary, and that now our shared experience, on a patchy, slippery football field, has brought us back together. I can't remember some of the games I saw last month. But I remember that game vividly. We all do.

We have different recollections and varied versions of just about every play in that game. But if the details change, one thing doesn't: what it meant to be part of the game itself. No matter what we've all gone on to do, whether we moved or returned to our old hometowns—some even returned to the same exact neighborhoods of their childhoods—each of us feels that in some way, shape, or form, that game defined us.

It's a funny feeling to take yourself back in time. It's tough. After playing for a dozen years, and talking to millions of people on television for nearly four decades more, it turned out that staring at a little black tape recorder is a very difficult thing to do. And as I interviewed more and more of the men who played in that game, I began to understand the real reason why it was so hard for me to revisit the past: I came to feel a profound sense of loss, almost as if the family had split up. But writing this story has also given me a special gift: the chance to get us all together again.

**A**nother reason I found this book so difficult to write was that I never intended to write it. David Halberstam did.

I first talked to David late one afternoon several years ago, when I picked up the phone, fully expecting it to be a friend of my son Cody looking for a pickup game of football, or one of my daughter Cassidy's friends catching up on tomorrow's homework. So after my impatient greeting of "Hello?" I was more than somewhat stunned by this almost theatrical baritone voice, saying rather slowly, "Frank, this is David Halberstam."

At first, I didn't believe it was him. My immediate thought was to say something like, "Yeah, sure, of course, David. Frank isn't here right now, but would you care to talk with Jim Thorpe?" But it really was David Halberstam. Once we got through the formalities, and I'd told him how much I'd enjoyed his recent books, he told me that he was thinking of writing a book about Bill Belichick, and wondered whether I might be able to put the two of them in touch. I knew Bill, and said I'd be glad to do what I could. As it turned out, the two of them hit it off, and the result was a wonderful book, *The Education of a Coach.*

That call was the beginning of our friendship. Both my family and the Halberstams have homes on the island of Nantucket, off the Massachusetts coast, and during that summer while David was occupied with the Belichick book, we got together several times, usually for a lengthy lunch—a lot of football talk and a good bottle of wine. I was much more interested in talking about the book about the Korean War he was working on. But David always brought the conversation full circle—back to football.

He seemed to delight in the stories I told him about some of the truly remarkable and talented characters who had made up the 1958 rosters of the New York Giants and the Baltimore Colts. He was particularly interested in what I thought about the frequent reference to that game as "the greatest game ever played."

In the spring of 2006 David told me he wanted to write a book about the '58 game after he finished his book on Korea. I was thrilled that this brilliant writer and journalist was going to take this project on.

About a year later, when David was ready to begin reporting and writing, I told him that it was really the entire decade of the fifties, and not just that one game, that had set the stage for the unprecedented growth in professional football that followed. And so David began considering expanding his list of interviewees to include other stars of that era. David had made several contacts with players from the '58 game, but now he wanted to reach Y. A. Tittle, the great Giant quarterback. Tittle had not played in that '58 game, having come to the Giants in 1961 from the 49ers. But he went on to achieve his greatest stardom as a Giant before retiring in 1965.

The last time I ever talked to David, I gave him Y. A.'s number in Menlo Park, California, and knowing Y. A., I happily figured that David was in for a real treat. At eighty-two, Y. A. is a fun-loving, inquisitive, Down South conversationalist. I was certain he'd tie David up for hours, if not days.

Sadly, they never met. On April 23, 2007, David was killed in a horrific traffic accident on his way to Y. A.'s home.

I'm sure that David's book would have been a classic look at a great moment in history. I am sad that I'll never be able to read a book that, I'm sure, would have beautifully captured our moment of history. But it was not to be. And so, partly for David, partly for myself, but mostly for all of the men who played in that game, I decided to write the book that David never did—in David's memory, and in the memory of those players who are no longer alive.

With that in mind, what follows is not the work of one of the brilliant storytellers of our time, but rather the modest literary efforts of the guy who made the two fumbles, and scored a touchdown, and found himself on the frozen grass of Yankee Stadium on December 28, 1958—in the middle of the "greatest game ever played."

Was it really, as *Sports Illustrated* headlined a story a few weeks afterward, "The Best Football Game Ever"? I'll let you decide.

Here's to you, David.

# THE GLORY GAME

# INTRODUCTION

It was third down and four yards to go, the ball on our own 40-yard line, less than three minutes to go in the fourth quarter. We huddled up on the bare dirt, where the field had been worn down by a season's worth of football, and waited for our quarterback, Charlie Conerly, to call the play that could win us the 1958 championship.

The stadium, to a man and woman, was on its feet—men in coats and ties, in fedoras and overcoats, screaming their lungs out next to guys in hooded sweatshirts and ski caps and women in fur hats and overcoats. Colt fans in Colt jackets. Colt banners being pulled through the packed stands, dueling with Giant banners, exhorting their respective teams.

Semicircular red, white, and blue bunting hung from the facades of every deck: Giant colors. The winter sky was a fading blue, the stadium lights bathing the field in an eerie, early dusk. The steam rising from plastic foam cups of coffee mingled with frozen breath and with the pall of the smoke of the cigarettes and cigars that thousands of fans were nervously puffing.

The whole crazy afternoon—the fumbles, the tremendous

swings in momentum, the spectacular plays, the artistry, the fights, the injuries—had come down to one play. If we got the first down, we'd run out the clock, and we'd win the title and become the "world champions of professional football," as they called it back then.

I didn't care what they called it. I just wanted the ball. I knew I'd get it. The Colts knew I'd get it, and I didn't care. I knew I'd make the first down. Everything in my career had prepared me for this play.

"Power 47," Charlie said in the huddle, in that calm Mississippi drawl: the four back, going off right tackle, with our fullback, Mel Triplett, leading the way into the hole. But I thought the 49 sweep would work better. This was a once-in-a-lifetime play, everything on the line., and the way I figured it, our off-tackle power plays hadn't had much luck all day long against the Colts' huge defensive line: Artie Donovan, the round tackle from the Bronx who'd grown up forty blocks to the north of the stadium, now playing the game of his life in front of—and against—his hometown; Gino Marchetti, the undisputed best defensive end in the league; Don Joyce, the combative right end who was always itching for a fight; Big Daddy Lipscomb, the astoundingly agile giant who loomed at the line of scrimmage as big as his legend.

The sweep was our bread and butter. The play would give me a chance to slide outside and pick my hole. That was always my strength: not the head-on stuff, but the chance to slide, look for an opening, slip into a crack for a few extra yards. They always said I had "deceptive speed." To be honest, I'm not sure I had much speed at all, but what I did have was a way of finding a hole. Our offensive coordinator, Vince Lombardi, called my running "fluid." I just called it running, and sometimes I did it well.

The Giants were exhausted, physically and mentally. We were hurting: cracked ribs, bad knees, chipped bones. We'd just played two of the most emotional games of our careers: a dramatic last-second win in the snow against the Cleveland Browns two weeks before to force a play-off, and an inspired shutout of the Browns the Sunday before to get to this game. We'd come too far to lose it now.

"How about the sweep?" I said. That was the way things always were in our huddle: We could tell Charlie what we thought would work—and what we thought wouldn't—and he'd listen. The cotton farmer from Mississippi—my roommate, my best friend—wasn't in it for his ego. Charlie just wanted to win. And so the old goat changed the play: "Brown right, over, 49 sweep": both guards pulling, leading me around right end, just as Vince Lombardi had designed it.

We lined up, as we had a thousand times before. Everyone knew exactly what they had to do. Lombardi had drilled it into us, and by now this sweep was second nature. We were professionals, and we'd been well trained, by the best.

Across the line, the Colts lowered into their stances, breath visible beneath their white helmets, ready for one final defensive stand. They wanted to stop us as much as we wanted to get the first down. We'd already won a title, two years earlier; at stake for the Colts was nothing less than the first major pro sports title for their proud port town since Wee Willie Keeler and the Orioles of the 1890s.

The Colts' season had been just as dramatic as ours—they'd clinched their division with an amazing come-from-behind victory against the San Francisco 49ers one month before. While we'd played the play-off game for the Eastern Conference title against the Browns the week before, the Colts had had an extra week off to get ready to win the title they felt they'd squandered with a couple of late-season West Coast losses the year before.

Man for man, they were the best team in the NFL. They were rested. They were primed.

Could these Colts snatch away our title? We didn't think so. I didn't think so. There was no doubt in my mind that I'd get the first down.

Then, as we broke the huddle, we didn't think that the next few minutes of the game would change professional football's history forever.

# CHAPTER 1

# THE BEGINNINGS

On December 28, 1958, the National Football League grew up. From Madison Avenue to small-town living rooms, fans began to pay attention to our weekly battles on their small-screen televisions. On that long Sunday afternoon, a nation began to recognize the unique appeal of a sport in which any one play could bring extraordinarily athletic feats or grimace-inducing collisions. Or both.

It wasn't complicated, our game, and this was a big part of its appeal. Professional football had speed and it had brutality. We didn't have a legion of reverential sportswriters covering the game, as the national pastime did. Covering the Giants were off-season baseball writers, guys who didn't understand the nuances of the offenses or the defenses—or even some of the rules. But you didn't need to know about nuances or rules when you saw a man carrying a football, looking for running room—and then watching our linebacker Sam Huff meet him head-on, pick him up, and slam him to the ground.

Sam, of course wasn't the only man on the field that day who began to capture a nation's imagination: Kyle Rote, Johnny Unitas,

Big Daddy, Rosie Grier, Donovan, Marchetti, Conerly—these were guys who did things on a football field that the common fan could understand. Could *feel*. Could get excited about. The hypnotizing rainbow passes, the open-field sprints . . . these were exciting, but just as compelling was the violence: the hits, the man-to-man contact that echoed into the rafters—all interwoven with the highest level of individual athleticism any sport could offer.

And after that day, the advertisers and the television programmers could feel it, too: how, in a very real way, the men who brought beauty to brutality every week on a football field could be seen as a new breed of the old American frontier ideal of ruggedness, and individuality, and—above all—toughness and resilience. We were men who made a living on physical contact, who could endure pain of some sort—a blow to the face, a cleat crushing your hand, a limb being twisted in a way that nature never intended—on just about every play, and then rise to our feet and do it again. And again, and again.

Crowds began filling stadiums across the country, in cities whose stadiums had been half-empty in the years before. Television ratings began to climb. Athletes who'd once labored in a lunch-pail league were now the stars of prime-time television shows and graced the covers of the weekly magazines.

On December 28, 1958, everything changed.

**B**ut for the Giants, the final day of the old era began the way it always did, game day or practice day: by walking to work three blocks down the hill from our hotel home, in a working-class neighborhood in a working-class borough of a mighty city—a fitting starting point for a team that really *was* a band of brothers.

Star running backs, obscure linemen, punters and kickers,

the oldest quarterback in the league, and a couple of brand-new rookies—we all lived in the Concourse Plaza Hotel, a twelve-story redbrick building planted atop a hill above Yankee Stadium, on a wide, ambitious avenue called the Grand Concourse, optimistically modeled on the Champs-Elysées in Paris.

We loved the hotel, we loved the neighborhood, we loved the time, and we loved our team.

In the late fifties, the Bronx was a pretty vibrant place—and the heart of a working-class football team was camped right in the middle of it, five months of the year. Most of us were making just about as much money playing professional football as the electricians, cops, and subway drivers who lived all around us. A lot of us were making less.

The rest of the year, we lived back home, working at our other jobs: as teachers, insurance salesmen, plumbers. Bert Bell, our colorful commissioner—a Philadelphia and Jersey Shore guy with no pretense—used to tell the new crop of rookies every summer: You are not going to make a living playing pro football, so don't quit the day job.

For me, the off-season before '58 had meant a brief movie-acting career that was winding down and a broadcast career that was just starting up. I'd always had my eye on the next thing I might do with my life. I'd always known—as any football player knows—that one blind-side hit on a planted leg, one searing jolt of pain as you feel the ligaments tear from your knee, could mean the instant end of a career.

But during the football season, we were residents of a proud borough, living in a giant, friendly boardinghouse, surrounded by our parks, our restaurants, our coffee shops, our subway stop—and our stadium. There was no disconnect between where we lived and where we played. We didn't have to fight traffic, or leave a suburban gated community, to drive to some stadium with an Internet company–sponsored name that would change as soon as the company declared bankruptcy. Our home and our workplace sat side by side. Our commute was by foot: down the hill a few blocks, past the shops and bars, under the rumbling el, through the glass doors.

I'd stop for a cup of coffee at a deli on my walk to the stadium, like any other guy on his way to work, and walk through the players' entrance and down the stairs to the locker room. After the game, I'd take a shortcut home: I'd walk back up through the dugout, across the scarred field, flanked by empty stands still smelling like beer and liquor and cigar smoke, then leave the stadium through a door tucked underneath the bleachers and go back up the hill to the hotel, maybe stopping to pick up a pack of cigarettes, a quart of milk.

Perhaps a fan would stop me and say hello, more often not. None of us played football for the fame, and none of us had much; celebrity hadn't really yet attached itself to professional football back then. The Giants were beginning to grab attention, but the individual players were still pretty faceless. Hell, half the time our friends back home didn't even know what we did in the fall. During my first few seasons, when I'd go back home to Bakersfield, California, after the season, people would ask me where I'd been all those months.

Until 1956, games weren't even locally televised. In Charlie Conerly's first few years, in the early fifties, when he'd disappear from Clarksdale, Mississippi, for months on end, his wife's friends would wonder whether Charlie had left her, or maybe gone back into the military. In the early years, Perian Conerly, Charlie's widow, remembers now, the public equated us with professional wrestlers. What kind of guy would graduate from college, then find work playing in a sport that paid less than working as a master plumber?

There were some perks to being a Giant in the Bronx, of course. If you were our starting left guard, Al Barry, for instance, you could enjoy your own squad of neighborhood bodyguards on your walk to the stadium. But Al's bodyguards weren't like the bodyguards who surround today's players; Al had his own private escort of dead-end kids.

"This one local boy got about three or four other kids, about ten or twelve years old, and they formed the 'Al Barry Guards Club,'" Al told me when I reached him at his home in Georgia. "I don't know why, but at some point this group of kids started walking down to the stadium with me. Then they'd sneak into the games. They used to send me postcards at the hotel, stuff like, 'Saw you play in Cleveland. Signed, the Al Barry Guards Club.'"

History remembers the bold-faced names from the 1958 championship. But most of the men who played in that game, in that glory game, in those glory years—the men who made up the small, blue-collar fraternity of the National Football League— weren't bold-faced guys. They weren't prime-time stars. They were men of their time: war veterans, Depression small-town kids who took on work in the NFL as a second job. They were the down-to-earth Al Barry, the always-laughing rookie lineman Frank Youso, the tough coal-town tackle Dick Modzelewski: men who had unexpectedly discovered in college that they possessed a talent for a game that they loved, and who'd been lucky enough to find someone who would pay them to keep playing it—as long as they could find gainful employment during the off-season.

Al's story was pretty typical for the mid-fifties NFL player.

Al's dad lost his furniture business in Los Angeles during the Depression. Al's dad died when Al was a kid, and his mother moved the family to an apartment in Beverly Hills to get her children a good education, and it paid off. Al got a scholarship to my alma mater, USC, graduated two years behind me in 1954, then played ball for the Air Force—on a team that featured several all-American football players. The Packers drafted Al in the thirtieth round. (If the NFL still had a thirty-round draft, it would take ESPN a month to televise it.) When the Giants traded for Al from the Packers in 1958, he was living in Wisconsin farm country on a two-lane road on the outskirts of Green Bay. Cows grazed across the highway.

When Al and his wife moved into the Concourse Plaza, he was happy as hell to be living in a big hotel, to instantly become part of the family.

It wasn't fancy by New York City standards, but the Concourse Plaza had some class. When the place opened in 1923, Governor Al Smith spoke at the dedication. The Concourse Plaza would "enable the social life of the borough to assemble amid luxurious surroundings, in keeping with its prestige as the sixth greatest city in the country," wrote a local paper called *Bronx in Tabloid*. New York governor Franklin Delano Roosevelt campaigned for the presidency at the Concourse Plaza. Its ballroom ceiling soared twenty-eight-feet high.

Our rookie kick returner that year, Don Maynard, merited only modest lodgings at the hotel—"a couch made into a bed, a bathroom, and the kitchen on the other wall," as Don remembers it now—but still found the place a little overwhelming. "When I got to the city," he told me from El Paso, the town he's never really left, "the first building I saw was the Concourse Plaza Hotel. That hotel had more bricks than some of the towns I lived in."

Today, Don swears he didn't even know where New York was when we drafted him out of Texas Western in the old Border Conference: "I had to look it up in *National Geographic*." Knowing Don, a Texan tall-tale-teller to the core, he may be slightly exaggerating this account. I do know that in 1958 Don would often ask himself why he was spending most of his time sitting on a bench in a huge New York stadium when he could be making more money as a master plumber back in El Paso.

When I think about the men on that field that day, some of them remembered as being among the best football players who ever played the game, I picture guys whose talent was all the more remarkable considering how humble their roots had been—and how few of them ever expected to find work in our equally humble league. They hadn't been groomed every step of the way to be in the NFL. They were hoping to get shoes on their feet—in Sam Huff's case, literally. The man around whom our defensive coordinator Tom Landry had designed an entire defense grew up in a West Virginia mining town—literally barefoot. Like myself, Sam had been embarrassed at times, growing up, by how humble his home was: no plumbing, a four-room mining house.

Jack Stroud, our sinewy, tough offensive lineman, was a Depression kid from Fresno, California, who worked the docks in San Francisco as a teenager to help his single mom with the finances. Our captain Kyle Rote's dad worked WPA jobs during the Depression in San Antonio.

Charlie Conerly's dad, down in Clarksdale, Mississippi, was a deputy sheriff who ran the town jail for a while. Harland Svare, our swift and scrappy weakside linebacker, was a farm kid from Washington State. Colt quarterback Johnny Unitas's dad drove a coal truck in Pittsburgh, and died when Johnny was five; his mother washed office-building floors at night. Andy Robustelli grew up in a tough neighborhood in Stamford, Connecticut, the son of a barber, playing football in the streets—not that he thought he'd end up in the pros. None of us really did.

Well, check that: one of us did. Maybe that's why Raymond Berry, the wide receiver, was destined to dominate this game. He'd been preparing for it in his mind—and no one prepared for a football game like Raymond Berry—for a long, long time.

"I don't think any of us knew in those days that we might end up playing in the pros," Raymond told me. "Games weren't nationally televised. But I'd thought about it—in a movie theater in Paris, Texas. I'll never forget the movie. It was a movie about [Elroy] Crazy Legs Hirsch. It was released after the Rams won the championship. I'm sitting in a movie theater, spring of 1952. I've never seen televised pro football or college. Elroy came into my brain, and I was thinking, *Man, I'd like to catch passes like that guy.*"

Me, I lived in thirty-seven different towns when I was growing up, according to my mom's Bible, where she recorded each and every move, as my dad followed the work. We lived in apartments. We lived in the back of the car. We lived in a small house next to the railroad tracks in the San Joaquin Valley, where I'd watch the big freights, pushing an endless line of boxcars, start their climb over the Tehachapi Range, on their way to Los Angeles, letting out their long, wailing whistle that traveled through the clear air for miles.

My dad was a roughneck, to begin with. Later on, he was a driller, and then finally a tool pusher. As a teenager, I'd worked in the oil fields too. I'd known what it was like to feel proud of earning a little money, and putting a nickel into the basket at church at Christmas for the families who didn't have much of their own, families who were struggling—and then, a few days later, finding one of those baskets at our own front door.

When I got to high school, I settled down. I went to Bakersfield High, about a hundred miles north and inland of Los Angeles. My junior year, my mother got sick, and I stayed in Bakersfield with her. My brother had dropped out of high school to work in the oil fields with my dad, so I was the man of the house. I did the shopping and the cooking, taking care of my mom. I enjoyed the responsibility.

In high school, I majored in wood shop. I wasn't embarrassed by it. Everyone in my family had always worked. But no one in my family had finished high school, and I wanted to graduate. It wasn't as if I was trying to get out of poverty. It was a noble, proud thing to work in the oil fields. To be a driller was to *be* something—certainly in my family, anyway: glamorous, macho work, using machinery that cost hundreds of thousands of dollars.

But I wanted to play football at a major college, so after I graduated, I attended Bakersfield Junior College to get my grades up, then transferred to USC, where I got my first taste of a very different kind of world. My classmates were the sons and daughters of lawyers and other white-collar professionals. My girlfriend, a doctor's daughter, was the Rose Bowl Queen, the Homecoming Queen, and a Phi Beta Kappa art major. I'd pledged a fraternity, but I had to drop out; I couldn't afford the dues.

Maxine and I married in January of my senior year, in 1952, and she was soon pregnant with our first child. On the day I was drafted into the NFL, I wasn't huddled around a TV or waiting by the phone. No one thought much about the draft back then; I wasn't even sure I'd be drafted. I was skiing with Maxine up on Mount Baldy. I was more comfortable on the mountain than down in the valley; I knew the guys up there. I loved to backpack up there. I enjoyed the wilderness.

Maxine and I were driving through San Bernardino, and suddenly, on the radio, I hear, "And the New York Giants took USC's Frank Gifford in the first round." What the hell? New York? Are you out of your mind? I wasn't even thinking about it. But Maxine liked the idea. She was excited by the idea of living in New York. We decided to give it a shot.

Maybe it was my itinerant upbringing that made those early hotel years in New York so enjoyable. First we lived in the Commander, in Long Beach; we couldn't afford the city at that point. Then the Whitehall, on 100th and Broadway, and then the Excelsior, with a few other Giants, across from the Museum of Natural History, just down the street from Central Park.

Sam Huff lived at the Excelsior too: "Our kids loved the park," Sam told me recently, as we traded stories in his office in Middleburg, Virginia, down in the horse country where the old coal miner's kid has found a beautiful life. Plaques and photographs adorn the walls, tokens of the considerable fame that has come his way through the years. But Sam, like me, seems to reserve his fondest memories for the beginnings of our journey.

"To me," Sam said, "the whole damn city was a playground. We didn't have anything like that in West Virginia."

Or Wink, Texas, or Kermit, Texas, or Hobbs, New Mexico, the towns where, as a little kid, I'd stand down at the end of the field on a Friday night and watch the football team head for the locker room after a game. God almighty, those high-school guys were huge, with these big pads, these helmets catching the lights. They were special.

And now, we were them: living in big-city hotels, but wide-eyed as hell just the same.

We moved to the Concourse Plaza for the 1958 season, joining a dozen other Giants and their families in the big hotel with the maroon awning, across the street from the huge, gilded Bronx County Courthouse. To us, the Concourse Plaza was like a big dormitory. We'd hang out in each other's rooms, play cards at night. We'd do our own laundry, wash our own jerseys—and the white uniform pants they'd make us pay for out of our own pockets. We'd have cocktail parties after games, crowding into our cramped quarters, thrilled when someone famous would show up—David Niven, who would win the Oscar as Best Actor for the '58 film *Separate Tables*; Gordon McRae; Ernest Hemingway. When the football and baseball seasons overlapped, we might get some Yankees up to our rooms: Yogi Berra, Mickey Mantle, Whitey Ford. "We'd have a packed house at those parties," Dick Modzelewski remembered, the coal-town man now living in Ohio. But I didn't need reminding: New York celebrities, wanting to hang at *our* place? It was something I could never get over. It's something I still can't get over.

"The Concourse Plaza was called 'the business and social center of the Bronx,'" Perian Conerly recalls now, in her distinctive, classy, Mississippi lilt. It was definitely the latter for us—just not the kind of society the hotel was talking about in its brochures.

Perian Conerly was our resident *true* socialite, historian, and literary light—a beautiful, blond Mississippi deb back then. Perian's book *Backseat Quarterback*, published in 1963, provides as lively and hilarious an account as you'll ever read about pro football in those early years. In the fifties, she was writing a social-notes column for the Jackson, Mississippi, paper, sprinkled with her own wry and gentle way of seeing the world—"a little fluffy column," in her own words. Later, her "New York Newsletter"—dispatches from a quarterback's wife—earned a little blurb in *Sports Illustrated* and *Newsweek*, and the next thing she knew, the column was syndicated.

To this day, Perian is one of the most sophisticated and worldly women I have ever met—but it does her no disrespect to say that she enjoyed her role as the queen mother of our redbrick, dim-corridored den. Perian loved the Concourse Plaza, and the place loved having her. Each December, the hotel staff would pack up her kitchenware and save it for the next season—if there *was* a next season. Every year, Charlie said that this season was his last. And every year, he'd come back for more.

"At one point," Perian told me, "there were twelve couples and twenty-seven kids in the place. Of course, we wives all knew each other. I was always looking out to see if we had any new wives, so I could make them welcome. Roach would always forget to tell me about a new player who might have a wife, so we had to try and seek them out on our own and make them feel welcome." (Roach was Charlie's nickname. "He wasn't sure why," Perian says. "He thought maybe it was because he used to catch roaches back in Mississippi, as a kid, and sell them to fishermen.")

Perian would try and squeeze us for the latest gossip for her column, but Charlie and I never gave her anything good to use, so she had to get her literary fodder from Don Heinrich, our other quarterback. Don was her husband's rival on the field, but football didn't factor into our home life; in the hotel, all the wives were sisters. It was Perian who told Don Heinrich's wife, Barbara, that the hotel provided another special service for Giant families, above and beyond storing the knives and forks for the winter: If cash was a little short, the front desk would provide an advance on her husband's paycheck. When Don's wife asked him about the service, she discovered that he had already been getting advances on his paycheck without telling her, and that was the end of Don's extra cash.

"We were just living the regular lives of wives," Perian says now, and there's no mistaking the delight in her tone at the memory. "When y'all would practice, we'd go over to the courthouse, across the Concourse, looking for trials. They were mostly divorce cases. Occasionally we'd get a juicy murder. And since we were just a couple of blocks from the subway, you could get downtown in fifteen minutes. Sometimes during practice, the wives would head downtown. We went to a lot of matinees. Standing room was a dollar and a half. I saw *South Pacific* before almost anybody."

Perian, Maxine, the other spouses living in our dorm—they weren't rich wives. They were housewives. They talked about their kids, they changed diapers together. The dads did, too. Our kids never strayed far from the football field, or the park. We couldn't afford a regular diet of Manhattan nightlife. Actually, some of my teammates couldn't afford *any* Manhattan nightlife. So we mostly stuck close to home. The parks, the stadium, these were our front yards—taking the families to Macombs Dam Park after practice, throwing the ball around, while the wives were pushing buggies.

"We all brought our children to Yankee Stadium," Sam recalled. "They all ran around and played with each other. John Mara, Wellington's little boy, used to show up wearing this little bow tie. Modzelewski's kids and my kids always wanted to take down little John. I'd tell them, 'Hit anyone else, but don't hit the owner's kid.'"

The rooms at the Concourse Plaza were nothing special; you were lucky if you even had a bedroom. Some of my teammates had to live on foldouts until the Yankees finished their season. "When Jack Kemp, the rookie quarterback, came to the team that year, he couldn't get a room that had a kitchen," kicker Pat Summerall remembers now, in that southern-tinged baritone. "I remember going to dinner with my wife, Kathy, to Jack and Joanne's room one night. We washed the dinner dishes in the bathtub, on our knees."

Kemp, our future statesman, remembers the place vividly today—as well he should. One night Jack and his wife discovered first-hand just how diverse the tenants of a Bronx hotel could be. Joanne was pregnant with their first child when the two of them arrived at their new home—"and every now and then she'd get woozy," Jack told me from his office in the nation's capital, where, after several decades of public service, "The Honorable Jack Kemp" now heads Kemp Partners, a consulting firm. "So Joanne and I are in our new room—not a suite by any means. I think it had a kitchenette.

"We're new to New York. We were excited. It's almost a second honeymoon.

"So we come home one night after being out with you and the Summeralls and the Conerlys, at the start of the season, and they've painted our apartment to get us into it. I went downstairs to complain to the front desk that my wife was pregnant, and she couldn't sleep there with fumes. They gave us another room. The next morning we came down to go into our new apartment. First we went out to get the paper. The doors were heavy. I had groceries, the *Times* in my hands. I open the door, shove it with my foot. Joanne went in, and the door shut behind her. Suddenly I hear a shriek like you've never heard. She's screaming bloody murder. I'm fumbling with the key. I finally get the door open. The hotel had rented the room to a drunken sailor, who's now lying in the bed. He was asleep, buck naked. He'd been throwing up.

"So how could I ever forget the Concourse? I spent a lot of time there. The only way I could go downtown with you guys was if I was a friend of Gifford's. Charlie did not speak one word to me the whole season."

Don't feel bad, I told Jack—Charlie didn't talk much to anyone. Including me. And I was his roommate for a lot of years. Most of the time Charlie just sat on the bed, cracking his ankles so loudly you could hear it in the next room. I did the talking.

Daily life wasn't all social at the Concourse Plaza—at least not for our all-business defensive coach, Tom Landry. Within five years of joining the Giants, the cerebral Landry had become a player-coach. In 1958, his room at the hotel was his film lab. "I learned more football in that one season in Tom's apartment than I'd learned all through high school and college," Sam once said.

While Sam was studying film reels, Maxine and I were learning a lot about bridge, playing with the Conerlys, and the Rotes, the Heinrichs. Financial constraints limited our social options during the workweek, and as Sundays would approach, I'd want to steer clear of our favorite haunts downtown, to keep a clear head. Maxine and I had a two-bedroom apartment—room 909. We needed the space—by 1958, we had three children: Jeff, Victoria, and Kyle, the latter named for my teammate. Charlie and Perian had a nice apartment with a view, sort of; if you leaned way out the window you could see the Harlem River.

If you were on one side of the hotel, you could see Yankee Stadium. If you lived on the other side, you looked out over the Bronx, and if you looked far enough, you could see a little bit of Manhattan. Punter Don Chandler's room was small, but he didn't care; to a Tulsa boy, panoramic views of Gotham didn't hold much appeal, and Don's room provided a view of the flags on top of the stadium, which told him, the morning of every game, what the winds would be like for his punts. Then again, as Don says now, you could never judge the winds coming in off the Harlem River, not once they started to swirl inside our huge home field.

• • •

**W**e didn't all live in the Concourse. The only two bachelors on the team—Cliff Livingston, our strongside linebacker, and Harland Svare, our other outside linebacker—lived in the Manhattan Hotel, downtown in Manhattan, across from Downey's bar and restaurant. They got a good rate. (All of us were always looking for rates back then—on anything and everything.)

We all envied Harland and Cliff to some degree, but not completely. They'd come to practice after what had been a long, hard night on the town, and we'd look at their bloodshot eyes and eagerly ask them what they'd done the night before. They'd just look at each other and shake their heads. Cliff and Harland always talked about how much better off we were—we had home cooking, wives to go home to, security. But a lot of us fantasized about being in their shoes.

Rosie Grier, our mammoth right defensive tackle, and Mel Triplett, our tough fullback, were roommates in an apartment over in Jersey: "We caught the bus, over and back," Grier says now, as if it were yesterday, from Los Angeles, where he's lived for years. "We couldn't afford a car." It wasn't that the black players weren't welcome at the Concourse Plaza; it was just that the fifties were simply a different time. Rosie and Mel felt more comfortable living across the river—and preferred the cheaper housing prices.

But Rosie and Mel did draw the color line, and set a Giant precedent, at an exhibition game in Dallas in 1956. Down there, the hotels *were* separated by color, and one day Rosie and Mel made a statement for our team: "We were going to go to some hotel for a luncheon, and the black players on the club said they weren't going to go to the luncheon," Rosie told me. "We talked about it, and Mel and I decided we wouldn't go. A couple of the older black players were on the bus. (The Giant roster had four black players in 1958: Mel, Rosie Grier, Rosey Brown, and Emlen Tunnell.) Mel and I wouldn't get on. We figured, 'If we can't stay in the hotel with our teammates, then we're not going to the luncheon.'

"So Wellington came out and said, 'You guys never said anything about this before.' We said, 'We shouldn't have to say anything about this.' Wellington said, 'I promise you we'll never again have to separate our team.' So we got on the bus, and we never stayed in separate hotels again."

Some of the local guys preferred home cooking to dinners warmed up on a hot plate in a hotel. Andy Robustelli, our elder statesman on the defense, commuted every day from Stamford, Connecticut, the hometown he's never really left. When we traded stories over lunch at his Stamford restaurant not long ago, diners filed by to say hello to the man—not because he was once a great Giant, but because he was a Stamford guy, a man who never forgot his roots, and never wanted to.

Jim Katcavage, our intense defensive end, commuted from Philadelphia every day—by train, if you can believe that. We called him "Choo Choo." He'd come racing in just before practice, checking his timetables to see what train he could catch to get home. As soon as practice was over, he'd give it a quick swipe in the shower, and then he was gone.

My fellow halfback, Alex Webster, lived down in Jersey, in East Brunswick, that year. Alex had always been a Jersey guy anyway. He'd grown up in a factory town just across the Hudson River, in Kearny, a tough guy with a reputation for barroom brawling. He'd lost his dad when he was nine, and turned into something of a renegade. He'd been cut by the Redskins after his first training camp. After the Skins let him go, his friends encouraged him to give football one last shot. He'd gone to North Carolina State on a football scholarship, and the Montreal Alouettes' coach had been down at Wake Forest when Alex was in college, so Alex got himself a tryout in Montreal. He made the team, was named the league MVP in 1954, and the Giants welcomed him home in 1955.

Webster tells me today, from his home in Florida, that he moved down to the Jersey Shore back then in order to stay away from the temptations of the big city. "I was glad I was commuting," he told me in that distinctive rasp, a voice worn down by years of heavy smoking. "The nightlife up there would have killed me. When I got home, Louise put the axe on me, and that was the end of it. So it was a lot easier coming home from practice every day than going back to a hotel room."

But no matter how long the commute, whether it was a five-minute walk down the hill or a two-hour ride by the rails from Philly, every one of us enjoyed meeting up in that locker room every day. We liked our work, and we liked the people we worked for. We liked knowing we were playing for a first-class organization—no, a first-class family. We knew that, rain or shine, during practice we could look over to the sideline and see our beloved owner Wellington Mara's tall, familiar figure, dressed in sweats, that ever-present smile visible from beneath that distinctive little cap.

Back then, the NFL was a league of family owners, and the Maras were the head of the family. When he bought the team in 1925 (for somewhere between the probably apocryphal sum of $500 and the likelier figure of $2,500) Wellington's dad, T. J. Mara, was thirty-eight, and a very well connected man in New York City. As a kid, T. J. had run bets down in his Irish neighborhood—legally—as early as the age of twelve. By the time he stumbled across the chance to pick up a franchise in the pro football business, thirty years later, he was a renowned boxing promoter and a highly respected legal bookmaker at the New York tracks, with booths on the infield at Belmont and Saratoga. If it wasn't exactly an honorable profession, bookmaking wasn't dishonorable, either; horse racing was still the sport of kings, and T. J.'s profession offered the perk of his being able to mingle with the likes of Vanderbilts and Astors and Belmonts.

T. J. once said he'd never passed up a chance to promote anything—just for the challenge. I guess that explains why, on one August day in 1925, in the office of his sports-promoter friend Billy Gibson, he took a flier on a business about which he knew absolutely nothing. Joe Carr, the commissioner of the five-year-old National Football League, was trying to convince Gibson to invest in a New York franchise. Gibson declined, and not surprisingly: In the first ten years of the league, thirty-five franchises went belly-up. By 1925, the league had eighteen teams, most in small Midwestern towns and coal towns—Modzelewski's towns. Unitas's towns.

Carr understandably wanted a presence in the sports hub of the universe. T. J. Mara wrote the check. "The Giants," he would say many years later, "were founded on brute ignorance. The players provided the brute strength and I provided the ignorance."

T. J. kept a fairly low profile around the team, but there was no questioning his devotion. Modzelewski remembers the old man making an unscheduled appearance before a home game, in our locker room: "He had two cops with him," Dick recalls. "He looked like he was looking for someone. Apparently there was some reporter who'd been saying negative stuff about the team, cutting us up. So Mr. Mara comes in, sees the reporter, and says, 'Take him out. If you can't say anything good about my team, get out.' We all cheered like hell: '*Ma*-ra, *Ma*-ra!'"

I never knew Tim well. But I know he was a gentleman; the first time I met him in his office downtown, he rose from his chair, in shirt and suspenders, and pulled on a jacket before he shook my hand. And all I needed to know about his generosity can be summed up by one night in 1953 after I'd played both offense and defense for the last five games of that terrible season. We'd just played our final game of the year—a loss to Detroit. I was sitting in the locker room, and seriously thinking of hanging it up then and there. Maxine and I had booked tickets on a night flight west. I wanted to get the hell back to California.

I grabbed a quick shower. And when I got back to my locker, there was T. J.: tall, wearing a dark suit and tie and, as always, a hat; he always had a real presence about him. I didn't know him, other than that first meeting in his office. He came up to me and gave me a folded bunch of bills—not a wad of bills, merely a folded bunch of bills. "I just wanted to thank you for getting us through the year," he said.

I thanked him. I didn't look at the money at first, just put it in my pocket. Later, I pulled it out: several hundred dollars. I said to myself, *Can you believe this?* That was a lot of money for someone who, two years earlier, had to borrow fifty cents in his senior year at USC one day to do the laundry.

By 1958, though, it was Wellington's team, and had been for many years; T. J. had transferred the ownership of the Giants to Wellington and his brother Jack in 1930, when Wellington was fourteen. Jack handled the business end; Wellington ran the team that had been his life's obsession, from his days as a kid when he handed out free tickets to his elementary-school classmates, into his twenties, when he scouted for the team by reading the out-of-town dailies, to his mid-thirties—when, Giant-obsessed, he was still single. It's been written that Well briefly contemplated joining the priesthood, and while all of the Maras were very devout Catholics, it never would have worked: Wellington never missed a Giant practice, never missed a Giant game.

In 1954, he married Ann Mumm, a young woman from the Upper East Side—a woman I now count as a dear friend. "The Giants were his whole life," Ann once said. "It was his faith, his family, and the Giants." They would remain married until his death in 2005.

It was Wellington who scouted me at Yankee Stadium when I played against Army for USC in 1951, and it was Wellington who took care of me the rest of the way. I've always felt that I played my career for the greatest owner in the history of the game. And I wasn't surprised to hear that, to a man, my teammates share my sentiments. I've never had to ask them what they thought of the man; they volunteer the memories themselves. Modzelewski, who played for four different teams, never experienced the kind of unity in Washington, Pittsburgh, or Cleveland that he enjoyed as a Giant: "We all got along—no one was jealous of anyone—and the Maras were the ones who kept us together, made us feel that way."

"I'll never forget first getting there," Webster told me. "I thought I might have a hard time with these guys—war veterans, guys from all over the country, me a Jersey guy. I never expected the love we ended up showing one another, from the top down. The way we talked to one another. The way we shared what was on our mind. All of us."

"It *was* always like family," Perian remembers. "They were special times. Especially our group. And our owners contributed to that feeling. I think they thought the group was special. It was like a family: Once a Giant, always a Giant."

That may sound like a cliché. But in 1958, it was true. It was a different time, a time when the bond between a football team and its owners, between a team and a city, felt almost neighborly. Today, I can't quite imagine reading, in a Giants game-day program, the words I found from a Giant program from those years: *"Alicia*

*Landry lost a charm bracelet, probably at the stadium, on Oct. 27, when the Redskins were here. The bracelet doesn't have intrinsic value. However, it means a lot to the Landrys. Its return will be greatly appreciated."*

Not that Wellington wasn't always looking out for the bottom line, especially when the team was struggling at the gate in the early fifties and we all worried that it was going to fold; some of the family's other interests, like the coal business, were struggling as mightily as the Giants. Wellington was the one who sat down with you at contract time, and my teammates tell me that Well could be a very tough bargainer at contract time. Of course, back then, every owner was a tough bargainer.

"When I first signed in 1956," Don Chandler told me, "I said, 'What'll you give me?' Wellington offered $7,200, with a $500 bonus. I said, 'That's not much.' He said, 'That's all you're worth.'" (Modzelewski was making $10,000, which represented a big leap up from the first contract his brother, Ed, had signed in 1952 with the Steelers. Dick recalls, "I'll never forget the photograph he had of the day he'd signed: It's a shot of all of us, and the family dog, and he's holding the check—for $3,000".)

In 1958, his third year, Sam Huff made $8,000—the equivalent of $56,000 today—after being named All-Pro in 1957. That's not a lot of dough, even if a steak downtown only cost four dollars. In 1960, when CBS miked Sam up for a documentary called "The Violent World of Sam Huff," he tells me now, he lied to Walter Cronkite about what he was making: "I told him I was making twelve. I was too embarrassed to tell him I was making nine."

I was making $25,000 in 1958. But then, the Maras had always been gracious to me, ever since the first signing bonus they gave me in 1952. And when I look back at those miserable early years, I have to say I probably earned every penny of it. We were playing in the low-rent Polo Grounds, the bottom of the barrel, where drunken fans taunted players *and* their wives.

At the Polo Grounds, across the Harlem River from Yankee Stadium (really, it's one thing to have to play on a field designed for baseball—but a field designed for *polo?*), the field sloped downhill for drainage, but after a rain the water would collect into this huge pond that circled around the baseball infield. "I remember one game where they couldn't even mark the ball," our bachelor linebacker Cliff Livingston told me from his home in Vegas, where he's still living the high life. "It would literally float away. Somebody almost drowned." That someone was me: On one play in the Polo Grounds, I was tackled and held underwater.

But if the Maras could be tight with a contract, they never treated us as anything but friends. We were guests at their home. Our kids would play together. We didn't feel like employees; we felt like Giants.

"The Maras would have us for Thanksgiving, Christmas parties," recalls Modzelewski—Mo, to me, now and always. "My son Mark was just a youngster, and he kept picking on our coach Jim Lee Howell's kid at one Christmas party. Jim Lee came to me and said. 'Mo, your son is picking on Pumpkin.' I told Mark, 'Leave Pumpkin the hell alone, or your old man will be playing back in Pittsburgh.'"

For Dick, that would have been a return to Forbes Field, where, before we traded for him in '56, he had to dodge beer bottles as he walked into the tunnel after the Steelers' eighth loss in a row. Mo doesn't carry too many fond memories of his years with the Steelers. His coach in Pittsburgh was a guy named Walt Kiesling, apparently a semi-sadist who, Mo swears, used to fill the team's water buckets with oats to torture them after a bad practice. At least old Jim Lee Howell, our head coach in name only, was just ineffectual.

"Coming from the Steelers, going to the Giants where they

treated you so well, honest to God, I felt like I died and went to heaven," Mo says now. "To be in Yankee Stadium? Oh my God."

Along with Katcavage, Modzelewski anchored the left side of our defensive line. Dick was the archetypal fifties tackle: wide as a tank, more or less immovable. He was known to sing the occasional Polish folk song for his teammates while they were gathered over duck soup at his mother's house when we were on the road in Pittsburgh. Like all of us, Dick was a small-town guy. He came from the cradle of pro football—western Pennsylvania, a coal town called Natrona, twenty-four miles outside of Pittsburgh—and he tackled like a coal kid . . . with leather shoulder pads. In Dick's time with the Giants, he had operations on both shoulders, maybe from years of tackling Jimmy Brown—the most powerful running back the game has ever known—and from having to practice against Jack Stroud, the toughest lineman I ever knew. One of Mo's legs is still black from that weird black salve that our trainer Johnny Johnson used to use as a cure-all for everything back then—including knees that locked up.

(Our other cure-all was the Scotch that our team physician— Doc Sweeny—would carry in that little black bag. You'd be sitting on a plane ride home—aching, bruised, hurting—and you'd tell Doc about it. He'd pull out a bottle of Scotch: "Here, have a nip." He believed there was no injury or illness that a good shot of Scotch couldn't cure. It didn't help your knee, but it sure made the flight back home more bearable.)

I t wasn't every owner who treated his team like family, of course. Hearing about the exploits of some of our '58 refugees from the dark side of the NFL, the always-woeful Chicago Cardinals, made me appreciate the Maras even more. To hear Summerall tell it, he

was lucky to get out of aging (even then) Comiskey Park alive. Today, as I go to Giant games on the road—a guest in a luxury box in
some huge, gleaming stadium with amenities we never dreamed of,
watching players who dress in spacious, carpeted locker rooms—
it's almost surreal to think of what an NFL player in a second-rate
organization had to go through back then.

In Chicago, of course, the Bears were the big show, the team
of the fabled George Halas—a guy who, legend has it, would visit
the saloons on Rush Street on a Saturday night, watch a bar fight,
and sign the winner up to play on his line the next day. The Cards,
playing in crumbling Comiskey, with its empty bleachers and flak-
ing paint, were simply a joke, top to bottom. In Summerall's five
seasons before joining us in '58, the Cards played sixty games—and
won seventeen.

"I think I would have quit if I hadn't been traded to the Giants
in '58," Summerall says now. "It was a totally low-class operation.
The equipment was bad. The trainers were bad. The field was awful. The locker room facilities were terrible; we were lucky to have
a nail to hang our clothes on. Traveling was bad. They'd say, 'Get to
the airport any way you can.' It was just a cheap outfit, in every way.
Even medically. I remember one time, we only had two offensive
tackles, and a guy pulled a hamstring during a game and we didn't
have anybody to replace him. So they gave him a Novocain shot
through his pants, on the field.

"This'll give you an idea of what it was like on the Cardinals:
Every Thursday, they passed out the cards so we could make bets
on the game that Sunday. One time our fullback Johnny Olszewski
and I played a parlay card together. Someone scored a TD that put
us over the spread. He said, 'You sonofabitch! We won't win our bet
on the parlay card!'

"Then, to have it be the Giants they traded me to? Things were a little different over there. For one thing, the guys were all reasonably intelligent. The thing that struck me about going from the Cardinals to the Giants was that on the Giants we had some really smart guys. We didn't have a lot more physical ability than the Cardinals, but the guys we had were bright. We had guys who could think about things, come up with solutions on the field, in the huddle. It wasn't just a collection of athletes. Our guys were smarter."

He's right. At least if we were betting, we'd have been smart enough to bet on our own team.

But history has proved Pat out: On the Yankee Stadium field that day, we didn't just have six future Hall of Fame players. The number of guys who went on to serve as coaches must rival any NFL's team's alumni: two head coaches (Webster and Svare) as well as a number of assistants, including Modzelewski, our tough safety Emlen Tunnell, and our big, cerebral tight end, Bob Schnelker—a substitute teacher at that time, with a fondness for mathematics. Not to mention a future general manager, Robustelli.

A t first glance, our opponents that day in 1958 seemed to have little in common with the Giants. The team had been in existence half a decade, hailing from an old, low-profile port town, with no championship pedigree. But we actually had a great deal in common. The Colt roster featured its own future head coach in Ray Berry, who would take the New England Patriots to a Super Bowl. Their owner, Carroll Rosenbloom, treated them as well as any man they'd ever worked for.

And their roster featured a few survivors from an even sorrier team than the Cardinals. At least the Chicago Cardinals knew what city their franchise belonged to.

The core of these Colts—among them, Gino Marchetti and

Artie Donovan—had come from a team most recently known as the Dallas Texans, a team that played the first four games of its only season in the Cotton Bowl in 1952 before its owners declared bankruptcy. (Before that, the franchise played in Boston and New York.) The NFL league relocated the team in midseason to Hershey, Pennsylvania, of all places, to finish out the season. They won one of twelve games, playing those last eight on the road, including a Sunday afternoon in the Akron Rubber Bowl. (Their one victory that year was against, of all teams, Halas's Bears. George started second-stringers for that one.)

"In Dallas," Gino Marchetti tells me now, "we were so bad the vets would hide on the bench 'cause they didn't want to go in. This is how bad we were: One day someone said, 'Who can play tight end?' I said, 'I can!' I said to the quarterback, 'Hey, Hank, hit me for six.' He threw a Hail Mary, and I caught it. I was so happy—until I heard the announcer say, 'Rams 42, Dallas 6.'

"Jimmy Phelan was our coach. He'd fought in World War One. Nice guy, but he never read a scouting report, hardly looked at film. You know how we made his last cut? He walks right into the locker room and points at various guys and says, 'You, out. You, out. You, out.' That's how Don Klosterman got cut. Don says, 'You can't do that to me.' Phelan said, 'Shit I can't. I just did.'"

No wonder the Dallas/Hershey guys lost eleven of twelve that year—especially if a legendary account of one of their practices is any indication. As the story goes, the week before a "Texan" game against the Eagles, the Philadelphia head coach, Jim Trimble, told John Huzvar, his fullback, "Don't come to practice Tuesday. Spy on the Texans." Huzvar sat in the parking lot in Hershey with his hat down over his eyes, trying to glean some covert intelligence. The next day Trimble asked him, "What'd you see?" Huzvar reported, "They were playing volleyball over the crossbar."

Artie confirms the volleyball story, and, as always with Artie, he insisted on sharing a few more memories of those strange days playing for a team without a home—like the one of an exhibition game against the Eagles in Hershey. "All the fans got so drunk in the stands," Artie told me, "the guards had to turn the water hoses on them.

"So anyway, Art Spinney—he was the starting guard in our game; his nickname was Pusbag—we told Pusbag to go get us some beer after the game. So he goes over to this bar, but the only thing he could find to carry the beer in was this sack that had horse manure in it. We didn't care. We just brushed the manure off the bottles."

In the meantime, while the Texans were bouncing around the country, the city of Baltimore had lost its own NFL franchise in 1950, the original Colts—named for the Preakness—or, depending on whom you believe, because "Colts" was short enough to fit into a newspaper headline on deadline. Those Colts folded after one year, but the fan base had proved unusually solid. So Bell turned to Rosenbloom, a personable, ruggedly handsome businessman who knew nothing about owning a professional football team, but was more than anxious to learn. Bell had coached Rosenbloom in the backfield at the Ivy-League University of Pennsylvania.

For his first roster, Bert gave Carroll some of the Texans. And the NFL's gypsies had finally found a home (until 1984, anyway, when they moved to Indianapolis).

Until Bell talked him into taking over the team, Rosenbloom had no experience in any front offices other than his family's businesses. He'd made his money manufacturing uniforms during the Second World War, running the Marlboro Shirt Company in Baltimore, downtown on Lombard Street. "He wasn't real excited about taking over the team—not at the start, anyway," his son Steve told me. "Owners back then, they had to be a little crazy, or civic-minded, or both, because no one was making money."

Rosenbloom paid $200,000 for the franchise in 1953, and put another $800,000 into getting it off the ground, in the renovated municipal redbrick horseshoe of Memorial Stadium, a few miles up the hill from downtown Baltimore, planted in the heart of a proud, working-class neighborhood. Rosenbloom expected to lose the whole thing. He wasn't alone. "This is Carroll Rosenbloom," a local radio personality told the crowd at a banquet introducing the new team to its city, "and it's lucky he's in the shirt business, because he's liable to lose it."

Bell appointed Rosenbloom's first head coach himself: Keith Molesworth, a man with virtually no professional coaching experience. Carroll wanted to fire him at the first training camp. He'd have to wait a year. Rosenbloom was also less than impressed with the players his buddy Bert had bestowed on him.

"It was a sorry bunch," Rosenbloom said years later, in Mickey Herskowitz's *The Golden Age of Pro Football.* "No discipline. No pride. Very few good players . . . All I asked of them was to let the other team know they'd been in a game. If you do that, I said, I'll look after you financially." Rosenbloom made good on his word. He figured that the most logical way to motivate his band of wanderers was through their wallets. He put in an incentive system, which was, of course, completely against league rules. He'd offer a certain amount of money for an interception, for example. "The other owners regarded me as a communist."

(Actually, Carroll wasn't the first owner to offer off-the-record bonuses. Before my time, T. J. Mara had been known to dangle cash-on-delivery for on-field exploits. As the story went—probably apocryphal, but not unbelievable by any means—some years before, he'd told an unidentified Giant defensive back before a game against the Browns that if he intercepted two Otto Graham passes, it would mean a new suit. The guy picked off one pass. Tim gave him a pair of pants. The next Sunday, goes the tale, he picked off another—and, the following Monday, got the jacket.)

It wasn't just extra cash that turned the Colts around. According to his players and friends, Carroll Rosenbloom had a way of pumping up the lowliest of underachievers. Today, an old friend of Rosenbloom's, who requested anonymity, speaks of the man's eloquent gifts of persuasion: "He just had this ability to motivate people," his friend told me. "He'd say, 'I want you to jump over the Empire State Building.' You'd say, 'No way can I do that.' But he'd say it often enough that, all of a sudden, you thought you could. He'd get people to do unbelievable things."

Rosenbloom, ever the entrepreneur, was equally concerned about advancing our game's overall image. He figured that the key to marketing what had been a second-rate league was to play up its connection with the college game everyone loved so much. Instead of reinforcing the public perception of the league as being a less dignified version of the college game—and its players as old, out-of-shape guys who played on the Sabbath, in half-empty stadiums in cities, instead of on autumn Saturdays with brass bands and standing-room-only crowds—why not promote the NFL as the land of glory gods, playing in a Valhalla to which the college stars people had loved had graduated?

Rosenbloom wanted his players to comport themselves as gentlemen. And in turn, he would treat them as such. To a man his players not only appreciated his generosity, but sensed that he regarded them as equals, and that he truly cared for the city of Baltimore.

"Carroll was a people person—he genuinely liked people,"

Raymond Berry says now. "And he definitely recognized that the fans were the most important part of the NFL. Without the fans, there'd be no league. He reached out. He hired a GM, Don Kellett, who was a great PR man, and they immediately set about making the players available to the fans, through the Colt Corrals."

The Colts already lived in and around the neighborhoods of Baltimore, and the Corral took them even deeper into those neighborhoods: they'd attend oyster roasts, dinner parties, cook-outs. "Fans would call and ask if so and so could come to the house, have dinner, sit down with the family," Andy Nelson, one of the Colts' starting safeties in 1958, told me from his barbe-cue place north of Baltimore. "You'd go to a kid's birthday party and have some cake, just because they asked you. We weren't look-ing for money or anything—it was just people trying to be nice to us, and we appreciated it. It's just being friendly. It's being homey. It's being down-to-earth. That's what we cared about. Not winning a world championship."

"We were the fans' friends," Artie says now, and Berry agrees: "It really was a unique relationship that was built between the team and the city."

Rosenbloom was known as a fair and generous negotiator at contract time. His son swears he once shoved a contract across the table to Gino Marchetti and told him to fill in the number. Rosenbloom's contract-negotiating philosophy was understandable: Happy employees made for a solid corporation. But Rosenbloom took it a step further. He made it a point to do whatever he could to guarantee the financial futures of his players. As a motivational tool, it was probably brilliant. Few of them were savvy with money, and fewer still had any great ambitions.

Despite being universally regarded as one of the best players to ever play the game, Marchetti, another small-town guy from Northern California, was content to go home when it was all over, helping to run the family service station and tending bar—until Carroll stepped in and began to look after his star's future: "Oh, yeah. He took care of my life," Gino told me. "This one time, I'll never forget, we were playing the 49ers in San Francisco. So after the game Carroll calls me into his room. I come in, and he says, 'I'm kind of worried.' So I sit down, and we talk, and he says, just like this, 'Hey, you dumb Okie, what the hell are you going to do with your life?'" (I'm not sure why Carroll called him an Okie. Maybe they didn't teach geography in the Ivies.)

"Well, I was happy to just be going home bartending in Antioch, California. He says, 'I want you to move to Baltimore. I'll help you in business. The people in Baltimore like you, and that's where you should be.' Then, after the game, he went up to my wife, told her the same thing. We stayed in Baltimore. And for years after that, if anything came up, and I needed something or wanted something, I'd call him, and no problem."

"At one point," the Colts' cornerback Milt Davis told me from his farm in Oregon, "Carroll Rosenbloom asked us all to invest in a mutual fund, the Dreyfus Fund, and all of us invested." For the veteran Davis, investing a paycheck represented a remarkable milestone for a kid who was born of black-Indian blood on an Oklahoma reservation, before his family traveled west in a Model A in the thirties, when Milt was three years old. In south-central Los Angeles, Milt's dad dug ditches in front of the school Milt attended. The boy fought off street gangs to get food from a local commissary. And now he was playing for a man who was guiding his investments. "Our money doubled in something like six years. Rosenbloom really did care. We had some leadership from the top."

If, as Mo says, the Maras made the Giants into an organization where "the whole team just molded together," then Rosenbloom clearly had the same effect on his own team. To hear the Colts tell it, the 1958 team was as tight a group of guys as you could imagine. "We didn't have cliques," says Artie, and the preponderance of nicknames on that team says a lot about the close relationship the players shared. Carl Taseff, the bandy-legged cornerback, was "Gaucho." Artie Donovan was "Fatso." Eugene Lipscomb was, of course, "Big Daddy." Lenny Moore was "Spats" but Unitas called him "Sput" for Sputnik, the Russian satellite, because of his speed. Steve Myhra, their erratic kicker, was "Mumbles."

The running back Alan Ameche, of course, was famously "The Horse." Milt was "Pops." And the mammoth All-Pro offensive tackle Jim Parker was "Boulevard"—"because his butt was as wide as one," Davis told me. "In that championship game, I remember Unitas in the huddle, saying, 'Boulevard, this is critical—a 32 trap, right over your ass.'"

The two most revered men on the team, Gino Marchetti and Johnny Unitas, didn't have nicknames. They were always Gino and John.

"I never saw so much love between a group as I saw back then," Big Daddy Lipscomb's wife said, years later. "They wanted to play for each other."

That's a sentiment I can fully understand.

The Colts and Baltimore enjoyed a distinctly different relationship with their city than the Giants did with theirs. In New York, the highest-profile stars are easily lost amid the glitter. But Baltimore is a small town at heart, and from the day these new Colts arrived in 1953, the town wholeheartedly took them in. To

hear the Colts talk today about playing at Memorial Stadium—
being introduced as they ran up an angled plywood ramp laid over
the concrete steps in the Oriole dugout—is to experience the bond
that only a small town of a city can share with its sports heroes.
Berry insists that Memorial Stadium was the first field where the
roar of the crowd was so intense that opposing teams couldn't hear
their quarterback's signals. (That sure wasn't the case in the Polo
Grounds. We used to play in front of eight thousand people.)

Today, Ernie Accorsi likens the bond between the Colts and
Baltimore to the relationship between Brooklyn fans and their Dodgers. Ernie was raised in Hershey, Pennsylvania, joined the Colt front
office in the seventies, and went on to serve the Giants as a general
manager, so he's obviously given all of this some thought. "In both
cases, the team was the city's identity. In both places, you'd hear them
talk in the neighborhood about their team—Brooklyn, overshadowed
by Manhattan, Baltimore always overshadowed by Philadelphia."

The night before a home game, the Colts would generally stay
at the Hotel Belvedere in Baltimore—the jewel of that city, built at
the turn of the century. The Belvedere had its own storied history:
Woodrow Wilson was staying in The Belvedere when he was nomi-
nated for the presidency; it hosted a half-dozen other presidents,
from Taft to Kennedy. But in the late fifties, the Belvedere's most
storied guests were named Marchetti, Unitas, and Donovan.

For the most part, the Colts lived in homes and apartments
in neighborhoods all over their friendly city. They immediately became part of the town's fabric—and thanks to that game, they still
are. I was amazed to find out how many of them stayed in town, or
returned to live in the area.

"We always considered New York the place where the big
money was," Gino says now. "But Baltimore, to me, well, it just
seemed like a genuine place. It was the people in Baltimore who

really made it so friendly. And being a Colt, I guess there was a certain mystique."

The night before we faced off against the Colts to fight for the 1958 championship, we weren't the only football players staying in the Concourse Plaza. The Colts were sharing our dorm. They'd gotten into town on Saturday afternoon and walked down to the Stadium for practice.

Talk about a different time: Can you imagine the two Super Bowl teams staying in the same old brick hotel these days, the night before the game? In the week before last year's Super Bowl, the Giants took over an entire resort, south of Phoenix. The Patriots populated *another* whole resort, east of the city. Each luxurious lodging place was replete with Jacuzzis and golf courses.

Back then, the Colts and Giants were just another seventy guys staying in a dorm—a dorm that Artie Donovan happened to know well. For Artie, checking into the Concourse Plaza on Saturday afternoon was like going back in time. Artie tells me now that he'd spent more than a few nights bending a few rules down on the Grand Concourse: "When I was a kid, we used to steal beer off the tables during dances in that ballroom. The couples would get up to dance, and there were these pitchers of beer on the tables. We'd hang out outside the ballroom, then go in and steal the pitchers. The maître d' was a guy named Jerry. He was from my neighborhood, so whatever we wanted, we got. All the big-shot lawyers would be hanging at the bar."

Artie had returned to his favorite borough—only this time, he was the enemy. And a couple of men outside a cafeteria near Jerome Avenue let him know it.

"These guys are standing there with their baby carriages with children in them," he told me from the suburban Baltimore country club he's managed for decades, "and these guys are yelling at me, 'You're gonna get killed tomorrow.'

' "Yeah, right,'" I said. ' "We're gonna stick it up their rear ends.'"

(Through the years, Artie has become, in many ways, the face and voice of the old Baltimore Colts, but Artie himself did everything he could to stay in his hometown. Even after he became a Colt, he was always looking for work in New York. He considered the police force. At one point, he wanted to be a teacher. After reviewing his application to get some teacher's credits, Columbia advised him to stick with professional football.)

Back then there was nothing unusual about staying in the same hotel as your adversary. Because the guys in the other uniform weren't your enemy. There wasn't any showboating, one-upping. The whole league was made up of just a little over four hundred guys, and a whole lot of them became friends. We didn't think of one another as opponents so much as members of a special fraternity. Through the years, we'd all crossed paths: played together in Senior Bowl games, in Shrine games, in Pro Bowl games. We'd played each other during the endless six-game exhibition season, in small cities, where we'd hang at the hotel bars together. We'd even brawl together; Marchetti once remembered teaming up with Alex Webster—his archfoe in our championship game—in a barroom melee against a couple of guys who clearly didn't know who they were messing with.

"I really don't think we looked at the players on the other teams with any animosity," Andy Robustelli says now, sitting at a table in his restaurant in Stamford. "Back then, there wasn't a hate signal anywhere, or anything that caused you to get rough with opponents. You wouldn't talk about who was better than who. You just said, 'I'll do what I can do, and hope I can do it to the best of my ability.' No one said you were playing on a better team because you were a better player. You played as a team. We emulated the Colts. It was like that back then. We had a capacity to reach out to other teams and say, 'You're a good team. We want to be like you.'"

Weeb Ewbank, the Colts' coach that day, may have captured this feeling we had for each other better than anyone, in an interview years later: "The thing I miss about the fifties is that people seemed to have more respect for each other—even if they disliked you. There was more of a purpose, less selfishness. People talked about doing their share. Whatever happened to that?"

We were all bound by being members of a small, special club: athletes in a league that was still playing its games in relative obscurity, fighting for a decent paycheck, playing in half-empty stadiums. In the fifties, the World Series was a huge event; the NFL championship game was anything but.

No story about the 1958 Giants would be complete without a brief visit to the streets of the team's *other* neighborhood.

By day, we were residents of the Bronx. But by night, on occasion—on many an occasion—we had another neighborhood we called our own: downtown, where bars were still saloons, and the streets were festooned with the neon nightclub signs that lit midtown Manhattan, beckoning us all—athletes, admen, businessmen, journalists—to the sanctuary of several well-lighted places. That world, for the most part, has disappeared now, of course—not just the bars and restaurants, but the feel of a city in its prime. Today's players are the poorer, I think, for playing in a city that has lost that feeling, but even if all of our old haunts were still around, I think something would still be missing: the camaraderie of a bunch of teammates working their way east across that most hallowed section of midtown—the streets that had been crowded with speakeasies during Prohibition.

Whole books have been written about the area that centered on 52nd Street—"*The Street.*" For the Giants, all of midtown Manhattan was *our* street. Anyone who lived through our glory days knows that we didn't just play them in a sacred stadium. We lived them on our nighttime tours, bathed in a glow that was very different from the lights of Yankee Stadium.

Drinking was simply a part of society back then, and it was definitely part of the professional football player's routine. Of course, we were hardly alone. Television advertised hard liquor. Any gathering—from a Park Avenue cocktail party to a gathering at a bar under the el—involved some sort of lubrication. "That was just a generation that drank" is the way that Nina Rote, the widow of my friend Kyle Rote, remembers it now. "Drinking was normal. When people would come to our apartment, the first thing you'd say was 'Would you like a drink?' It was the polite thing to say. That was the generation when it was okay to drink. And you were expected to hold your liquor."

We were encouraged to loosen up; one of the many cocktail invitations we got during the '58 season, from some friends downtown, read, "Let's Get Plastered." We would do our best not to, but back then, it would have been strange to *not* drink at a party.

Liquor was definitely part of our society. Our announcer, Bob Sheppard, told me he had a weekly routine of stopping for a few drinks at a little place in Queens on his way back to Long Island after the games. Doc Sweeny had that bottle. Even our team *chaplain* bent a few elbows downtown with the rest of us—and frequently. Father Dudley, in fact, could mix a mean Manhattan.

I should know. Earlier in the '58 season, I had to spend a

few days in the hospital after I'd messed up some of my knee ligaments in our fourth game, against the Cardinals. I'd had a rough
first month, medically speaking: A couple of hits to the head had
briefly sidelined me in our first two games. Now, on Sunday after-
noons, Father Dudley struck a reassuring figure on our sideline, in
his black suit and his white collar. When he visited me in the hospital that week, though, he wore a slightly different uniform; Father
Dudley was a Franciscan monk, and when he came to my hospital
room, he was in full Franciscan garb, from the robe, with its deep
folds, right down to the sandals.

He showed up in my room and said to the nurse, in that slow,
deep, authoritative voice that I'll never forget, "Will you leave us
alone, please?" She agreed, probably figuring he was going to lead
me through some special mass—a prayer to the saint of torn knees,
perhaps. Father Dudley had a different ceremony in mind.

He reached into one of the folds of his robe—and brought
out the bourbon. Then he reached into another fold—and pulled
out the sweet vermouth. Then, the cherries. Then, somehow, from
somewhere, he pulled out a couple of glasses. And some ice. And
we had our Manhattans. Chilled and straight up. Just the way he
liked them.

In a very real way—in a very liquid way—our evening prowls
across midtown Manhattan were just as historic as our games uptown: more than simply a tour of popular watering holes, but a tour
of some shrines that echoed with the vibrancy that had made the
city such an amazing place in the previous decades, with the growth
of the theater, of the sports teams, of Madison Avenue.

Our uptown and downtown neighborhoods shared something
in common for me, too: in both places, I was becoming a (small)
part of New York history myself. At Yankee Stadium, we were playing in a stadium that really did put New York on the sports map.

It might have been called "The House That Ruth Built," but it was a place that Conerly, Rote, and Huff—after our 47–7 championship win over the Bears two years earlier—were beginning to claim for their own, too. And downtown, where the soul of the great city truly resided, we were walking in another set of historical footsteps: The Street, where jazz was born and speakeasies once ruled.

Our path didn't touch on the haunts of the real royalty of midtown Manhattan. We didn't hobnob at the Stork Club, or drink on the roof at the St. Regis. The high-end hotels weren't for us, nor could we have afforded them. We haunted saloons. Our half-dozen regular stops were peopled by New Yorkers of all stripes—not the New Yorkers who lived in the penthouses, but the folks who brought the town to life, including its less-than-legitimate entrepreneurs. In a way, we were kind of silent heroes to the people who ran the colorful side of New York.

And believe me, some of them were pretty colorful. Back then, the city wasn't littered with "clubs"—it really was still a town of saloons, and the guys who loved to have us come into their places were saloonkeepers at heart. They recognized us, and they welcomed us as part of the community. We weren't superstars looking for a VIP room, just football players who liked to drink, and talk, under a cloud of cigarette and cigar smoke, gathered around a circular bar, chatting with friends and strangers alike, nighttime New Yorkers who felt like and treated each other as neighbors.

We enjoyed hitting our regular places, but we didn't frequent any of them to be recognized, or celebrated. Most of the time, no one knew who we were. In 1958 we were starting to claim some of the Yankees' high-profile turf around town, but the erratic attendance at our home games made it abundantly clear that we were far from superstars. Except for our regular-season game against the

Colts in November that year, we didn't sell out any of our games. When we beat the Eagles in the ninth game of the season, on a cold day at the Stadium—a must-win game—we drew exactly 35,458. (Unfortunately, they weren't treated to much of a game, either: Four of the first five plays featured fumbles. The next day, in the *Mirror*—one of the nine dailies that were on strike when we played the championship game—one of the biggest headlines read, "Frigid Weather Couldn't Stop High-Stepping Gals." A story about the Bergenfield [New Jersey] High School band's bare-legged female members offered far more intrigue than interviews with the participants in a lackluster football game.)

But the saloonkeepers in our downtown neighborhood knew us well; more often than not, we chose our destinations based on which proprietors might be willing to take care of some of the check—or all of the check. It seems almost bizarre now to think that the players on a New York team would have to watch their budget. But somehow that sense of perspective made life better. Somehow, it made more sense. On our team, there were no super-stars, and no superstar salaries. We didn't have to deal with becoming rich overnight and not knowing how to handle all the pressures of sudden wealth—because there *was* no sudden wealth. We were all in the same boat, and it wasn't a yacht.

We appreciated the city in a way that the modern players probably don't. Today, they all seem to live in Jersey, apart from one another. Do they take advantage of New York the way we did? Do they get to appreciate the things about New York that we knew were special—the parks, the museums, the galleries, the theater? Do they know what it's like to be part of the fabric of a place that can be so huge and so much like a village at the same time? I don't think so.

So on the good nights, after the good games, we headed downtown to our second home—"by subway on the way down," Summerall recalls, "and taxi on the way back, when we were a little more *relaxed.*"

The big nights out, of course, would follow a home game—bigger if we'd won. That year, we broke out of the gate slowly, losing two of the first four games, but we won our last five. The temperatures and snow of the frigid early winter had the city in buoyant spirits.

This was the postgame routine: We'd make our way back to our various apartments at the hotel—or cramped rooms. Depending on the number of guests we'd invited to our cocktail party, and the need for ice bags on bruised and battered bodies—as well as the need for drinks—we'd spend a couple of hours getting ready to hit the town.

We'd get organized, get our coats and ties on. Me, I kind of liked that guys wore coats and ties, and women wore dresses and furs back then. It was harder to get Charlie dressed up. Charlie couldn't have cared less, of course. In fact, I don't think he actually owned a coat. This was not a man who had much use for ceremony. (The next season, the team gave Charlie a day in his honor, and showered him and Perian with gifts. One of them was a season's worth of cottonseed and a ton of fertilizer.)

Nor could I blame Charlie for being less than enthusiastic about hitting the town on some of those Sundays; in our loss to the Cardinals at home that season, the crowd was all over him. ("His parting shots were such duds," Gene Ward wrote about his passes in the *Daily News*, "that the stadium virtually rocked with derisive boos at his futile fourth-quarter flinging.") But we'd clean him up, drag him out—and he'd be the toast of the town.

After a few cocktails at the Concourse Plaza, we'd walk the three blocks down 161st Street and up the stairs to the elevated subway, wait on the wooden-planked platform with its view of the empty field beneath us as the December wind whipped our over-coats, and head for downtown. The subway was our 1958 limo, the D train our stretch car.

I'd gotten my first taste of the city in 1951, when I played at the Stadium with USC against Army—the first time the Trojans had played in New York. If USC was where I got my first hint of privi-lege, of a world above and beyond my own, my first glimpse of the real New York, as a USC player, was astounding. The university did it up right for us. We stayed at the Waldorf, that grand palace gilded in gold paint, planted on Park Avenue. The night before the game, we saw *Guys and Dolls* on Broadway, back in a time when the theater crowd dressed to the nines. I remember thinking, "Man—this is unbelievable." I had no idea that, a year later, I'd be calling New York my second home.

But in 1958, the city's offerings were even more unbelievable. On the long nights, we'd hit every spot, and make a night of it. Our first stop would be at Downey's, for a quick one, on West 45th Street and Eighth Avenue, where the price was always "right"—if there was even a check at all. Downey's was a theater crowd. We could meet and mix with some Broadway cast member, or crew member, or a stage director, or lighting guy: *real* theater people. Now *that* was big-time. That season, Maxine and I caught a couple of Broadway shows, including *West Side Story.* Even back then, tickets for two to a Broadway show could run you pretty high, so the tickets we got usually came in exchange for tickets to a Giant game—or, sometimes, were just plain free.

Another favorite spot was, Mike Manuche's. I can still remem-ber the phone number at Manuche's, Judson 2 5483, and the red interlocking *M*'s on the pink matchbooks. Manuche's was next door to the longest-running jazz joint on the Street, the Hickory House. But the Giants preferred the nonmusical ambience of Mike's saloon. Mike was a big, handsome, affable former Air Force pilot whose own Giants roots were deep: he had tried out for the Giants once. I'm glad he didn't make the team. We wouldn't have been able to enjoy his saloon, where, after any game, Mike would relive the game for you—or anyone who would listen—right by his circular bar, where people could drink, talk, and smile. Funny how the circular bars have disappeared. Now everyone just seems to sit and stare at the bottles behind the bartender as they check their cell phones or caress their BlackBerries.

Vince Lombardi *loved* Mike's. But the real star in Manuche's was Mike's wife, Martha Wright, a pretty reddish-haired singer and actress with sparkling eyes. Martha had set the record for consecutive Broadway performances when she played Nellie Forbush in *South Pacific* for more than one thousand performances in a row. The city's high rollers could catch Martha's act at the Waldorf and the St. Regis. We'd see her at Mike's, when she wasn't on a stage somewhere. Between them, Mike and Martha had a pretty wide reach into the city's more interesting folks.

For *really* interesting folks, though, there was Eddie Condon's, the jazz club on 55th between First and Second Avenues, home to a lot of great musicians. The funny thing is that the people at Eddie Condon's bar hated the music; we could never hear each other, and a lot of the time the clientele were people who definitely had something interesting to say. You'd run across Roy Cohn, or the mayor, or a hooker, or a gambler, or someone who might have been a member of the mob. Condon's was the one place that, a few years later, Pete Rozelle would insist I stay away from. I usually abided by my friend Pete's requests. I ignored that one.

Eddie Condon's was presided over by a classic New York host

and gatekeeper—Peter Pesci. Peter was an Italian guy who had these great, expressive hands, which he was always clapping or rubbing together. And he always wore red socks. He never struck me as the kind of guy who should have been working in a jazz joint. Through the years, Peter took care of a lot of players. Peter was pretty connected with the people one shouldn't know, but he never apologized for having a very diverse set of connections. Peter was a huge Giants fan, and, I must admit, a huge Gifford man. When I'd show up at Eddie Condon's, Peter would always announce, "The fabulous Mr. Gifford arriving," which would embarrass the hell out of me, but he didn't care.

Peter was eventually stricken by a long, lingering illness. To bolster his spirits, I gave him my '56 championship ring. He lost it. Years later, his wife, Slatsy, gave me Peter's old pocket watch. It had an engraving of a train on the back of it. It reminded me of the one my father had carried. I still have it. At the funeral home, Slatsy and I discreetly checked to make sure that Peter was wearing his red socks. He was: the Fabulous Mr. Pesci, departing in style.

At the other end of the social spectrum was the 21 Club, a real highlight, another temple to New York history. It was at 21 West 52nd Street, the classiest address on the Street. But for most of us, 21 wasn't a regular spot, and you'd have been hard-pressed ever to call it a saloon. But on the days we were feeling flush enough, we'd drop in—maybe on the more cultural evenings, for dinner before or after the theater. I didn't go to 21 much; we just couldn't afford it. But it was one of the places Maxine always loved to go.

In its days as a speakeasy, when it was known as Jack and Charlie's 21, it had a mythology all its own. Federal agents knocking on the door looking to bust the place were thwarted by an ingenious system. The bouncer would press a buzzer, and a moment later, inside, the bar would move into the wall and the glasses and liquor would plummet down into a pit of sand, to muffle the sound of glass breaking. Meanwhile, in the basement, five thousand cases of liquor were automatically sealed behind a huge masonry door designed to look like part of the basement wall. (That subterranean room is now available as a private dining room.)

When alcohol became legal again in 1933, 21 was a joint that attracted the well-connected—"a Tiffany's window onto society," in the words of a writer for *Fortune* magazine.

By 1958, that description still seemed accurate to me. The patrons of 21 tended to be on their best behavior. Bogart was known to hit 21, El Morocco, and the Stork Club, in that order, but as the story goes, while Bogey would occasionally cause a scene at the two other places, he was known to never do anything even slightly improper at 21. Its policy of not catering to the press made 21 feel a little higher class than its brethren; during Prohibition, the joint even barred the newspaper writers, to ensure that its patrons could drink and eat in peace. (Not that they didn't eventually welcome writers of a different sort; Hemingway and John Steinbeck were patrons of 21, too.)

Another quirk of 21: they took only cash, no matter who you were. No checks, no credit. There was the occasional exception; when a man named George Humphrey signed his check one night, and the waiter politely informed him that cash was required, Mr. Humphrey produced a dollar bill, and pointed to the signature on the bill: it was his. The credit of Eisenhower's secretary of the treasury was deemed sufficient.

Maxine and I paid cash—21 was one place where it wasn't likely anyone was going to take care of your tab because you lugged a football up in the Bronx. But we'd always have a table at 21, although the maître d' would never make a big deal out of it. No one announced you at 21, where I always felt a sort of thrill that I never felt at our other regular haunts. Today, my helmet still hangs amid the bullfighters' swords and the toy cars and the muskets. That's pretty cool: you can sit beneath Frank Gifford's helmet. And I often do.

On most of our cross-town rambles, our last stop was over on Third Avenue, up on 55th Street: the venerable P.J. Clarke's—in many ways our favorite spot, and still going strong. The history of P.J.'s was nearly as storied as our other watering holes. Its bar had been featured in the classic Ray Milland movie *Lost Weekend*; the Giants preferred to visit on winning weekends. And we often did. Clarke's was another old speakeasy, owned by a gentleman named Danny Lavezzo. He was the key guy. You'd get through the front bar, with its tiled floor and dark wood, if you could, then work your way back to the "main" room, run by Frankie Rebundo. You had to know Frankie to get into the back room. And Frankie knew us. If any of us had to go to a cocktail party, or a postgame commitment, or a dinner commitment, it'd always be, "See you at P.J.'s later." That would be around midnight—or sometimes later, depending on how you felt after the game. I was usually pretty well beat up. But I could usually make it.

"21 was out of my league," Pat Summerall recalls. "P.J.'s was always good to us, though. We got thrown out of there many times."

There was one spot that we never missed: a three-story redbrick building whose distinctive emblemed awning beckoned us in, its vertical neon sign flashing a name into the night: Toots Shor's, the mecca of our kind of New York nightlife, presided over by one of the most remarkable men I have ever met.

Bernard "Toots" Shor was a hard-living, life-loving mythic

figure. He offered no apologies for some of his more questionable friends, and felt no regrets for living a long and roller-coaster marquee life, during which he squandered everything he'd ever had, just for the sake of being New York's number one saloonkeeper. "A Damon Runyon Land" is what the writer Nick Pileggi once called Toots's place, and that pretty much says it all. Toots rose from speakeasy bouncer to a guest in five different White Houses. He counted Supreme Court justices, presidents, TV stars, and gangland capos among his friends. And I was lucky to be able to count him one of mine.

I'll never forget the first time I went to Toots Shor's in 1952, my first year in the city. Maxine had read a lot of things about the city. She came up with all these places I had never heard of, and we'd go exploring together. "Toots's is where everyone goes," she'd told me, so we got all dressed up one night and walked through the door underneath the big awning with the interlocking T and S emblem on the front. Toots greeted me at the door: hair slicked back, a big broad nose, a wide smile. I'll leave it to more eloquent and artistic types to describe my friend Toots—as so many have been tempted to, at one point or another: "This huge man, one of the biggest men I'd ever seen," remembered Peter Duchin, the son of the famous bandleader Eddie Duchin, "with a huge, rubber face that had crinkles. It looked sort of like putty in a way." Novelist Don DeLillo, as cited in Carlo DeVito's biography of Wellington Mara, *Wellington,* added a true writer's touch to his portrait of the man: "The slab face and meatcutter's hands . . . a speakeasy vet, dense of body, with slicked-back hair and a set of chinky eyes that summon up a warning in a hurry."

Toots was big, all right: 6 foot 3, increasingly wide, with a waistline that ever expanded—270 pounds, at one point—in direct relation to the brandy he'd consume in mind-boggling quantities, night after night, as he moved from table to table. But Toots was big in another way: He was larger than life. He could be standing between Crosby and Sinatra and, somehow, it was Toots standing in the spotlight.

As Gay Talese once put it, Toots's place was the first Elaine's—the first truly marquee hangout in the town—and if that's true, make no mistake: The Giants were hardly the marquee drinkers. Jackie Gleason, Toots's great buddy, was a regular. Mantle and DiMaggio were hanging out there when I first started going. One night I saw Frank Costello, the mob guy, on one side of the room, and Justice Earl Warren on the other. Harry Lavin, the captain of the waiters back then, used to say that Toots could pick up the phone and get Truman or Eisenhower on the other end. (A few years later, I was drinking with Paul Hornung at Toots's the night before he met with Pete Rozelle, who was about to suspend Paul from the league for a year for gambling on NFL games. Meeting Paul there that night was fittingly appropriate; according to a wonderful film documentary of Toots's place, produced by his daughter, at one point it had been a drop-off point for shady characters running the numbers rackets.)

Whitey Ford loved Toots. Whitey had a custom on day games when he was the Yankees' starting pitcher: After his eight warm-up pitches at the start of the first inning, he'd always look over at Toots, in his box, to let Toots know he saw him. Toots wasn't a fixture at only the Stadium; he'd be at every sports event in town. You'd see him at the Garden for fights, where he invariably had a wager on the contest. He lost $100,000 on the Billy Conn–Joe Louis fight in 1941, one year after he'd opened his place.

I'd even see him at the Polo Grounds, where he'd talk to the players, because our bench nearly abutted the field-level seats on the sideline. (You'd be standing there, watching the game, ready to go in, and someone would just reach out, tap you on the shoulder, and introduce himself. Neal Walsh, a man who later became a dear friend, tried to sell me an insurance policy while we were playing the Bears one day.)

But if there wasn't a prizefight or a game at the Garden that night, you'd find Toots at his place, with Phil Silvers, Wilt Chamberlain, John Wayne, Dempsey, Hemingway. Toots would bounce from one table to the other, pausing to insert himself into a conversation between Whitey and some politician, or Yogi and some writer. (It was at Toots Shor's that Toots famously introduced Yogi and Hemingway to each other. "Yogi," Toots said. "This is Ernest Hemingway. He's an important writer." Yogi's reply: "What paper you with, Ernie?")

He'd always stop to talk to you, and somehow having Toots greet you—"Crumb Bum" was one of his favorite labels; anyone Italian, like Sinatra, would be "Dago"—would make you feel important. Toots himself would usually introduce himself as "I'm Tootsie, the Pretty Jew"—which was *really* a reach.

We'd drink with cops, working stiffs, copy editors from the Associated Press across the street—their drinks already poured, waiting for them—with their visors still on their heads, garters holding up their sleeves. At the circular bar, admen would bump elbows with the star of some TV quiz show.

But no matter who you were, or what you did, Toots could make you feel special. That's another one of the big reasons we'd go to Toots's—me, Charlie, Kyle, Heinrich, Summerall, Mo, Sam. It wasn't just that we might not have to pay the tab. It wasn't just for the chance to see all these famous people. The truth is, most of the great athletes I know are shy people. Toots received us all with open arms and a big bear hug, and that made an insecure guy feel pretty good. When I came out of USC, I was shy. Still am, believe it or not. I could always run faster, jump higher, and I'd always, constantly, been athletically ahead of where I should have been. But I was just an athlete, born and raised in the oil towns. I'd gotten to where I was because of innate athletic talent and hard work. Now, here I was mingling with Supreme Court justices, and great writers, and actors who'd worked at their crafts to rise to the top.

And the man who oversaw them all—the man who certified greatness in our town, who almost single-handedly decided who was a star in New York—was certifying me. In New York, I was coming to realize, it didn't matter where you come from—and I'd really come from nowhere. I'd had been a pretty rootless upbringing. And now Toots was saying, in a way, that I had a home. That I was really a New Yorker. And it felt pretty good.

I suppose it may be surprising to people now to think I ever felt this way—I guess I seem pretty secure in the eyes and minds of most people. But I never was. Having the guy who presided over all those celebrities acknowledge you as one of his friends was a very big thing.

But then, Toots knew what it was like to rise from nothing. His mother was killed in a freak accident when he was fifteen, down in Philadelphia, and his father committed suicide five years later. He was sitting in a bar in Philadelphia when his uncle told him, "You'll never amount to anything." So he came north, and got work as a bouncer in his first speakeasy. He worked in four different clubs during Prohibition. He was strong, and he was tough. He was perfect for the job description—although, truth is, Toots liked to pretend he was tougher than he was.

Toots's bar was a huge, circular affair, the first thing you saw when you walked in the door. It had more than a dozen seats, the drinkers three-deep, surrounding a couple of bartenders in white jackets and black ties, and, in the middle of the circle, a two-tiered tower of glistening bottles. Circular bars were great. Eight or ten guys could stand around, friends and strangers, and you could see each other while you drank and smoked.

And Toots was always there—from opening to closing, with a break to go home to his town house for dinner with his two daughters and his wife, Baby. She was a former Ziegfeld Girl. Toots was huge. Baby was tiny and blond and pretty. And she was the only person I've ever seen him afraid of. When Baby talked, Toots would listen.

But there weren't too many other women at Toots's. Women had a different set of rules. If you swore in front of a woman, or insulted her, Toots would throw you out. He threw a lot of people out, for a lot of reasons. If you ordered white wine, you were gone. (He always gave Father Dudley grief about his Manhattans, but he never threw him out.) If he didn't like you, you were gone. He didn't have to explain; some people Toots just didn't like.

Toots was a little sexist, too. He had a rule about women and their drinking: He'd want to know anytime a woman ordered two martinis. That wasn't right, as far as Toots was concerned; a woman shouldn't ever drink too much. Meanwhile, his own head would be lolling over by the end of the night.

Whitey Ford once said Toots's place took two years off his career. I don't think he took any off mine. In fact, he might have added some—that's how good he made me feel, because when Toots took you in, he took you in completely, literally and figuratively.

He always saved a space for the Giants, no matter how packed the place was. He'd hold tables for us. He didn't care who you were—senator, congressman, ambassador—it didn't matter. The Giants would get a table. "He'd say, 'Defense up front, offense in the back—the offense doesn't score any points'" is the way Sam remembers it. (Of *course* Sam would remember it that way.) "I was a special guest, up by the bar," Sam recalls. "In the number one booth were Toots and Gleason. I remember one time when Fat Jackie and Fat Toots got into an argument over who could run faster. 'You ain't fast,' Toots said. They had a race around the block. Toots went one way, Jackie caught a cab. Jackie was waiting on him."

Back then, a cab could beat someone running around a block.

Sam has good reason to remember Toots's generosity. The big man offered Sam tickets to a World Series game in '56. Sam passed—and missed Don Larsen's perfect game.

"After the games," Modzelewski recalls, "it seemed like everyone would go their way—then at about nine or ten everyone could come to Toots. I remember coming in one time, after a loss. Toots said to me, 'What the hell are you laughing about? I saw you knocked on your ass the whole game.' He'd keep it up till midnight—when he couldn't talk."

It's true that Toots had a habit of overimbibing. He drank way too much. But it was also true that he was the best friend a man—a football player—could ever have.

Not everyone on our team drank. Rosie Grier abstained. That didn't mean he didn't hang out with those who did partake, usually up in Harlem: "I'd go out with the guys, but when they started drinking, I'd say, 'See you guys later.'" Rosie's main vice was eating.

Rosie was funny about things like that. During games, he could be a terror—his body immovable, his long arms swatting runners down. But in person, he could be as meek as a lamb. Most of us wished Rosie would bring a little more intensity to his practices, but one thing he could never be accused of was a hangover.

"My dad gave me something to think about a long time ago,"

Rosie told me. "He'd say, 'Trouble is easy to get into, and hard to get out of.' So when I saw guys losing control, guys yelling, that would be my time to leave. See, I never forgot the night we were playing an exhibition game in Oregon. There were a bunch of us in a nightclub that night—all these guys making a bunch of noise. An older guy started giving the waitress money. They made fun of him. I said, 'Leave him alone.' I went and stood outside. Next thing I know, I saw the guy coming back with a shotgun. I went in and said, 'The guy you been making fun of is coming back. With a gun.'

"But I'd still go out in New York. Sometimes we'd go up to the Red Rooster in Harlem, next to Big Wilt's. Emlen would swing on the chandeliers. Emlen loved the Red Rooster, and the Rooster loved him."

Everyone loved Emlen Tunnell, our veteran safety—the Giants' first black player, signed in 1948. Em often tried to talk me into joining him at a nightclub up in Harlem called Jack's. I deferred for a while, but Em was one of the truly great guys, and he kept at me, so eventually, Charlie and I went up there—and, of course, we had a great time. But I can't say I ever became a regular.

**N**ot everyone wanted to spend their time pub-crawling across 52nd Street. A lot of the guys stayed close to the hotel to do their drinking; there were more than enough bars and family restaurants in the Grand Concourse neighborhood to accommodate every taste in liquor and food. Guys like Don Chandler and Al Barry and Frank Youso, our big rookie lineman who would play a huge (literally) role that day, had their favorite spots, low-key, laid-back places where their profile was as low as the prices.

Youso remembers one particular night when he was dining at

his favorite place under the el, its name long lost to history (and Frank's memory). He'd just bought a brand-new topcoat, and he'd put it on his chair so it wouldn't get stolen from the coatroom. The place was full of off-duty cops and a couple of priests. Frank was delighted when a guy came up and introduced him to his friend: "This is Frank Youso; he plays for the Giants." Frank rose to shake the guy's hand. When he sat back down, his coat was gone.

"Figure that out," Frank says now. "Twelve policemen sitting there, and two Catholic priests, and someone had stolen the coat. When I got off the plane in International Falls the next day, it was twenty below zero—and no coat."

Downtown, if you were a Giant, you could usually count on someone picking up a tab. Back in the neighborhood, they picked up your coat. Such was the so-called celebrity surrounding the New York Giants.

Not surprisingly, Maynard, the Texas receiver who'd never seen a tall building in his life, never ventured too far from the Concourse Plaza. To hear Don tell it now, I'm surprised he even left the hotel. Don saw malice and danger around every corner, lurking in the alleys and shadows of our big city. "See, my dad used to tell me, 'Always come home before dark,'" Don says now. "So when I got to New York, when I was on the streets, I learned to walk close to the parking meter—close to the curb, where I wasn't worried about outrunning anyone. I always walked down the curb."

In his one season in a Giant uniform, mostly returning kicks, the only time Don set out to find Toots, he never arrived. The occasion wasn't an evening of hitting the spots after a game; Lombardi had summoned us for a meeting at Toots's place. "But I didn't know where it was," Don told me. "I went down on the subway. I couldn't find the place. 'What do you mean you couldn't find the place?' Lombardi asked me the next day. I told him what happened. See, after I came up from the subway station, I'd gone two blocks north and two south, and I didn't see the place. But I wasn't about to get too far away from that hole in the ground, so I'd know how to get back. When I didn't see the restaurant, I just went back to the subway and back up to the hotel."

How could a New York Giant not know where Toots's was? Because he was the kind of Giant who never left the small town inside of him. The first time I called Don down in Texas, to talk about this game, we had to reschedule our conversation; the lunch special at KFC was calling his name.

The Colts, of course, didn't do their drinking at places like Toots Shor's. Baltimore didn't have places like Toots's. And didn't want them. The Colts were a true neighborhood team, and they drank in the local watering holes. Some of the black players would visit bars like The Alhambra, down on Pennsylvania Avenue, but for most of the Colts, neighborhood bars near their stadium provided all the ambience—and beer—they needed. The players tell me that their favorite spot was a friendly hangout named Kusen's, near Memorial Stadium. I guess Ivan Kusen, a beloved Yugoslavian immigrant who also worked in Baltimore's shipyards, was the Colts' Toots, in a way.

"Ivan didn't know anything about football, but he became a season ticket holder," Artie Donovan recalls. "He'd always say, 'You goddamned football players!' I'd take him home and drop him off at night after he closed. I'll never forget those rides—he'd have all the receipts and money on top of this patent leather bag; he'd put string beans and corn on top of the case to hide the money.

"When my mother would come down from New York, I'd go

down to Penn Station, and she'd have a box of Schrafft's for me, and the first stop was always Kusen's. My mother would have an old-fashioned."

Artie must have done ample time at Kusen's; he became the executor of the old man's will.

"Then there was Andy's, a little further up York Road," he told me. "There was no 21 club, like in New York, and all that stuff. We went to regular bars."

No one went to Toots's the night before the championship game. Artie didn't even go back up to his old neighborhood in the Bronx on Saturday night. Instead, he brought the neighborhood down to him: "After practice Saturday, a guy from my neighborhood brought down some pizzas. Jerry's Casa Villa. I never ate the meal. I had the pizza on the TV all night, to keep it warm, so I could eat it for breakfast. We stayed up until one watching TV— me and Art Spinney."

Ray Brown, the Colts' safety from Mississippi, went to Charlie's hotel room that afternoon, and they watched the Gator Bowl together, before the Colts convened for their customary hamburger team dinner downstairs. Ray and Charlie had both grown up in Clarksdale, Mississippi. Like I said: At some level, we were all part of the same gang.

Maxine and I played bridge with the Conerlys later that evening—the perfect image of your typical fifties couples. Charlie and I went over our impressions of the regular-season game we'd played against the Colts that year—a hell of a game, and one that the Colts weren't likely to have forgotten. We'd been struggling, and they'd been undefeated. I had no doubt they were looking for some special revenge after that game.

• • •

Sunday, November 9, had dawned dark and cloudy, but by 10 A.M. the sun was out—"Mara weather," they used to call it, because of the legendarily uncanny tendency, through the years, of the clouds to part and the sun to burst out and bathe the Stadium field whenever game time rolled around. By noon the bleachers were full, and by kickoff the place was completely packed: 71,163 fans—5,000 more than the Yankees had drawn for the final home game of their World Series against the Milwaukee Braves a month earlier.

This was our first really crucial game of the year. We were 4–2, one game behind the Browns in the East. An estimated ten thousand Colt fans had come up from Baltimore, carrying placards that read, simply and emphatically, "I'm a Colt." That day, Colt fans had to settle for a backup quarterback—George Shaw, their former starter. Unitas had hurt a couple of ribs. This would give us an advantage, we figured. We needed one.

The Colts came into the Bronx that day with a 6–0 record, and they were not only undefeated, they'd been dominating. They'd scored 50 points in two games, including a 56–0 rout of Green Bay the week before. They were playing like a team possessed. Most of them felt as if they'd been the class of the league in 1957, but with a 7–3 record they'd embarked on a final two-game West Coast road trip and dropped both games, handing the Detroit Lions the Western Conference title.

Shaw wasn't much of a downgrade; he was one of the first of the running quarterbacks in the NFL, and he had a pretty good arm. He also had Berry and Lenny Moore. It never mattered much who was throwing to Lenny Moore; he'd catch it. And when he wasn't catching, he was running. Moore was as good a back as there was in the league—versatile, fast, running wild in our secondary, beating every defensive back who ever tried to cover him. He did it all. I don't know if he ever threw the option pass. But I'll bet he could have if he had to.

George Shaw had a great day. Charlie had a better one. Charlie knew how to rise to the occasion. I didn't have too bad a game either. I hit Bob Schnelker with a 13-yard option pass to set up our first touchdown—a play set up by something Vince had seen on film that week. I also ran for a touchdown, 13 yards, behind a block from Conerly, of all people.

In that game, the Colts were driving for a fourth-quarter go-ahead score when Sam picked off a Shaw pass near the goal line. Summerall kicked the game-winning field goal a few minutes later, and we won it, 24–21. The locker room was a madhouse. We were pretty giddy after knocking off an undefeated team in front of the largest crowd the Giants had ever played for. "How about a moment of silence for good old Charlie?" Jack Mara said, mocking the naysayers, as Charlie stood nearby—with a cut nose and cleat marks on his left chin, maybe from his block on my TD run.

Jim Lee Howell courted the press from his leather-upholstered swivel chair—not that Jim Lee had anything to do with the game. As usual, the day belonged to Tom Landry and Vince Lombardi. Landry's defense had foiled a key Colts trick play—a fake field goal. And Lombardi, no doubt trying to one-up Weeb Ewbank's strategy, called a trick play for us—Chandler ran for a first down from punt formation in the second quarter. "The odds against making first down from punt or field-goal formation," Vince told the press afterward, with obvious glee, "are ten to one."

That day, Lombardi also explained his overall strategy to the writers—and looking back, I wish he hadn't. He explained to them that he'd wanted to run to the outside, to get away from the Colts' inside linemen. In hindsight, it's hard not to believe that the Colts didn't file that intelligence away, for use six weeks later.

Until that game, I hadn't been aware of any feud between the two franchises; the Browns were our real rivals. But to hear the Colts tell it today, they had us in their sights—both during and after that game. Today, Artie still swears that following the Summerall field goal with three minutes left, he saw us smiling and laughing on our sideline. I kind of doubt it. But Artie swears he can still see me laughing.

"You rat bastards," he says now. "You were standing on the field laughing at us."

"No we weren't," I said.

"Yeah you were. I threw a rock at you."

"A rock?"

"Well, it was clumps of dried field or something. Maybe it wasn't a rock. But you didn't even think we had a chance to get back in the game. Gino was next to me. I was so goddamned mad at you, standing over there laughing. You rat bastards."

Bad blood was brewing elsewhere, too. Johnny Sample, the Colt cornerback, claimed that Perian, in a column, wrote that Charlie had said we'd "outgutted them." Perian doesn't remember anything like that. But Artie says our quotes fired the Colts up for our final meeting.

"After that, during the rest of the season," Artie says, "we had all these clippings posted around the locker room, things the Giants had said about the Colts. Every day Weeb would go around the locker room: 'Look what they said about you!'"

**S**ix weeks had passed. But the Colts hadn't forgotten anything, and as they came down the hill from the hotel on the morning of December 28, 1958, they were riding high. This time, they had Unitas. They were much healthier than we were. To a man they thought they had the better team, and they were right.

"Honestly, I always felt we were going to win that game," their starting center, Buzz Nutter, a coal-town West Virginia man, told me. "We were a better offensive team than y'all were, and we were equal to you on defense, even though you got more publicity."

In our apartment, we just played your average bridge game. Perian's column was the furthest thing from anyone's mind, and we tried to put football aside, and everyone retired early. Hardly the stuff of glory, or high drama, but definitely the stuff of everyday people living everyday lives: workingmen, about to put in another day—a day that has stayed with us the rest of our lives.

## CHAPTER 2

# GAME DAY

The temperature was cool—nothing like the previous two Sundays, when we had to beat Cleveland first in the snow, then in subfreezing temperatures in the play-off. Actually, it was one of the warmest days of the month. That December had been the coldest December in the city in thirty years, but as I walked down the hill to the stadium at 10 o'clock, it was in the low forties. A few hours later, as the sun set and dusk rolled in, all of that would change.

I'd already started to think about game stuff—in particular, what sort of defense I'd be up against. On the runs, I was wondering if Big Daddy would bring his A game today or "just show up," as he sometimes did. If it was the A game, we'd want to forget the 47 power—our short-yardage bread-and-butter play off tackle: He could eat it alive. You never wanted to be tackled by Daddy. (To this day, I can remember the pain in my ankle from a game where Big Daddy grabbed me and wouldn't let go. I thought he was going to break it.)

Pass coverage? I had to worry about their little gnat of a cornerback, Carl Taseff. I'd always wonder, *How can Taseff cover me like that?* Taseff got an enormous amount of mileage out of that funny little body. You'd make a good move, drive to the inside, break it out, he'd still be with you, and you'd be asking yourself, "What the hell is going on here?"

The rest of the Colt secondary weren't flashy: Milt "Pops" Davis the vet, Andy Nelson the barbecue king from Alabama, Ray Brown the brain—Ray was already studying law in the mornings back in Baltimore, sowing the seeds for a postfootball career. Not a single big name among them. But they'd managed to intercept an incredible thirty-five passes that year. In twelve games. Do the math: that's three picks a game. (The following year? Forty.)

So my work would be cut out for me when I lined up at flanker. But then, my work was going to be cut out anyway. The Colts had made headlines behind Unitas that year, but, as with us, it was their defense that had made them what they were—in their case, a power of the NFL. Our guys had shut out the Browns in the play-offs to get us here, but nearly as impressive was the Colts' defensive performance that had clinched their title a month before. In the second half, they'd shut out a 49er offense that featured Hugh McIlhenny and Y. A. Tittle—in no small part because of the play of the Colts' linebackers: Don Shinnick and Leo Sanford, real pros, and Bill Pellington, the madman.

With Pellington, my strategy would be to just run to the other side of the field whenever possible. But like Big Daddy, Pellington was great at pursuit, and I had no doubt he'd end up piling on anyway at the end. Bill was deadly in a pileup—elbows, knees, insults all flying at the same time. Against Pellington, being tackled was just the start of it. In the pileup, anything could happen, from a jab to the ribs to an X-rated reference to your ancestry, your mother, you name it. Intimidation was what Pellington was after. But the way Pellington played just flat pissed me off.

Then, the Colts probably felt the same way about Sam when

*he* was piling on. "Sam was the only guy who should have had his number on the bottom of his shoes, he piled on top so many times," the Colts' Buzz Nutter told me before he died in the spring of 2008. "Sam knew where the camera was. He'd get on top of every pile so everyone would have to get out from under him. He had that number 70 pointed right where the camera could see it."

The rest of the Giants arrived by their usual routes. Cliff Livingston and Harland Svare took the D train up from the Manhattan Hotel. Andy Robustelli drove down from Stamford. Alex and his wife hired a babysitter and drove up that morning from East Brunswick, up the turnpike. Rosie and Mel crossed the George Washington Bridge. So did Bob Mischak, our backup lineman—a Newark guy, living in Union that year, just across the bridge. "As I got ready to leave to go the ballpark," Bob remembers now, "all the people where I lived were already congratulating me. Everyone was anticipating a win. So was I."

As Artie walked into the stadium, he heard a New York fireman shout, "I hope you're better than you were at Mount St. Michael's!"

That's all we needed: more motivation for Fatso.

One of the Colts went right to the locker room, dressed quickly, and then went straight to the field, before any other players and before any of the fans. Raymond Berry did not rank among the league's best because of great athletic talent—he had poor eyesight, a bad back, average speed. The man who'd dreamed of being Elroy Hirsch had honed his craft by leaving nothing to chance. He ran precise patterns. He was the last to leave the Colt practice field. And he checked out the conditions of each and every field he played on. Andy Nelson swears today that one time on the road, Ray walked

off the width of a field before a game and discovered it was too nar-
row by a foot.

So while the rest of his teammates were still back in the visitors' locker room, Raymond was out surveying every inch of the
field that morning, looking for ruts, wet spots, frozen spots, bald
spots—anything that might interfere with his almost-scientific approach to a football game.

"I went from one end of the field to the other," Raymond told
me, "because I wanted to know what kind of cleats I'd have to wear.
I noticed a couple of things. The field was dry, except for a few
frozen spots, two or three. Inside the five-yard line at each end it
was pretty hard, and there was one spot near the Giant bench, and
that was the worst.

"I was trying to figure out whether to wear shoes that had
normal-length cleats. I always carried extralong cleats for the ball
of the foot on each shoe, because I did all the cutting on the balls
of my feet, and when I saw these frozen spots, I thought I couldn't
afford to take a chance—I'd go right on my butt if I wore normal
cleats. So I wore long cleats on the ball of each foot that day. I didn't
like to wear them, as a rule, but on that day, I did."

As he stood alone in the vast emptiness of the stadium, Berry
took in every detail—the piles of dirt-colored snow, shoveled up
against the stands; wooden barriers that looked like cattle fences set
up behind the end zone at the open end of the field, to keep the
fans at bay. Ray was reassured by the attempt at added security; it
had been just a few weeks since his own home crowd had rattled
him down at Memorial Stadium. The Colts had just finished that
remarkable comeback from a twenty-point deficit against the 49ers,
clinching their first division title with a 35–27 win. But as soon
as that game ended, Berry remembers, a mob stormed the field.
"It was a crush," he told me. "It was absolutely crazy, and I can

visualize the epicenter: all these people heading for the center of the field. The noise was deafening—you could not hear yourself scream. People started falling. It was frightening. They lifted us up. I was above it all, and as I got lifted up, I was aware of people going down."

Berry told me his radar picked up on something else that morning, too, as he looked to the clear sky and savored the mild temperatures: "I noticed that it wasn't that cold, and that there wasn't any wind, and I knew we'd gotten lucky for December 28 in New York. All of that played into what we needed to win that day, because Weeb had told John that we weren't going to be able to run on the Giant defense; we were going to have to pass. So no wind, no real cold, a pretty dry field—all of that favored us going in."

Milt Davis, the Colts' veteran cornerback, had come out early, too, to test the turf. He saw that the baseball diamond was exposed, and that there were torn-up spots—and he grew worried. Milt had broken the fifth metatarsal of his right foot the week before against the Rams. After he saw the frozen spots, he figured he had to go with long cleats, too. He didn't like the idea; covering Kyle was as tough as covering Berry, and long cleats cut down on your mobility. "Kyle Rote had great quickness, in and out of cuts, and the ability to drop his weight down when he cut; he got great separation," Milt remembers. "I think Kyle was the number one receiver I ever had to cover. So I'm asking myself, How can I do this with a broken foot?"

The trouble was, wearing the cleats hurt Milt's foot. He could backpedal, he could cut, but he couldn't come forward. "I told Weeb I couldn't go," he says now. "He said, 'You have to.'"

So Milt went out for warm-ups with one tennis shoe and one cleated shoe.

●●●

**O**ur spartan locker room had carpeting, and hot and cold running water, and that was about it. It smelled like socks and laundry, and it was our sanctuary. I liked the closeness. I liked our two clubhouse guys—Pete Sheehy and Pete Previte—who took care of everything; our pads and jerseys would be in our lockers, waiting for us. Mostly, I liked that each day, Charlie would be by my side, and your buddies would be in their lockers, before and after practice. With Charlie cracking his ankles. With Katcavage checking his timetables to see what train he could catch to get home.

The only remarkable thing about our locker room was its unbelievable aura of history. When we first came over from the Polo Grounds, in 1956, one of the locker room attendants had given me Mickey Mantle's locker. Well, that's the way I remember it; Sam, of course, remembers it completely differently. Today, Sam still insists *he* had Mantle's locker. (That figures. To this day, the offense and the defense seem destined to disagree.)

I'd been acquainted with Mantle's talent for a while now, even before his pro days. Back at USC, once in spring practice, on our football field, adjacent to the baseball field, I remember that a baseball came banging into our huddle, and I distinctly recall walking around the bleachers thinking, *Who the hell hit that ball? No one could have hit that.* Someone said, "Some kid from Oklahoma named Mantle." It had carried over the fence and the track. That had to be the longest ball ever hit at USC. Now, five years later, I was dressing in his locker. Or Sam was. (Or Mantle was dressing in ours.)

We all had Yankee lockers, and considering how great the baseball team was—and how much of a second-class citizen our league seemed to be in the nation of professional sports—it's not surprising that we all remember whose pinstriped locker we occupied. "I had Berra's," Mo says now. "He kept complaining his hooks were getting bent from my equipment." Summerall remembers his locker well: it belonged to "Bullet" Bob Turley, who had won the Cy Young that year—"but as I remember," Pat says, "you still had to wash your own jock."

To be sharing the lockers of a team that routinely won world championships was a thrill, in a lot of ways—but it wasn't as if we were starstruck. From 1949 to 1956, New York baseball teams had won every major-league championship, but now things were shifting. After all, we'd won a title in '56. I'd been the league MVP that year. Before the '58 season, two of New York's baseball teams, the Giants and the Dodgers, had carpetbagged their way out west, leaving a wound that still hasn't healed. The football Giants weren't going anywhere, and everyone knew it; the Mara roots were way too deeply interwoven with the fabric of the city.

And to be completely honest, we didn't have a hell of a lot of respect for baseball players anyway. Just about every player in the NFL went to college, which wasn't always the case in baseball. We might not have learned a lot, but at least we were exposed to higher learning.

Was I awed to be in the same stadium as the Yankees? Honestly, no. All I knew each season was that we were going to be able to get into Yankee Stadium full-time when these guys got through playing, and the quicker they did, the better off we'd be, the sooner we'd be able to call the place our own.

Nothing personal. I'm sure they couldn't have cared less, either.


We did have a little extra equipment that modern dressing rooms don't carry: cigarettes and beer. The cigarettes were cartons of Marlboros, thanks to one of our biggest fans: Jack Landry, the Marlboro brands guy at Philip Morris. He'd sit on our bench during the games, and over the next few years, he'd give a lot of Giants off-season work: Huff, Lindon Crow, Chandler, Cliff Livingston, and Mo went on the road, marketing the brand. In front of the camera. Charlie would become almost as famous as a Marlboro Man as he was as a quarterback. He had the perfect face for it, kind of expressionless—a frontier guy squinting into the sun. ("The cowboy represented an antithesis—a man whose environment was simplistic and relatively pressure-free," Jack once said. "He was his own man in a world he owned." No wonder Charlie became one of the most famous Marlboro Men. Living in his own world was just fine with Charlie.)

Me, I endorsed Luckies. I had a lot of endorsements in those years, from contact lenses to orange juice to sweaters. Why not? I needed the money. But when the Surgeon General's Report came out, I stopped the cigarette ads. It's the only ad campaign I ever felt guilty about.

But back then, our whole backfield smoked. Kyle was a heavy smoker. And Webster. Alex would smoke on the bench, during games. You'd see the smoke curling out from under the hood of his cape. Heinrich, too; we were a very nervous backfield.

We had two kinds of beer in our locker room that year. Ballantine, our sponsor, gave us each a case per week. Maynard didn't drink, so he gave his case to Webster. It was probably because of the beer, Don figures, that Red helped the rookie out, sitting next to him and explaining defenses during film sessions.

We had Rheingold that season, too. Al Barry's sister had married into the family that owned Rheingold Beer—"We got a case from Rheingold to go with our Ballantine," Al recalls.

...

The Colts? They never had beer. Artie remembers drinking Nehi Orange. Buzz Nutter remembers Coke—"except when we were in Dallas, when you had to have Dr Pepper."

The Colts tell me that they felt the same affection for their place, down in Memorial Stadium. To a lot of guys who'd seen much sorrier locker rooms, it was a revelation. "We had a guy whom everybody paid ten bucks a week," Jackie Simpson, their backup defensive back, told me. "Your locker was spick-and-span. Your T-shirt was folded, your socks were there, your shoes cleaned up. When I got traded to the Steelers? They brought a big box out—all the jocks and socks were in a box. You tried to grab ones that didn't have holes in them."

As a rule, our pregame locker room scene before the warm-ups was pretty much the same week to week. Most of the time we were quiet: "We just got suited up when the time came, and went out to play" is how Alex described it. Nothing special usually, and I didn't expect anything different that day. We'd been there before. You could count on a little intensity from the handful of guys standing by the locker room door waiting impatiently for word from Coach Jim Lee "High Pockets" Howell to hit the field. You didn't want to get near Cliff Livingston, not when he had his game face on—his eyes all dilated, mouth set grimly. Katcavage would be standing by the door, champing at the bit to get out there.

The eyes of Bill Svoboda, our veteran linebacker—one of our honorary captains that day, playing in his last game after a nine-year career—would grow as big as saucers.

"He was one tough guy," Sam says now, and coming from

Sam, that's no small compliment. "He'd hit so many people, he didn't have a bone in his nose anymore. Bill was a wildman. One time, in the off-season, he couldn't get his lawn mower started. So he just picked it up and threw it into the bayou. Then he calmed down, realized what he'd done, and bought another one. He probably chucked that one, too."

My own usual pregame ritual involved no superstitions, no special routine. For one thing, I'd been doing it all since high school: pull on the equipment, lace up the shoes, grab the helmet, and go. It's second nature. I never relied on rituals to get me ready for a game. I always felt that if you have to rely on superstition, you're in trouble.

That day, as always, Johnny Johnson taped my ankles. I kept the tape to a minimum, because I didn't like it, but it was mandatory. I pulled on my shoulder pads, which were plastic, not the leather pads of old—although, down the hallway that day, the Colts' Don Joyce's *were* leather: after going against tackle Rosey Brown in the regular-season game, his pads had torn, and he'd taken them to a Baltimore shoemaker to have them sewn back together.

Then the blue jersey, and the white pants.

There was one other unspoken element that added to the silence: we were tired. If I said I was pumped up and crazy that day, I'd be lying. We'd just played the toughest season we'd ever played. For the last month, every game was a must-win: we'd had to win five straight games just to be here. That takes it out of you physically, and it takes it out of you emotionally. And speaking of physically, a lot of us were hurting. Grier had been on crutches that week after getting hit from behind on his knee in the last game. Huff had a cracked rib. Our backup guard, Buzz Guy, had chipped an ankle bone. Jack Stroud was hurting all over, after a particularly tough season for him: "I tore up my knee three times," he told an interviewer years later. "Each time, I'd get it taped up and go back and play and tear it up again. So for that game I had a bad knee, plus I had been kicked in the ribs in Detroit so that it was still tough to breathe."

Kyle always had two bad knees: "We'd tape both of them each week," Johnny Johnson recalled, just before his retirement at the age of ninety. "Kyle's knees were both pretty bad. So we'd tape both, solidly, and he was able to run pretty well."

My own knee was as good as I could expect, after getting hurt in the fourth game of the season, on October 19; after I'd caught a Heinrich pass, a Cardinal cornerback named Charlie Jackson hit me below the knee, just as I'd planted the foot to cut, and I heard something pop: stretched ligaments, which prompted a brief hospital stay. Obviously, there was no question I'd play—or that anyone else would, either.

"It was a different kind of guy who played the game then," Johnny Johnson tells me now. "We'd just try and do whatever we could to put you guys back together. We would tape up guys with a sprain or strain, do whatever we could to put them together well enough so you could go out and at least make an effort.

"In those days, there were no MRIs or scopes or anything, so you'd tape and improvise. We'd put a patch on the back of the knee, wrap it up tight, and you guys would just go out and do the best you could. Unless the ligament couldn't handle it, you'd go to the end of the year before you'd do anything about it."

With thirty-five guys on the roster, the idea was to patch the players up as quickly as possible and get them back on the field—limping or otherwise. Believe it or not, our roster was so thin that day that we didn't have a backup defensive lineman—and that would come to haunt us, in a big, big way.

In fact, we were so banged up that earlier in the week we'd

practiced down at the Armory, indoors, because the weather was so cold that the coaches didn't want us out there at the Stadium, where the cold, windy conditions could help worsen the injuries.

On other days we'd have taped up and headed out to the field an hour before the game. On the morning of the championship game, though, we veered from custom. We had a meeting to vote on championship shares. And this team meeting was one for the ages. It was also about the worst way you'd ever want to start one of the biggest days of your life. It was players-only, and it wasn't laid-back. It's hard to believe now, but we spent our last minutes together, before a championship game in our home stadium, having a heated shouting match that almost came to blows. And I would have been on the receiving end.

When I saw Ray Berry last year at a Colt dinner, he couldn't believe it when I told him about our meeting just before the game. While the Colts were pumping themselves up a hundred feet away down the hallway, Sam and I were fighting about whether first-year quarterback Jack Kemp should get a full share. The shares in question? According to the Associated Press, it was $4,718.77 for each winner and $3,111.33 for each loser. Sam's own book, written twenty years ago, says the winners got $4,674.44 and we each got $3,083.27. Seems like peanuts, right? Hardly worth fighting about? Wrong on both counts. A few grand was a huge amount in 1958. It could mean taking the summer off from work. It could mean the down payment on a house (and it did, for a lot of the men in that game). So giving a full share to a player meant everyone else's share would be diluted by more than a hundred bucks. And that was still big money. Twenty-five steaks at Toots's, for instance. A thousand subway rides. It was a sum worth fighting about, as far as I was concerned—and I was the most vocal guy in the debate, in favor of getting Jack a full share.

But this argument wasn't all about principle. Our shouting match had an underlying theme. The animosity that was always simmering just below the surface between the offense and the defense was coming to a head.

As any Giant fan knows too well, the team has never been an offensive firepower, never made its name by running up the score—or even scoring many points. In our case, it was no different. On defense we had an all-star middle linebacker who stood behind a tremendous front four. On offense, we couldn't even figure out who our starting quarterback was—Heinrich or Conerly. We'd scored the third-lowest total points in the league that season, averaged less than 20 points a game, and won our games by an average of 5 points.

We had no speed to speak of. Kyle was playing, basically, on one knee. Our fastest guy, Maynard, only returned kicks, because in our offense, a halfback had to be able to block, and Don was a skinny speed guy, period (with great hands, as the world would discover in a few years, across town in Shea Stadium, where he played with a quarterback named Joe Namath). Alex was tough, but he wasn't fast. Our other starting end, the workmanlike Schnelker, had great hands, and was faster than everyone thought he was, but he couldn't leave a defensive back in his wake, the way Lenny Moore could. I was the fastest back, and Rosey Brown, our tackle, was probably faster. But then, Rosey was the best athlete on the team.

All of which accounted, in part, for Sam's blatant disregard for anything and everything our unit had ever accomplished.

The tension between the two units obviously was magnified by the certainty that our real head coaches—Lombardi and Landry—didn't really like each other. I honestly don't think those two spoke more than three words to each other a day. Their coolness toward each other stemmed from many factors: They helmed different units, and they had a much higher profile—at least with the players, if not the media—because of the void in the head coach's office. It was like having two head coaches, and how could that ever pave the way for pleasantries? Jim Lee, the old Arkansas native, may have sat in an upholstered head coach's chair in his tiny office off the locker room, but it was an empty chair as far as we were concerned. By Howell's own account, in fact, one of his few roles was to mediate between the two assistants: "One day one of them would come in and tell me he hadn't been given enough time, and the next day the other would," Jim Lee once said. " . . . They were fussing all the time."

Then, add the factor of their two completely different personalities—the stoic, mechanical, unsmiling Landry and the volatile, grinning, exuberant Lombardi. "You could hear Vince laughing from five blocks away," Wellington once said. "You couldn't hear Landry from the next chair."

Their rift filtered all the way down to their units. "We were always separate anyway," Sam says now, when we can laugh about it—and we do, today. "We were always divided into two groups, and that's the way we got along. We had different dressing rooms at Fairfield, when we practiced up there. At the Stadium, we had to take the training room for our [the defense's] meetings. That's where we met—in the training room. But hell, we didn't need much room anyway. We had twelve guys who could play defense. Seriously. Maybe thirteen was the most we ever had. Anyway, offense was always what Wellington favored."

He was right, at least when it came to our first-round draft picks. Every first-round draft pick the Giants had between 1940 and 1959 was either a running back or a quarterback. And the numbers on our team *were* skewed. Our roster was almost two-thirds offensive players, which meant that in that endless six-game exhibition season substitutes and soon-to-be-cut rookies could play offense during blistering, meaningless warm-up games. Meanwhile, the defense had to play most of the time, in every game.

"Plus, you had Lombardi," Sam says. Another good point. Not that Landry wasn't respected by Wellington; he'd been a player-coach in the early fifties, the ultimate vote of respect. But Wellington and Lombardi had gone to college together, at the Giants' favorite university—Fordham. By some accounts, Well and Vince weren't close at Fordham, but it's hard to believe that bond wasn't impor-tant when Wellington later hired Vince away from Army.

"Our team was always divided into two groups," Sam says now, "and that's the way we got along. We were two units, and we were different. But on game day we were one."

But on *that* game day, before the game, we were definitely two.

Like all the confrontations we had in those years in the "friendly" rivalry between the offense and the defense, the confron-tation was probably going to be between me and Sam. We were the high profiles on each unit. We weren't the captains, or the lead-ers—that would have been Charlie on offense and Robustelli on defense. And Charlie and Andy would have sooner broken out into a Broadway duet than have an argument in public, or an argument of any kind.

No, this was between me and Sam. This one got personal, and it got ugly.

Jack Kemp had been the seventeenth-round draft pick of the Lions in 1953. They traded him to the Steelers—"for two Cokes, a chin strap, and an old Frank Gifford helmet," Jack says now. The Steelers cut him after the last preseason game in '58, and the Giants picked him up. He was making $100 a month, until, in an early practice, he threw a rollout pass about eighty yards—twenty yards over Maynard's head. And he happened to do it right in front of Jim Lee. "Howell said, 'Gee,' just like that," Jack remembers. (That does sound like Jim Lee.) "We did some more passing, then Lombardi came up and said, 'You got a hell of an arm, kid. We're going to sign you. How much you making?' 'I'm making a hundred.' 'How much do you need?' I say, 'Like, a thousand.' They gave me four-fifty."

Jack had been active for a few of our games that year, and that was enough for me. He was in on all the practices. He was a neighbor at the Concourse Plaza. He had been part of what got us here, and I thought he should be paid accordingly. Sam's point was also a simple one—and based upon his pure and open dislike of anything connected to the offensive team. The defense had turned in huge performances in our final three games. The old story about Sam coming off the field in games and saying to me, "Would you assholes go out and hold them for a while this time?"—it wasn't a joke. He said it. He was only half kidding, and it stung because it was at least half-true.

And here I am in the locker room, a few minutes before a championship game, defending a full share for another offensive guy—who wasn't even active that day. Hell, everyone in football knew the defense was our strength. (After our play-off game against the Browns, the Pulitzer Prize–winning columnist Red Smith had called our defense "those slightly cannibalistic characters who were simply devouring the Browns: the yeomen of the guard" who "came to glory." No one ever wrote about the offense that way.)

"Hell, Frank," Sam says now, "you wanted to vote shares to the kids sitting on the bench, for chrissake. You could afford to. You got so much of a bonus, we didn't have any left. I was making eight grand that year, man."

Some of our argument that day was probably personal. No, not probably; it *was* personal. "Jesus Christ, did I hate you," he says now, laughing. "I didn't want to hate you—I wanted to *be* like you. We were jealous of you. You did *everything*. That's why we were all jealous of you. We really were. You made all the money. You're doing all this broadcasting and TV work. Number-one draft choice. Glamour boy."

Maybe our fight was just a strange way to let off some steam. Whatever lay behind it, here I was, minutes before a championship game, ready to fight a teammate. Finally, somebody said, "Shut your mouth!"—it wasn't Sam; maybe Mo—and I got my ass out of there.

And Jack got his share.

So, less than an hour before our one o'clock start, as we piled out through the door for calisthenics and warm-ups, we weren't exactly a gung-ho, unified squad. I wasn't nervous. But on game day, the stakes were for real. Most of the time—five days a week— the walk through that dark, damp tunnel, the sound of my cleats echoing off the concrete walls, then down to the dugout, then up into the burst of sunlight, meant a practice, a workout in front of a hollow stadium where you could hear the echoes of the kidding and the whistles and Lombardi's barks bounce around the vast old park. Not that practices were easy—Vince ran a serious practice, never afraid to keep us late after the defense had gone in. So did Landry. You'd hit hard, you'd be exhausted, and you never thought about being injured in practice.

But on Sundays, the first thing you'd see was the crowd. The first thing you'd hear as you came out of the first-base dugout was the background noise of tens of thousands of voices, even more excited than you were, and the butterflies would begin. In a twelve-game schedule, every game is huge. And every Sunday could also bring that career-ending hit. I'd try to put it all out of my mind, and I usually could.

The usual pregame routine gave us a chance to get loose both physically and mentally: you'd do some stretching, run through a few plays, engage in some friendly chatter. I'd usually look up into the stands to spot a friend or two—maybe Toots.

On this day, though, as I came out for the warm-ups, things were different. For one thing, the tension between the units was still there; none of the usual banter. I also noticed something else. This time, there was an added dimension to the feel of the crowd, an unfamiliar one: a lot of them were Colt fans. Wearing a lot of blue and white. By one estimate, there were fifteen thousand of them—by another, twenty thousand. Add the Colt band, with those bass drums that never seemed to shut up, and the Colt cheer-leaders in their cowgirl outfits, and it was obvious that our opponents weren't going to be alone that afternoon. It seemed like half of Baltimore had come north, thanks to Rosenbloom's offer to pick up half the travel fare. The newspaper deliveryman strike that had muted the publicity in New York had left all those tickets available to Baltimore fans.

Of course, their fans didn't concern me. But the Colts did. Baltimore had enjoyed a mini-vacation while we'd played our play-off game against the Browns; they'd had a week off. Ewbank had given the team three or four days to rest. They'd scrimmaged that previous Saturday, then gone through their normal routine the past week.

For most of my teammates, stepping out onto the field, even that day, was still part of a routine. That's not to say they weren't feeling something special. On his ride up from Jersey, Alex hadn't said a single word to his wife. But I know I speak for Charlie and Andy and Kyle and the rest of the veterans when I say that I felt no overwhelming sensation of nerves.

Of course, for some of the rookies—even the ones who wouldn't play more than a few minutes—that first moment endures. "Even as a rookie," Bob Mischak, our lineman, told me, "during the regular season sometimes you come out for the intros, and you sense the crowd and all, you know it's there, but you're kind of oblivious—you're getting prepared in your own head. But that day? The feeling was something spectacular. The crowd was already loud. Of course, I'm sure they were well lubricated."

The guys in white were feeling their own emotions—except the even-tempered Berry: "At that point, I couldn't have told you who the president was," he told me. "I was just thinking about the game." And eying the turf. Raymond's folks were in the stands; Raymond's dad had coached him in Raymond's only other championship game, in high school in Paris, Texas.

Ray Brown's dad and stepmother had driven up from Alabama to watch him play, which just fueled the thrill of the occasion for a man who, although he would clerk for a Supreme Court justice within a few years, counts our game as one of the true highlights of his life: "As I'm warming up, I'm thinking, 'Pinch me—I'm dreaming. I'm on the field at Yankee Stadium, with all these guys who are future Hall of Famers, and I'm a rookie, and going to start?' It was just unbelievable."

Like the Giants, there were a lot of southerners on that Colt squad, too, all of them a long way from high-school fields surrounded by cotton and bayous, and they were the ones who told me of a special sensation, inside each one of them, as they took the field. The day before, they'd been working out in a big, empty, storied cavern. Now, twenty-four hours later, they were on center stage in front of more fans than any had ever played for.

"I tell ya—and remember, this comes from a guy from Louisiana, who didn't usually play before a whole lot of people," their linebacker, Leo Sanford, told me. "It's a feeling I've never had before and haven't had ever since. I recall running onto the field there in Yankee Stadium, and I guess if a guy is in athletics, that has to be the top thing he'll ever do: playing in Yankee Stadium in a championship game—with so much background, thinking of the number of great athletes who'd been there before . . . It was just an outstanding feeling."

Even some of the stars, the guys who should have been jaded, remember being thrilled at the sight of the stadium as it filled up to the rafters. Marchetti had come a long, long way from Antioch, California, from the bench of the old Dallas Texans, to his status as, arguably, the best defensive player in the game—a perennial Pro Bowler, beloved in Baltimore. And as he glanced around the stadium, scanning the wings of the upper decks, and all the bunting, he took a moment to soak it all in. "Remember, I'd played on some bad teams," Gino says now. "I played on some teams where a first down was a victory. But getting primed up for a championship game in New York? I was in heaven."

Andy Nelson, the safety from Alabama, was concentrating on his footing: "The field was in rough shape. Slick and frozen. Looked like if you got close to the sideline your feet would go out from under you. It had clearly been played on quite a bit." He was right about that. Our ragged home field had already taken the beating of a full season.

Artie's dad was there, down from the Bronx neighborhood. He was a world-famous boxing referee who'd refereed a lot of Joe

Louis's fights, and bouts Charlie and I had seen at the Garden or St. Nick's Arena—if someone could comp us some tickets. (Eight years before, when Artie's mother had leaned out from the second floor of their apartment building to shout that Artie had been drafted into the NFL, his dad had shouted up, "Those big guys will kill him!")

Typically, though, Artie had a slightly different memory of stepping onto the field that day: "It stunk in the stadium. Maybe they'd put fertilizer on it, to keep it warm. It reminded me of an exhibition game against you guys in '54, in Louisville. It was a brand-new stadium, and the only thing they'd had before that game was a circus, with elephants and horses crapping all over the field. That day, when we were on defense, your offensive line would pick up a pile of horseshit and flip it at us. 'They're throwing horseshit at us!' "

Mone of the Colts had as emotional a warm-up as Milt Davis. Back when Milt was a teenager in Los Angeles, he told me, his family put him in an orphanage. In 1958, Milt hadn't seen his father in fifteen years. As he was warming up, testing that broken foot, he heard an usher call his name.

"I remember it distinctly," Milt says now. "The sky was sun and broken clouds. I heard my name. I walked over to the usher. He told me my father was up there, on the third-base side, and I looked up about thirty rows, and there he was, waving. He was in the shade, way back up there. My daddy had never seen me play a game. He hadn't told me he was coming."

Milt waved back. When the game was over, his father was nowhere to be found. Milt never saw him again.

My own father was in the stands, too, sitting with Toots in

his mezzanine box. My father had come down from Point Barrow, Alaska, earlier in the week, where he'd been drilling oil wells, to see me play professionally for the first time in his life. During the days, he'd watched the team practice, and listened in on our interviews. On a couple of nights, I'd taken my father down to Toots's, where my friend had taken him under his arm. It had been a great week for my dad—and a great week for me. Over those few days, we'd become closer than we'd ever been before.

I'd never really known him because he was always away working. But I'd always been proud of of him, and that day, I hoped I could make him proud of me.

**N**ow came a sort of calm before the big storm, and I remember that, somehow, the scene was moving as if in slow motion. We went back into the locker room after warm-ups, and the atmosphere grew thick, serious. Jim Lee checked his watch and bellowed out in his Arkansas twang, "Twenty minutes now; let's be ready."

These were the last few minutes. Some of us liked quiet and privacy. Alex sought out Kyle, as he did every week. "I was always trying to find Rote," Alex recalls, "because sometimes I'd feel like throwing up, and Rote would tell me a joke to get me over it."

We said a prayer, of course. All the teams did. Father Dudley led the prayer—minus the robes and the cocktail condiments. Each time we prayed, I always remembered the time I went up to Father Dudley before a game and said, "Father, we're over here praying, and they're over there praying. How do you know who God favors?"

"Frank, over the years," he said to me, "I have found that God seems to bless the team with the better personnel." Made sense to me.

That didn't bode well for us. We had our share of future Hall of Famers, but man for man, you had to feel the Colts were a better team. And I wasn't alone. One man who probably knew us better than anyone agrees with me now.

"Frank, I have to tell you," Bob Sheppard told me. "On that day, I thought the Colts were the better team."

And as anyone who ever set foot in Yankee Stadium knows, that was voice of God speaking.

Lombardi wandered by my locker, to talk quietly about a pass we had been working on, just a quiet reminder for both of us to go with it early; the Colt secondary was quick and aggressive, and even though they knew we loved play action, Carl Taseff would probably play the run. Meanwhile, Landry and Huff were quietly finalizing what they'd do on third and long—a situation that would come up a lot, with less-than-hoped-for results.

As usual, Jim Lee didn't have anything to do with strategy. Even with the title on the line, it was business as usual, which meant that this day was more or less like the day when a New Jersey sportswriter asked Jim Lee about a certain play after a certain game, and Jim Lee responded, "Go talk to Vince, he runs all that stuff."

The Colts went back into the visitors' locker room for their final preparations. Milt decided to go with two tennis shoes. Don Shinnick, the linebacker, led the prayer. Lenny Moore made sure he had his miniature Bible in his thigh pad: "I already had God's word with me," says Lenny. "I had that Bible in my right thigh pad for every year of the twelve years I played. It's in my wallet right now. That same Bible. I always carry it with me."

But while the Giants were still trying to ease our pregame blowup, the Colts were listening to Weeb Ewbank, who pulled a rhetorical rabbit out of his hat and delivered a strange pep talk that was, I guess, psychologically brilliant. Little Weeb, brush-cut, frowning, stood up and faced the men who had dominated the league that year, on both offense and defense, and who'd clinched the division three-quarters of the way through the season—and told them about how they were all nothing but a bunch of castoffs.

"I think about that pep talk a lot," Don Joyce says now. "You know, there were two Weebs. There was the meek and mild-mannered guy, but sometimes he was a tough guy. And that day, he had something derogatory to say about all of us.

"Ameche: 'I didn't like you. I didn't want you. Go see if you can do it.'

"Unitas: 'Pittsburgh didn't want you. We got you for a seventy-five-cent phone call. You've had some success here, but I don't know if it's temporary or not. We'll see.' Taseff: 'We tried to trade you; they didn't want you.' Lipscomb: 'The Rams were glad to get rid of you. We got you for a hundred bucks. You've been a problem here. See if you can straighten yourself out today.' To the kicker, Myhra: 'You've been awful. You've had an awful year. You've got to put those balls through the uprights.'

"And I'll never forget what he said to me: 'Joyce, the Cards couldn't control you. They were glad you came here.'

"It kind of silenced us. I remember this quiet descending. He'd really hit us where it hurt. Nobody said anything; they just listened. I think that had something to do with us winning that game, I really do. I don't think I remember any pregame speech before that."

"To me he said, 'You were too small,'" Andy Nelson remembers. '"No one wanted you. You weren't big enough to play this game, but we gave you a chance.'

"He went right on down the line, made it sound like we were all a bunch of guys nobody wanted to have."

"That was one of the better speeches he ever made," according to Gino. "He said to me, 'Marchetti, they said you weren't going to get any better, but you did. See if you can show up today.' To Ameche, he said, 'We had to draft you because the Bears didn't take you, because they didn't want you. But we took you, so get it done.'"

Weeb even poked at himself: the Browns hadn't wanted him, and they'd let him get away to coach the Colts.

For Berry, Weeb dragged up the usual stuff: that he wasn't fast, that one of his legs was shorter than the other (which, Raymond insists to me now, it wasn't; his bad back was chronically out of line, prompting him to put a lift in one shoe). But Raymond wasn't listening: "Me, I was a guy who wasn't paying attention to coaches talking before any game. My mind was in another world. I'd heard too many comments and speeches by then, and I was only motivated twice by speeches in my lifetime, and those had happened a long time before: Bully Gilstrap at Schreiner University in Kerrville, Texas, and Rusty Russell at SMU. So maybe what Weeb said had a positive effect on a lot of them, but it wasn't my bag."

To this day, I can't ever recall a coach saying anything that fired me up. But almost to a man, the Colts will tell you now that that talk may have made a huge difference. Whatever communal fire needed to be lit, the little man had lit it.

Artie, of course, has his own version of that talk. Artie insists that he wasn't even in the locker room: "I never heard the speech. I was in the bathroom throwing up.

"I swear to God. Our kicker, Bert Rechichar, was in there with me. Weeb wasn't going to let him play. Bert said, 'I'll get in that goddamned game.' Weeb didn't like him."

As usual, Artie was half-right: Weeb didn't like Rechichar, but today Bert insists he was there, and that he recalls vividly what Weeb said at the very end: "He closed the whole thing out, after chewing everyone's ass, by saying, 'Remember this: If you want to do anything, you got to do it in New York.' Nothing else needed to be said."

U p in the press box, the announcers and reporters were settling into their cramped, cold perches. "I was right about the fifty," Dave Anderson, who would later win a Pulitzer for his column writing in the *Times*, told me. "I was doing sidebars for the *Journal-American* that season, but I wasn't writing that day, because of the strike. I just wanted to be at the game. Where else would you be?

"To get to the press box, you had to walk up a ramp from a mezzanine box, and you'd walk down into it. I think it was enclosed in plastic that day. What I remember best about that press box was Wellington up on the roof during games, taking Polaroids of the other team's defense, and putting them in a sock weighted with something like a golf ball. We saw these things flying down. We didn't have the heart to tell him no one looked at them."

In the radio booth, getting ready for their national telecast on the GE network, were Joe Boland—the voice of Notre Dame and, of all teams, the Chicago Cardinals—and his partner, Bill McColgan. Their call went coast to coast—sponsored, of course, by Marlboro.

On another mike, Bob Wolff was getting ready to call the game for a broadcast syndicated by National Bohemian Beer. "That press box was cramped," Bob told me. "You couldn't walk back and forth. I had all my notes from the Baltimore papers, and they were obviously playing it up big: If a guy had the sniffles, would it turn into pneumonia? Baltimore was all over it."

Sheppard prepared for his pregame introductions. He was in his third year with the Giants—his third of fifty. He'd come a long way, and quickly, from his first pro bono pro-football call a few years earlier at an exhibition game of the old Brooklyn Dodgers of the All-America Football Conference.

On the wall of Bob's home in Long Island today hangs a framed print of the *Daily News* cartoonist Bill Gallo's cartoon citing Gallo's five favorite moments in the Stadium: three Yankee moments—Larsen's perfect game in '56, the year we went to the Stadium; Maris's 61 in '61; and Reggie's three home runs in a World Series game in '77—and two Giant moments—Summerall's kick to beat Cleveland in the last regular-season game that year, and this game. But Bob can't hide his real priorities, even today. In his backyard grow four rosebushes, named for our front four that day: Andy, Rosie, Mo, and Kat. Like I said, the offense never got much respect.

The day of the game, Sheppard was wearing the special stadium boots his wife, Mary, had given him.

"The old football press box hung down from the mezzanine, above third base, and it was all steel," he recalls. "That press box was a horrible place. I'd come home one night earlier that season, and my feet were frozen. So my wife Mary bought me some stadium boots. It was cold that day—clear, but cold."

Then, finally—and for many of us, the highlight of so many Sundays—the world-famous introductions. If you couldn't get excited by the sound of Bob Sheppard introducing you in Yankee Stadium, you had to be dead. Sometimes, in the dugout, we'd imitate his call of our names before he did the actual calling. But not that day.

"When you came out of that dugout," Sam says now, "and Bob said, in that deep, drawn-out baritone, 'Ladies and gentlemen, number 70, Sam Huff,' you'd run out onto that goddamned field, and you were ready to play. That was inspiration."

That sentiment is still shared by any athlete lucky enough to hear Bob announce his name. Before the Yankees-Padres World Series of 1998, when the great hitter Tony Gwynn was asked what he was looking forward to, his answer was "I'm waiting to hear Bob Sheppard say my name."

The Colts took the field first, all in white—with the Colt band flanking them in a gauntlet as the team ran out of the visitors' dugout, the bandleader thrusting his baton rhythmically into the air.

Finally, and fittingly, Bob introduced our defense.

"What I remember most at the start of the game," Bob says now, "was the crowd. The Stadium was full. They were standing behind the seats; they were standing on boxes, filling the bleachers."

Andy Nelson remembers the sound of the crowd, just before kickoff: "It was like a buzz, like you're inside a beehive."

It wasn't a sellout. We'd sold 22,500 tickets in the twenty-four hours after our play-off win, but there were 5,000 empty seats, apparently. Somewhere. I couldn't see them.

The two coaches made for an interesting study in contrasts as they met with referee Ron Gibbs to go over the ground rules: for the Colts, the squat Ewbank, like a well-dressed bulldog, in a fedora and a light-colored coat, looking ready for a football game, clutching a couple of pieces of paper. I found out later that one of those sheets held his thoughts on what it would take to beat us. Two sentences said it all: "One of our keys to winning this week will be predicated on how well we pass-protect, pass the ball, and how well we catch it. Run good patterns—study your opponent— make him wrong."

How accurate it was. And how simple.

Representing our side? Tall Jim Lee, in a white shirt, a thin, dark tie, long black topcoat, and black fedora. He looked a little like an undertaker who had his pants pulled up too high. He was also clutching some paper. I doubt it was a game plan—the game plan was locked in the heads of our two real coaches, Vince Lombardi and Tom Landry. Maybe it was a program.

Then the captains met with Gibbs at midfield—Marchetti for the Colts, Kyle and Svoboda for us. The lights were already on, making for a strange effect—daylight in the sky, but lights bouncing off the helmets, like in a night game.

We won the toss. Kyle chose to receive the ball.

In the radio booth, Boland set the stage: *"They've got a lovely day for it. It's a great tribute to pro football that seventy thousand fans will show today, with the city barren of the normal means of communication and newspapers. Radio and TV have done a great job . . . It seems that New York is one big village today."*

The game was broadcast nationally on NBC. Chris Schenkel, our announcer, and Chuck Thompson, the Colt announcer, shared the booth.

The size of the audience? By the end of the game, 45 million people were watching us, in 11 million households: a larger audience, by far, than any of the top-rated shows on television that year, and infinitely larger than any audience for a pro football game, ever since the first championship game was televised nationally in 1951.

The Wayne High School band and the Colt band serenaded us with a noncelebrity version of the national anthem—heavy on the bass drums.

Bert Rechichar put the ball on the tee. Maynard and Phil King, our number one draft pick from Vanderbilt, waited at the goal line.

At one o'clock, Eastern Standard Time, Ron Gibbs blew his whistle. Bert Rechichar took five steps, booted the ball, and put it in the back of the end zone.

Maynard took a knee, and we were finally under way.

As I trotted onto the field, my instincts took over. I just felt ready.

## CHAPTER 3

# FIRST QUARTER

One of the commentators in an NFL documentary about the 1958 championship game likened those first few minutes to a title fight between heavyweights feeling each other out in the early rounds. I'd liken us to a couple of lightweights who looked as if they'd never been in a ring. Yes, we made history that day: we played the worst first quarter in the annals of championship football, before or since. It was ragged, it was chaotic, and it was downright ugly. The major metropolitan area could feel fortunate that those first fifteen minutes were blacked out. The only difference between the offensive play in the first few series of this game and an August preseason game in Louisville or Portland was the location. At the start, the most legendary stadium in the land was treated to some of the most forgettable football every played.

The climate didn't have anything to do with it, and we couldn't blame the mistakes on the hype—there weren't any newspapers being delivered in New York, and, outside of Baltimore, this game, like all NFL championship games before it, had garnered little national attention. (*The New Yorker* didn't list it under the week's sports events, but then, we probably didn't have a lot of fans who read the *The New Yorker*.)

It wasn't nerves, either. The Colts were playing in a championship game for the first time in the team's short history, but they were a confident team full of veterans, and they'd rolled through the NFL's Western Division. Besides: I don't think Johnny Unitas ever experienced a nervous moment in his life.

As for our guys, we had no reason to be nervous. Two years earlier, when we might have had reason to be rattled, we'd broken out of the gate in our first title game in eighteen years—and our first title game in Yankee Stadium—and rolled to a 47–7 victory over the Chicago Bears. Our key players had been here before.

But we stumbled all over the place at the start of this one, and much of the reason, to my way of thinking, was that we had the wrong guy at quarterback. We began the first series of the game of our lives with our second-string quarterback. You read that right: our starting quarterback was Don Heinrich. Now don't get me wrong: I loved Don Heinrich, as a friend. We welcomed him into our inner circle. He was a drinking buddy. He even played quarterback pretty well, setting all kinds of records at the University of Washington before coming to the Giants in 1954. But Don Heinrich was no Charlie Conerly.

So on the first series, instead of leaning in to hear the Mississippi drawl of my old big-eared buddy, it was Heinrich calling—to my surprise—three passing plays. We had worked, of course, on the pass during the week, with the idea of getting away from our traditional run-heavy tendencies. The strategy sure didn't fool Marchetti. Not for nothing did a rival coach once call him the single greatest player in the NFL. On the first play, a flare pass to Alex out on the right side, Marchetti blew past Frank Youso's block, blew past Mel Triplett's attempted pickup, and batted down Heinrich's pass as if he were swatting a fly. On second down, we called a screen to Alex, and it looked like a great call—until Marchetti got into Don's face. Heinrich had to float a balloon over Marchetti's upstretched arms, and Alex was held to seven yards.

As a chant of "G-I-A-N-T-S" reverberated throughout the stands, the Colts called an unexpected timeout; my guess is they were confused that we'd come out throwing. On third and three, I was hoping to get the call on a sweep, but Don, with orders from Lombardi, stayed with the pass, a square-out to Kyle: hurried, high, and incomplete.

The punting team came on, and we slumped off the field. We'd set the tone on our first series, and it was in a distinctly minor key. No, you can't lay our three-and-out all at Don's feet. But teams just play better for a man they believe in. The opening series did nothing to boost our confidence.

A lot of theories have been floated about key moments of strategy in this game. But I have yet to hear anyone point out the obvious: that the Giants, as we had all season, began the game with the wrong quarterback.

I found the whole Heinrich-Conerly system, which called for Don to start a game while Charlie watched from the bench so that he and Vince could get a look at our opponent's defensive schemes, to be just downright weird. To start with, the sidelines are the worst seat in the house. You can't see *anything* from the sidelines. And if Charlie was on the sidelines, he was like anyone on the sidelines: struggling to get a view of what was happening. This strange system had never been used before on a good football team, as far as I knew, and it's never been used since. But we'd been starting Don all season. In fact, we'd been starting Don for three years. A story in a game program against the Steelers that year gave the front-office version of this peculiar arrangement: "Don reached star status as a quarterback in 1955 after a year of apprenticeship. He and Charlie Conerly now give the Giants a one-two punch that keeps the attack moving in high gear. Don's particular genius is as a field general who has the knack of spotting and exploiting enemy flaws. For this reason he generally starts."

Well, for one thing, Don never reached star status, and certainly not in 1955, when we won all of six games and his completion percentage was under 50 percent, with two TD passes. Hell, *I* threw two TD passes that year, from the option (they were two of my only three completions). In our championship year of '56, Don started all twelve games—with a completion percentage of 40 percent. Charlie replaced him in every game, as well as the play-off game against Cleveland.

Yes, Don had brains—he would later coach for four teams—but if he was so adept at spotting and exploiting enemy flaws, how come we had to replace him in every game, as early as the first quarter? While I always heard that the two-quarterback idea was Vince's, this thing had Jim Lee Howell's fingerprints all over it; in some games, the pattern had no rhyme or reason. Sometimes Don would play a quarter, sometimes longer. For example, in our third game of the season, they'd started Heinrich, brought in Charlie, who threw an interception, then yanked Charlie for Heinrich again, then brought Charlie back in again in the third quarter—and he threw another interception. That's just crazy. It didn't look like a coherent plan; it looked like we were making it up as we went along, and that wasn't Vince Lombardi–style coaching. During the week, Charlie would practice primarily with the first string. We'd do an hour of practice with the offense, and Don would come in for maybe the last twenty minutes of it. And yet he would start. And Charlie would then get most of the playing time.

"Charlie couldn't understand it," Perian told me when I asked her if *she* had a clue as to why our coaches started Heinrich, and whether he ever talked about it. "Do you suppose it was in Don's contract that he got to play a little?" The arrangement still ticks her off after all these years, because, in all the records of all those great games, Don is listed as the Giants' starting quarterback. "But Roach just went with the flow. He didn't complain; he always did what they wanted him to. But it seemed silly to me at the time, and it seems sillier now."

I don't think the Maras ever put incentives into a contract. I never asked Vince about the quarterback system. We were good friends, but back then, no one questioned a coach's strategy, even Jim Lee Howell's. One has to think that this was all Jim Lee. Had it been Lombardi, why didn't Vince start Lamar McHan and Zeke Bratkowski when he got to Green Bay, and let Bart Starr watch the first quarter from the sidelines?

The Colts took over at the 30—and came out determined to one-up us in ineptitude. If we'd tried to cross them up by passing, Weeb tried to trick us: he had his guys come out in the weirdest formation we'd ever seen, with the entire Colt offensive line, except for one lineman, lined up to the left of their center, Buzz Nutter.

Nutter later confirmed to me that Weeb had called a trick play, hoping to run Lenny Moore wide to the left, from his right halfback position, behind a wave of blockers, hoping to break Lenny on a long run. I guess it would look good on a blackboard. On the field, everything that could have gone wrong for them did. It didn't fool our defense. We just thought it was dumb.

"You were in your defensive huddle," Buzz told me, "and we thought we'd catch you by surprise. The trouble is, the damned official wouldn't get off the ball. By the time we got him off the ball, you guys got it together."

But after watching the tapes dozens of times, I've figured out what actually happened: the Colts had ten men on the field—a screwup, pure and simple. By the time Lenny took the handoff, with L. G. Dupre and Alan Ameche blocking for him, the whole right side of our defense had played it perfectly. Lenny kept going outside, looking for room, and our corner on that side, Carl Karilivacz, came in to nail Moore for a 2-yard loss. Too bad they didn't stick with that formation all day; eleven against ten usually wins. Looking back, it's also too bad they didn't let Weeb keep sending in the plays.

Things grew uglier. After an Ameche trap for six, Johnny faded back on third down, facing a heavy rush; Landry had Cliff and Harland blitzing from their outside linebacker positions. Unitas stepped up into the pocket, tucked the ball in, and began to run. Johnny was always extraordinarily good at reading the rush. From a fan's point of view, you can't see the pressure as we see it. Actually, the good ones *don't* see it; they *feel* the pressure, and *hear* it—the sounds of pad on pad, cleats coming closer, tearing up the turf.

But the next thing Johnny felt was Livingston laying him out. Johnny coughed up the ball. Our tough little safety, Jimmy Patton, recovered.

Now we had the ball back on the Colts' 37—a huge break, and a great time for us to make a statement. On second down and eight, Heinrich called for a draw to Triplett, and it might have worked— if Heinrich hadn't bobbled the snap from Ray Wietecha. Don was cool enough to pick the ball up on this play, but then made his second mistake, something Charlie never would have done: he tried to salvage the play by handing off to Mel, who had no clue what Don was trying to do.

And now, here in the middle of a botched handoff, Artie swooped in, to wrap up both of them and force *another* fumble: the second fumble on the same play. Gino fell on it. Colt ball. The whole play looked like a seventh-grade fire drill. Artie may have looked like the overweight captain of a bowling league, but he was quick beyond belief. Beneath those layers of flesh was a really good athlete, schooled as a kid on the handball courts of the Bronx.

Mel couldn't be faulted for the fumble. He had a very quick first step, and once Mel got going, he didn't make too many turns. The only way Mel knew how to run was straight forward, and on his first carry of the day, I don't blame him for being eager, because in our last game, the play-off against the Browns, Mel had gotten kicked out of the game for getting into a polite swinging match with a guy named Don Colo.

That's kind of the way Mel lived his life: straightforward, no questions asked.

**M**el Triplett is not a name you hear a lot anymore—no surprise, considering he played with Webster, Charlie, Rote, and me. But Mel was our second-leading rusher that season, two yards short of my 468 yards, and he'd been the offensive star of our '56 championship game.

"Mel? Mel was down-to-earth, laughing and grinning and having a baby every year," our backup lineman M. L. Brackett told me, from his home in Alabama. (For the record, Mel had twelve kids.) Grier sizes up his roommate more succinctly, with that distinctive Rosie laugh: "Mel Triplett was a trip."

Born in Indianola, Mississippi, Mel was so prodigious a talent that as an Ohio high-school running back he received more than twenty scholarship offers for college. He chose to stay close to home, and went to the University of Toledo. We'd picked him up three years before—the first black running back for the Giants. We called him "Choo-Choo," too, because he always made this funny sound when he was running—sort of puffing, like a train. Come to think of it, that made sense. He ran as if he were on a track, banging into anyone—the opposition, his teammates—who got in his way. (Huff once described Mel's 17-yard TD run in the '56 game thusly: "With his head down he went straight over an official and into the end zone.") When Mel was in the backfield, the rest of us were always very alert.

Mel was very emotional about his play, very focused. "He used to say, 'If you need three yards, give me the ball, get out of the way, and don't get run over,'" Grier recalls. Rosie knew Mel better than anyone else. They were roommates. Rosie did his best to keep tabs on Mel, not always successfully; one night Mel disappeared, and came back to their room, real late—and talking about things that Rosie had never heard Mel talk about. Radical talk about relations between the races—"hate talk," as Rosie recalls it. Before too long, Grier realized that someone had taken Mel to a Black Muslim meeting and tried to convert him. By the next day, Rosie had unconverted his roommate.

I'll say one thing for Mel: he was his own man. Triplett cared as little about the coaches as he did about running over his teammates. I'll never forget the film session after a game where Triplett had missed a block. Lombardi, as he loved to do when you made a mistake, kept running the tape back and forth, back and forth, ragging on Mel.

Suddenly, a quiet voice emerged from the back of the room. It was Mel's.

"Run that again," he said, "and I'll cut you."

Vince, without a murmur, moved on to the next play.

We tended to give Mel his space.

**N**ow, in this sloppy seesaw early-game duel, the Colts again had great field position. And again, the immortal Mr. Unitas gave it right back again. No wonder no one remembers the first quarter of this game. I'm surprised the NFL hasn't deleted it from the records. Anyone who played that day has.

This time, our defense had something to do with the third turnover in four series. On third and five, Johnny faded back, with plenty of protection, looked downfield to his left for Berry on a simple turn-in, cocked his arm, and threw the ball right into Carl Karilivacz's hands. They'd obviously seen on film from our earlier game in November that Carl was going to play way off Raymond— which, unfortunately, for the rest of the day, he did. But on this one, Carl was all over it.

Carl had come over in that year from the Lions, where he'd played for two championship teams and had played the Colts twice each season. And he was well aware of what they liked to do with Berry working one-on-one with an isolated cornerback.

"We'd gone head to head against each other for three years," Berry told me. "So this time, on that first throw, he gambled and came in front of me to intercept the hook. But he didn't do it again. In our game against you guys earlier that year, he was crowding me, and we ran right by him on one play, picked up sixty or seventy. Maybe that's why he stayed off the rest of the day. After that one gamble, he didn't do it again."

Landry hated gambling on defense anyway. Tom didn't want any heroes. I wouldn't be surprised if he chewed out Carl after that pick. Landry didn't care how many interceptions you got, if you got them breaking the coverage. I should know. For my first two years, I played defense more than offense, which meant I was playing with Landry, who was even then a player-coach. So I knew how rigid, strict, and unyielding he was as a coach.

Actually, in one game against the Redskins, I made an interception and lateraled the ball to Tom, who ran it in for a touchdown. On the following Tuesday, we watched the film.

"Gifford, was that the coverage?"

"I know, Tom, but they were in a Brown right, L-split," I started to explain, "and—"

"There are no 'buts.'"

"But what if—"

"There are no 'what-ifs.'" If you didn't play the defense Tom's way, end of conversation.

"He had a computer mind," is how Huff remembers Landry. "He studied the opposition's offensive frequencies in various situations, and he taught them, and you studied them. He'd always say, 'You have to believe. You gotta believe. I'll put you in position to make the play, trust me.' If you weren't in the position, and making the moves he'd given you, he'd give you 'The Look.' He didn't have to say anything; you could read his mind, and what he was saying was 'You dumb-ass.'"

Again, we had the ball back, for our third series, starting at our own 45. Sooner or later, you had to figure, something would give. We still hadn't gotten a first down. And even though I was our leading receiver and rusher, I still hadn't touched the ball. That wasn't too surprising; Vince knew they'd be keying on me early on.

Unfortunately, we still had Heinrich behind the center. When I finally got the ball, on our patented 48 sweep, a quick toss around left end, Mel missed a block, and no one accounted for linebacker Don Shinnick, who nailed me for a loss. On second down, Big Daddy shed Al Barry's block and nailed Mel at the line. Daddy was just getting started.

About then the Colts started using an overbalanced 4–3, putting Artie right on Ray Wietecha, our center, which put the Colts, unexpectedly, into an odd-man line. They'd also made a personnel change: their outside right linebacker, Leo Sanford, had injured a knee, and Steve Myhra, their kicker, came in to play linebacker. I figured we could exploit that, and eventually, we would.

On third down and long, with Marchetti pursuing on every play, Don's checkoff to Mel got six, and the punting team had to come back. At that point, they were getting more work than we were. But the most important thing that happened in that series didn't happen on the field. It happened behind the bench, as Joe Boland was quick to point out to his radio audience: "*The veteran Charlie Conerly starts to loosen up in back of the Giant bench, right down in front of our broadcasting booth.*"

It was about time. The totals for Heinrich's day? Three three-and-outs. Two short completions. One or two fumbles, depending on who gets the fault for the botched handoff.

"With the two best defenses in the NFL," Raymond Berry says now, "you wouldn't expect an offensive juggernaut." Raymond is being generous. Their defensive line was beating up on our guys, big-time. And they seem to have scouted us very well.

What we didn't know was that during the previous week, Colts owner Carroll Rosenbloom had dispatched one of his scouts, Bob Shaw, to sneak into the Stadium and spy on a practice. As the story goes, Rosenbloom told Shaw that if he wasn't caught on his spying mission, he'd have a job for life. Apparently, Rosenbloom wanted to win that game badly—for a lot of reasons.

Supposedly Shaw reported that we didn't appear to be working on anything new. But it didn't take a rocket scientist to figure that out. We hardly ever did anything different on offense, and never on defense. In fact, we hadn't changed anything since the regular-season game in November when we'd beaten them. They didn't need Shaw. They just needed some film from our first game.

Spying has always been part of the game of pro football. When Bill Belichick and the Patriots were heavily fined for videotaping the Jets' coaches during a game to try and decipher their signals, Belichick's desire to gain an advantage represented nothing new—just the latest version of a practice that's gone on since the game began. It was certainly part of the Colts' history. According to Ernie Accorsi, a bottomless source of Colt lore, Weeb was as paranoid as they come. Memorial Stadium's field offered a view of several of the homes that surrounded it, beyond the open end: middle-class houses, a true neighborhood. To Ewbank, apparently, every one of those innocent, happy homes was the site of a potential telescopic espionage episode.

"When Weeb left [the legendary Cleveland head coach] Paul Brown's staff, and the Colts were going to play the Browns the first time in Baltimore, Weeb sent Fred Shubach, the equipment guy, to check out all those white houses with a view of the stadium to see if they were spying," Ernie recalled over a lunch in midtown Manhattan, several months after he'd departed his position as the Giants' general manager. He had plenty of time for stories, and I had plenty of time to listen; and as a veteran of both teams' front offices, Ernie has some pretty good tales to tell. "Shubach starts knocking on doors in this working-class neighborhood, asking, 'Excuse me, do you mind if I look upstairs?'"

As Weeb had come to the Colts from Paul's staff, he did everything the Paul Brown way—and Brown's way invariably involved trying to find any extra advantage. Paul's innovations went beyond the playing field; he was a pioneer in watching film—and a pioneer in football technology. Sam reminded me that the Giants were well acquainted with the technology part of Brown's playbook firsthand: "Remember Gene Filipski?"

How could I forget Gene? He'd been released a few weeks before we were going to play the Browns one year, and we claimed him, to see what we could learn about the Browns. And Gene told us that Paul Brown was using a radio to get signals into his quarterback Otto Graham (decades before that technology became mainstream). He also told us that Paul, being so meticulous and proper, had registered the frequency with the FCC. So in a simple stroke of counterespionage, we got our own radio and hooked it up to their frequency, and gave Filipski some earphones, standing next to Landry. He would interpret the plays, and we would flash the call into Sam. By the end of the first half, the Browns had zero yards on offense.

Unfortunately for us, something in the radio system broke. They went back to their unique system of calling plays by messenger, shuttling players in and out.

So Weeb was pretty well trained in the art of football espionage. Or, as Artie puts it now, "If they'd made Weeb and Paul Brown into spies, the United States would have ruled the world."

Come to think of it, before they renovated Yankee Stadium, a lot of our own field was in full view of all sorts of folks: subway riders, where the platform gave a good view of part of the field; denizens of the courthouse; residents in the apartment buildings. But I don't remember Jim Lee worrying about any spies. Maybe it was too many apartments to worry about.

So nothing has changed in the spying department. The Patriots were just following in a grand tradition. Something else hasn't changed, either, as far as football players' priorities are concerned. Those Patriot videotapes in Spygate didn't just film opposing coaches, I've been told; in the time-outs, they had their cameras on the cheerleaders.

O ur high-school-scrimmage level of play couldn't last for long. And it didn't. The Colts and Unitas took over on the 15. And Johnny U began to look like Johnny U.

I don't know if the next play was Johnny's call. I do know that Lenny Moore told me that he thought he could handle our cornerback, Lindon Crow, that day. And I know that, on this play, Moore was lined up split so far to the right he was practically standing on our bench. With that split in our defense, it meant man-to-man coverage by Crow.

Johnny faded back on first and, with lots of time, looked around, and looked around again. We had absolutely no pressure—particularly from Grier, who was hurting far more than any of us knew. On that play, he took a block from Alex Sandusky—and couldn't even get off the line of scrimmage. That season, the Giants had as good a front four as anyone in the league, but because of Big Ro's knee injury that day, it turned out we were playing with a front three.

Johnny fired a bomb to Lenny streaking down the right sideline, Crow right on his shoulder, step for step. Johnny underthrew Moore just a little, but Lenny, as only Lenny could do, slowed, waited, and, with Crow's hands in his face, pulled the ball in over his shoulder at our 40, leaving Lindon sprawled on the turf. Moore broke it back in and took off. Jimmy Patton saved the touchdown, but Lenny made it to the 25. The play had covered sixty yards. Incredibly, it was the initial first down of the game—seven minutes into the first quarter.

"He was one of the fastest guys I ever had to cover," Lindon told me. "I didn't want to play too tight, because he might outrun me. I was right on him on that play, but that golden arm swung that thing over the top, down on the outside. It was pretty hard to stop."

There was nothing else Lindon could have done. Crow was all over Moore, all day. History hasn't been kind to Lindon. I don't think I've ever seen a cornerback play a better game. Covering Lenny without a good pass rush, man-to-man, was impossible.

When Moore first arrived on the team, Johnny wouldn't throw much to Lenny—and wouldn't tell him why. "At the beginning of my Colt career, I was always just, 'Finish practice, and hit the locker room,'" Lenny told me. "Then one day Raymond came to me and said, 'Lenny, we need to get you a little bit more involved in the offense.' I thought, *What's he talking about? Johnny calls the plays.* But Raymond says, 'Listen to me now: You don't stay out after practice and work enough with Johnny on timing. Johnny's not going to throw to you because he doesn't have the confidence in you yet. You have to work with him.'

"So I did. And after that, Johnny started asking me, 'What do you have? What do you think you can do?' That day, I'd told him I could do whatever I wanted to do to with Crow. I could go deep, go in, go out, whatever."

On the next series, from our 25, after two running plays gained just four yards, Johnny took too much time changing the play at the line, then received the snap and was scrambling to his left when Ron Gibbs called a late whistle, stopping the play: too much time. As Unitas slowed down, Kat was still in hot pursuit of him, and the Colt center, Nutter, always looking for someone to hit, pursued, and laid a hit on Kat from behind. Kat wheeled around, and the two had to be separated. As I watched their skirmish, I was glad to see some emotion. It was easy to understand why tempers were fraying: both sides were getting frustrated.

And it was all legit, from where I stood. Nutter had done the right thing; you've got to protect your quarterback, especially with Kat chasing him. Today they'd say that Jim Katcavage "has a good motor." Back then, we just knew him as a guy who played football like a man possessed. "Kat did not know what 'slow up' meant" is the way Sam puts it. He had one speed, all the time. He was always in a hurry—to catch a train, to get on the field, to get off the field, to hit the quarterback.

"I remember one practice when we were getting ready to play the Bears in the championship a few years after that," Sam told me. "Katcavage blew through and hit Y. A. Tittle, our own quarterback. *Drilled* him. I said, 'Why the hell did you hit Y. A.?' Kat said, 'I've been fighting that tackle on every play. What did you expect me to do when I finally got there?'"

They didn't call Nutter for a late hit, of course. They didn't call much of anything compared to the way the quarterback is protected today. Things have changed dramatically; if someone lays a late or dirty hit on you today, the zebras are all over it. Most of the time they get it right. The rules may have even swung too far the other way. But back then, some guys got away with playing way over the edge. You got used to it. You didn't like it—especially when Pellington nailed you late, then pushed you into the dirt and uttered something about your mother—but you lived with it.

On third down, Unitas threw a quick pass in the flat to Moore. Moore liked that: a quick little flare, and let Lenny do the rest. But Livingston was there and collared Lenny after a 2-yard gain.

That was Cliff: he wasn't big, but with Harland on the other side, we had two of the fastest outside linebackers in the game.

That series had represented the first tough test of our defense, and they'd come through. The Colts had a chance to finally break the ice, with a field goal from 31 yards: a chip shot today, but definitely a reach for Steve Myhra, who had limited range. Actually, Steve had no range; he'd missed three extra points that year, as well as six of his ten field-goal attempts. Not surprisingly, Steve missed to the left. Also not surprisingly, considering how sloppily we were playing, we jumped offsides. We seemed determined to hand it to them.

Myhra got another shot from the 26. But this time, his kick never passed the line of scrimmage. Sam blew in, untouched, and blocked it—just swatted it out of the air. The stadium erupted in a roar.

As Modzelewski remembers it, Donovan was in there, blocking on the Colts' "big-butt" team, but Mo handled him, allowing Huff to blow right through.

Nutter, the snapper, who was still pissed about it when I asked about that play, remembers that the Colt line missed an assignment. Guard Alex Sandusky blocked out, instead of in: "*Christ*, man," Buzz fumed, as if it had happened yesterday. "The guard was responsible for protecting to the center. He turned out, and, shit, nobody touched Sam."

The real question, as far as I'm concerned, was why Myhra was kicking at all. Bert Rechichar, their other kicker, was better, at least as I remembered it, and I should have: When we both played in the College All-Star game after our senior years, I'd done all the kicking for USC, and I figured I'd do it again. Bert, from Tennessee, did it instead.

So what was Myhra doing kicking? Because Weeb didn't like Bert. Actually, according to most of the Colts, Weeb didn't like *either* of them; he just disliked Myhra less—even though Rechichar had been one of Weeb's stars, going to the Pro Bowl the previous three years as a safety. Bert wasn't starting in this game, though. All Bert was doing was kicking off, and muttering under his breath on the sideline.

"Weeb used to say to him, 'Bert, you can't possibly do all the things that people call me up and tell me you're doing, because there's only twenty-four hours in a day," Nutter told me. "Shit, Bert was in them bars all night long. He was a good football player, but Weeb wouldn't even use him as a defensive back. Weeb was like that."

Today, Bert reluctantly confirms his reputation: "Weeb . . . accused me of associating with undesirables, like I was riding around with a guy in a Caddie who was a numbers taker or something. He also figured that Myhra had a higher elevation at the start of the ball. That was bullshit. That was a real joke. But what the hell can you do with Weeb? He was the head man."

It's funny how, in any sport, but especially football, one play can shift the momentum so drastically. There's no way to quantify it. You can never reduce sports to its numbers.

If Myhra had made the second field goal, after we'd committed the penalty, maybe everything would have been different. We were a tired football team, from our stretch drive and play-off game, and we might have just folded and finished out the season. Instead, as we trotted back onto the field, we were a different team—and more important, we had Charlie with us. Even hearing his familiar, slow drawl in the huddle, on third and one from our own 31, seemed to make a difference: "Brown right, L-split, 48 pitchout, on three . . . *break*."

As we broke the huddle, I looked at our big left tackle, Rosey Brown, and said, "Okay, Ro"—that was it. Rosey knew, as I did, that we had to make something happen. Up to this point, our running game had gone nowhere: four runs for zero yards. But Rosey and I made a living sweeping left, with either the 48 sweep or the 48 option, where, if I pulled up to throw the option, he'd pass-block for me. On the option, I had the choice of passing it or pulling it down to run, and Rosey could read the coverage as well as I could. He always knew whether I was going to pass or run, usually before I did.

Rosey Brown was the best all-around football player on our team. I think Rosey could beat me in a 40. We had a couple of goes at it in practices. I pretended I wasn't even trying. I would beat him off the mark—a physics thing, I guess; mass, weight, acceleration, or something like that—but Rosey was closing in on me at 40. Truth is, had we gone 50, it would have been Rosey by a head, and if we'd gone 100, Rosey would have pulled away. (But how many times in your career do you run 100? Or 50? At least, that's how I could justify the embarrassment of losing a sprint to a lineman.)

This time, thanks to Rosey, the sweep went as planned—and then some. Jack Stroud pulled from the right side, cutting down on his guy. Rote made a terrific block on Shinnick, the outside linebacker; Kyle was known for spectacular catches, but people underestimated his blocking ability.

Then, there came Rosey in front of me. He laid a block on the cornerback and steered the guy right into the safety: two for one. Now there was nothing but daylight. I cut inside, and it was wide open.

When you try and remember what it's like to make a run that long, you can't. It all happens too fast. In the stands, fans are wishing you'd speed it up, but down there, everything is happening in hyperspeed, all flashes and blurs. You hit the hole, you hear all this noise, and there's a violence about it. You hear bits of sounds—the grunts, the "oomphs," the swearing—and suddenly all you're seeing is flashes of this and flashes of that, glimpses of arms and legs, hands reaching for you, they almost get you, but they don't, and maybe you're wondering for a mini-fraction of a second why they didn't, and then another guy's suddenly there. . .

. . . then, all of a sudden, wham! And you're down.

I'd gone thirty yards before Pellington, the outside left linebacker on the other side, used his angle to close in on me. I slowed and damned near made Pellington miss, but he got me by the ankle. I dragged him a few more yards and went down after a 38-yard gain—just as Rosey passed me, looking for someone else to level.

"The key to that play," says Maynard, who had a good view from the sideline, "is that you were running under control."

And I was holding on to the ball, tucking it in. I should have kept doing it.

Our first big play. Our first first down—twelve minutes into the game.

I flipped the ball to the official and ran back to the huddle. Was I celebrating? Even inside? Not a chance. After the run, I just trotted back to the huddle. On the field, I never thought about what I did. I thought about what I *almost* did. After every play, whether it had worked or failed, I always came back to the huddle wondering what we could learn from it: What can I do off that play the next time? If we fake it, can Triplett slide out to the flat, run a screen off it? Or could Schnelker get open downfield? Could I throw a pass off it? Can we do it on the other side with Webster?

The last thing you think about is yourself. We didn't have replays on JumboTron screens, of course, but I can tell you with a straight face that if we did, not a single member of our team would have stood around watching and congratulating himself. Besides, your own teammates would think, *What an asshole.* And the last thing you'd want to do is piss off a teammate. Your teammates are whom you're playing for. Not your coaches, not the fans. Your teammates.

Now we were on the Colt 31. And Charlie thought it was time to open it up. On second down, he rolled right and saw Kyle on a crossing route, but led him a little too far, overthrowing him at the right sideline at about the 5-yard line. Carl Taseff was right with him, but Kyle had a step, even with that bad knee. You have to wonder now if Charlie wouldn't have led him perfectly if Charlie had been warmed up, and had been in the game from the start.

On the next play, though, Charlie was on the money. Webster circled out of the backfield and cut back to the middle, behind the linebackers and in front of the safeties. Alex was deceptively fast. He was big, and he could look like he was lumbering, but he had long strides and great balance, and he was a good receiver. It was an unusual call, but Kyle had already told Charlie he could clear out the coverage on that side, leaving Alex open in the middle.

This would have been a game-changer. He was open. He was *wide* open—no one near him. Charlie led him perfectly. If he catches it, he has a chance to cut it up the middle and go all the way.

If he doesn't slip. If his home turf doesn't betray him.

The shadows were starting to cross the field as the sun disappeared behind the ornate façade of the upper deck, and as the temperature began to plummet, the traction on the field was changing. "The turf down there was getting loose," Alex says now. "It wasn't muddy, but the grass and the sod were starting to go. He threw a great pass. I just slipped."

If he catches it we're knocking on the door. As it is, we had to go for the field goal. Fortunately, our kicker was Pat Summerall, the hero of what was arguably the most dramatic play in New York Giant history.

**T**wo weeks earlier, we'd trailed the Browns by one game in the standings, going into the final game of the regular season. We had to win it, to force a play-off with the same Browns. With snow falling and the wind whipping through the Stadium, less than five minutes remained. We'd reached the Browns' 33, and sent out the field-goal unit for the kick that would give us a tie, and send us into a play-off game. Pat lined up for the field goal—and missed it.

"I didn't even want to go back to the bench," Pat tells me now, in that so well known, distinctive Arkansas twang. But four or five guys came up on the bench to tell him to forget it: he would get another chance. He did—but not until we'd dodged a bullet on my own phantom fumble, a play that made headlines from New York to Cleveland. On third down, with the snow blowing around our ears, and the footing treacherous, Charlie, throwing from the Brown 42, hit me with a 7-yard pass. As I caught it, I turned up-field, and I ran into their linebacker, Galen Fiss. The ball popped out. Another Browns linebacker, big Walt Michaels, scooped up the ball and began to run the other way.

But the head linesman, Charlie Berry, ruled it an incomple-tion—much to the dismay, outrage, and disbelief of Paul Brown. "There isn't a man in this room who doesn't think Frank Gifford fumbled that ball," Brown fumed afterward in the losers' locker room. I don't blame him.

On fourth down, Pat came out, and the rest, as they say, is history. Chandler put the ball down somewhere around midfield in the snow, and Pat coolly and methodically kicked the longest field goal of his life. How long was it? Well, we'll never really know what the yard line was—too much snow blanketed the field.

"It was over the fifty, from the still pictures I've seen," Pat says now. "Kyle always said it was fifty-three. I can still see Lombardi coming out and shouting at me, 'You sonofabitch—you know you can't make it from that distance!'"

I asked Pat if the ball was in Canton, in the Hall of Fame, where it belonged.

"No. Vinnie brought me the ball. I got all you guys to sign it. Then I left it in the house. The kids took it out on the front yard and all the signatures got rubbed off."

Compared with Pat's snow kick the previous week, this one was routine: 36 yards, perfect weather conditions. Pat trotted on and coolly nailed the field goal. We had the lead, 3–0, with three minutes to go in the first quarter.

It always feels good to draw first blood, and the momentum carried over to our special teams. Lenny Lyles, the Colts' rookie—their top draft pick, and tremendously fast—took Chandler's kickoff out to the 21, where Cliff, busting up the Colts' wedge, just nailed him. Cliff was a madman on special teams. Many was the time the rest of us would literally stand on the sidelines on kicks, just to watch Cliff go flying in there to bust up the wedge.

It felt as if we'd turned the tide—and, for the next few minutes, we had. In fact, we were set to seize the game right there and then, except for a couple of plays that never made the highlight reels—a couple of fleeting moments that have been buried beneath all the big plays that came later in this game.

The first play was the interception Johnny should have thrown on third down of that series: Landry sent Karilivacz on a blitz, and Carl got in Johnny's face, forcing him to hurry the throw. The ball floated way behind Moore. Crow read the play perfectly, broke back and reached out for an easy interception. But before the ball got there, Moore *tackled* Lindon, throwing both arms around his waist. It was a smart play by Lenny—Crow would have probably taken it in for a touchdown—but it was also blatant pass interference.

No whistle. If we get the call, they're penalized 15 yards, they're pinned on their 5, and we get the punt in great field position. Instead, they get to punt from their 29.

Now, the second key play, long forgotten: Ray Brown got off a weak punt. If Lindon comes up to catch it, we have great field position. Funny how in retrospect it's the little things that no one notices that swing a game. This swing was huge. For a moment, it would turn the tide.

Most coaches will tell you that the best barometer of how much a team wants to win is the play of its special teams. Bill Parcells always says that every football game is one-third offense, one-third defense, and one-third special teams, and he's right. But for me, the play of the special teams tells you the most about a team's desire, because these are the guys who hurl their bodies into the kickoff wedge, or break up a punt return and take unbelievable shots, time after time. You don't read about them, but if you're going to win in the NFL, you better have a bunch of these no-name overachievers on your coverage teams.

On this play, the Colts did. At least three Colts beat their blocks at the line, and they were swarming in on Lindon as the ball came down. Lindon, for right or wrong reasons, decided to let the ball bounce, then took it on the hop. And now, with Colts closing in from all three directions, he began to scamper around, looking for somewhere to run. He reversed his field, looked for daylight—and was nailed at the 17 by one Sherman Plunkett. Right—*that* Sherman Plunkett. The same 300-pound Sherm who played for the Jets some years later, and was best known for the enormous stomach that hung over his belt like a bowling ball (he wasn't a bad blocker, either).

On this day, he was the slim and quick version of Sherman Plunkett. With help from Ordell Braase, the Colts' backup defensive lineman, he tackled Lindon at our 17-yard line—23 yards behind where the punt landed.

The quarter ended. Instead of having the ball at the 40, we had 83 yards to go.

As we changed sides—nothing but a sixty-second pause for one commercial back in those days—and the offense took the field, I was thinking that, as badly as we'd played, it could have been worse.

Unfortunately, we had a halfback who had a bad habit of carrying the football like a loaf of bread. More unfortunately, I have to live with him every day.

## CHAPTER 4

# SECOND QUARTER

To understand the first real turning point in this game—my first fumble—you have to fully understand the play. To fully understand the play, first you have to understand what was happening on the right side of the Colts' defensive line. And to understand the right side of their line, you have to know about Big Daddy, and you have to know about Don Joyce and The Feud with Rosey Brown.

Let's start with the feud. Joyce was a big, athletic, scrappy defensive end from the rough streets of Steubenville, Ohio. Don had a history of what he describes now, with a proud laugh, as "roughneck" play. Don is best remembered by several of his teammates for having once devoured twenty-six pieces of fried chicken (with white gravy and potatoes) in a preseason eating contest—and then asking for artificial sweetener for his iced tea.

Lipscomb, Donovan, and Marchetti (who quit after twenty-two pieces) overshadowed him on that defensive line. But Don Joyce was one of a kind.

Across the line, at left tackle, stood our own Hall of Fame tackle. Named to the *Sporting News*' All-Time NFL 100. Inducted into Canton. Rosey Brown was one of a kind too—just another kind. And somewhere along the line, Joyce tells me, they'd developed a certain dislike for one another. Me, I had never found Rosey to be anything but the ultimate gentleman; he was a class act on the field as well as off of it. In other words, it would take something special to provoke him.

But then, Don had a way of getting under people's skin: "Yeah, I kind of had a lot of fights on the field," he admits now. In fact, it was Joyce's feistiness that had gotten him onto the Colt roster in the first place: Back when he was playing for the sorry Cardinals in a game against the Colts, on the kick return team, he blindsided a Colt named Joe Campanella, and knocked him under the Colt bench. Weeb grabbed Don and said, "Joyce, you're not going to last another week in this league."

Weeb traded for him the next day. That little episode tells you a whole lot about both Weeb and his priorities.

Today, Joyce isn't quite sure when the feud with Rosey started. He just knows it had some history. Joyce does remember the time his teammate Lenny Moore approached him with some news he'd heard from the Giant locker room. Moore had been talking with Rosie Grier (Moore and Grier were Penn State buddies) and Grier had told him that Rosey Brown had vowed to get Joyce—"and that if he had to, he'd carry a knife and cut my throat" is how Don remembers the particular wording of the message (this so-called message, which I don't believe). Don says that he and Brown "had a bit of a fistfight in the next game." Another time, Don says, the fight wasn't so little: "Rosey pulled my helmet off, and he started throwing bolo punches. I was dancing around, trying to throw jabs to his throat. The officials went into a huddle, decided to not break it up, let us go for several minutes (all of which none of us ever recalls actually happening).

"Then, that year, in 1958, before our regular-season game

against the Giants, someone put a clipping in my locker. Rosey'd said he was going to knock the shit out of me—in so many words. It was all about us being enemies. So I thought I'd get ready for him. A guy at Captain Joe's Crab House gave me his lacrosse pads for my arms. In warm-up, the day of that regular-season game, I'm hitting the sled, hitting goalposts. I got tape on my hands. The officials checked my tape. Then I put the left lacrosse pad on . . . and Rosey got his jaw broken in the first quarter. Big Daddy asked for the other pad."

Actually, it was a fractured cheekbone, on a play in which Rosey was blocking for me. But it took more than a fractured cheekbone to keep Rosey down.

Don told me that he and Rosey ended up good friends when they later scouted college all-star games for their respective professional teams and shared a few drinks. That's not the way I remember Rosey. As a player, Rosey didn't drink. And I have to question a lot of what Don has to say. I never saw Rosey get involved in any extracurricular activity that would have an impact on his two basic priorities: protecting Charlie, and knocking people on their butts so that I could get all the headlines. He was the best at that position I have ever seen, then and now—and a better friend.

As for Daddy? When it comes to Eugene "Big Daddy" Lipscomb, everyone has a story to tell about him. He was truly unique, in a lot of ways. But it seems fitting to let Daddy's play on my fumble start the discussion.

We had it first and ten on our 18. "Brown right, L-turn in," Charlie said, which meant, simply, an 8- to 10-yard turn-in to Kyle Rote, our split left end. I would flare toward the sidelines to pull the linebacker, or become the checkoff receiver if Kyle was covered.

The prime receiver, of course, was Kyle, but if Kyle was covered, Charlie would pump-fake and flip it out to me.

If he did, I'd be on my own, except for Rosey, who would pull out to his left and block for me. The trouble is, Rosey would first have to stand Joyce up at the line, then bounce outside and clear out the linebacker, or the safety, or whoever came into coverage. So for the play to work, a lot of things had to go right. None of them did.

Well, one thing did: Charlie flipped the ball to me, and I caught it. After that, everything came apart. We just hadn't accounted for the speed and the pursuit of the Colt defensive line.

I took the pass, and then tucked the ball into my left side, my outside hand, to protect it as I looked for room to the outside.

On the line, Rosey fired out and stood Joyce up, but he didn't stay with him long; Rosey immediately sprinted to the left to look for someone to hit, which was usually the cornerback. But Joyce had read the thing immediately. I hadn't counted on a defensive end's being that quick, and when I found myself in trouble on the outside, I turned it in. There was Joyce, coming at me full speed. I did a full 360-degree turn to try and avoid him. Unfortunately, I was stupidly waving the ball out there, looking for balance, and I had just started to break free of his hold. All of a sudden, here comes Big Daddy Lipscomb, face-to-face.

To this day, I don't know how he did it. He'd been rushing Charlie, but turned his 6-foot-6-inch, 306-pound frame on a dime when he saw the pass. He was coming full speed from his right tackle spot, and he just completely enveloped me with those long arms, huge hands, and wide body. The ball popped out. Then Daddy just fell on top of me. Their backup left tackle, Ray Krouse, a former Giant teammate, pursuing from the other side of the field, fell on the ball.

They had it on our 20. And number 16 had given up a score—
at least three points, and more than likely seven.

It damn sure wasn't my finest moment. I hadn't taken care of
the ball, and I'd looked like a stupid ballet dancer doing a pirouette
out there, trying to spin my way free. On the other hand, if Daddy
didn't make that astounding play, I had daylight. As the old saying
goes, "If 'ifs' and 'buts' were candy and nuts, every day would be a
party."

That one play said it all about Big Daddy Lipscomb: for an
enormous man—one of the league's few 300-pounders—he was
great at lateral pursuit. And when he got there, his strength was
surreal. Basically, he was as quick as a linebacker, and the size of a
mountain. And he *played* like a linebacker, roaming from sideline
to sideline. When you carried the ball against the Colts, you were
always subconsciously thinking, *Big Daddy: where is he?*

I never knew him personally, but it seems like everyone who
played with or against him has a Daddy tale to tell, and the stories
grew with each passing year, just like Big Daddy did.

If you believe Artie, Daddy never *wanted* to rush the passer:
"Daddy thought he was a black Tyrone Power," Artie said, laughing. "He didn't want to get hit in the face. One time we're playing
the Rams, and Big Daddy pulls up lame because he doesn't want to
play against Duane Putnam. I said to him, 'You better come in for
the second half, because if we lose, I'm gonna shoot you.' Hell, I'm
thirty-seven and I'm playing the whole game. Daddy stayed in."

"When I was first with the Packers," our left guard, Al Barry,
recalls, "I'd try to take him head-on, and he'd just kill me . . . I was
238, 240 . . . and 6-2, and he was 300, and 6-6. The only way to
block him was to trick him. On pass plays, where you'd normally
step back to set up, I'd rush at him. On running plays, I'd pretend
it was a pass. That was the only way I could handle him.

"I remember a game in the snow: someone stepped on my foot, I didn't pay any attention, and afterward I went in and my sock was full of blood. So the next week a story in the paper said I might be out with a bad toe. On the first play of the next game, I line up against Big Daddy. He says, 'Hey, Barry, how's your toe?' I say, 'Fine.' Then he says, 'Exactly which one is it?'"

Daddy hadn't gone to college. The Rams found him playing for the marines at Camp Pendleton. "I asked him once where 'Northern College' was," announcer Bob Wolff told me. 'That's what he'd written on a questionnaire—No College.'"

Off the field, though, Daddy's behavior belied his menacing on-field image. He was no tough guy. Inside that huge body lay a childlike, manic man whose glee was infectious. He called anyone he didn't know "Little Daddy," which was how he got his own nickname. Or "Sweet Pea." Daddy legendarily uttered his most-often-quoted words when someone once asked him how he made so many tackles: "I just reach out and grab an armful of players from the other team and peel them off until I find the one with the ball. I keep him." Too many times I was the one he kept.

Daddy could be the bully, says Barry: "He spit on me one time. I don't remember why he did it. We got him back. I got the center to help. On the next play, we got him on the ground and beat the shit out of him." But Daddy was more bluster than actual toughness, teammate Ray Brown recalls: "One day, after a game somewhere, as we're leaving the stadium, I picked up a cricket. I held that cricket out to Big Daddy. I guess he didn't know about crickets, being from Detroit. It hopped out of my hand, toward Daddy, and he jumped like it was a snake or something. He went berserk.

"He knew I was studying to be a lawyer," Brown says, "and after Emmett Till was killed in Mississippi, found in a river with a big cotton-gin fan on top of him, Daddy came up to me in the locker room, put his arm around me and pulled me in, and said, 'When Brown becomes a lawyer, I'm going to go down to Mississippi and he's going to keep me from being thrown in the river.' I said to him, 'They don't have any fans big enough to hold you down.'"

On this, everyone who knew Daddy agrees: he was a wounded soul. Daddy was known to carry two things in his pockets: wads of cash, and photographs of his mother, lying murdered in the street in Detroit, after being stabbed nearly fifty times at a bus stop when Eugene was eleven years old.

Teammates spoke of Daddy's dark side: crying jags, sudden depressions. "Daddy was a nice guy," Artie says. "A poor, unfortunate guy."

On this day, he was just getting started.

Now the Colts had the ball back, on our 20. Knowing Johnny—and keeping in mind Weeb's game plan to emphasize the pass, which we now know, but didn't then—one would have to figure he'd go for it all at once. Typically, Johnny did the opposite. He took them right in for the game's first touchdown—without ever going to the air. He ran it down our throats. It was line against line, and at this point, it was no contest. Our defense, "the finest in the league," wasn't used to being dominated. As a matter of fact, as I watched from the sideline, their dominating short drive was a little shocking.

On the first play Moore got four yards before Sam caught him, lifted him by the waist as if he were hoisting a sack of potatoes, carried him a few yards—and then literally threw Lenny to the ground. Of course, there was no penalty.

The play looked routine, but it probably wasn't. This was

likely the play on which Moore got hurt. Lenny remembers only that he was hurt in the second quarter. My guess is that Sam's face-plant did it. "What many folks don't know—it didn't even hit the newspapers—in the second quarter, I pulled something in my chest, and man, if I did certain things, I couldn't move: there'd be a sharp pain all the way through," Lenny says now. "This was in the second quarter. I don't know what caused it. I told Weeb about it. He said, 'Don't say anything, just shut up and leave it like that.' So we kept it quiet."

Two more runs put the Colts on our 10, first and goal. And then Unitas crossed us again: as we tightened our defensive line to stop the run, he faked to Ameche on a plunge, drawing Harland, our outside linebacker, toward the middle. But now here came Moore, crossing over from his right halfback position, heading left. Their left end, Jim Mutscheller, blocked in on Harland, who had moved inside to stop the run he figured was coming his way.

With everyone caught inside, Moore had a wide-open field, except for Karilivacz, the cornerback, alone out in the flat. Carl had a clear bead on Lenny—who sprinted right past him.

Jimmy Patton saved the touchdown by shoving Lenny out at the 1. On the next play they sent Ameche off left tackle. Parker just blew the injured Grier away, and Ameche scored easily.

The Colts had their first points, and their first lead—7–3—not on Johnny's arm, but on his play-calling, and the play of his line. At this point, they were dominating us in every phase of the game.

That Colt offensive line never earned a lot of attention. The only lineman whose name has gone down in history is huge Jim Parker's. But Sandusky and Spinney at the guards, Buzz Nutter at center, and George Preas at right tackle? They aren't exactly household names, but the Colts' margins of victory in 1958—by scores like 56–0, 40–14, and 34–7, and averaging more than 30 points a game—suggest that the line was doing something right. They also were giving Johnny a lot of protection, and opening holes for Ameche, Dupre, and, sometimes, Moore.

To hear the Colt linemen talk about it now, the unsung key to this game was Buzz Nutter. Buzz was an unusually athletic center, with an uncanny ability to read the defense and call out blocking schemes at the line. But his teammates remember him best for his determination never to give up on any play, and always looking for someone else to block. "He was the star of that game," Artie told me, and you don't often hear a defensive guy saying that his center was the star of a game. "He was all over the field."

Nutter came out of nowhere—from a Virginia Tech team that, by his own recollection, won fewer than ten games in his three years on the varsity. Buzz was stunned when the Redskins drafted him, and unsurprised when they cut him. He caught on the next year as a free agent with the Colts. "Christ, first day of camp I weighed 200 pounds," he told me. "Everybody said, 'Man, you must be an end.' I was faster than hell. I said, 'I play center.' 'Not in this league,' they said. Within three years I was up to 235. No weights—we didn't have weights. We just ate and ate and ate. And drank beer. By then Ewbank was on my ass about drinking too much beer."

The talent of the Colt line told only part of the story of that short drive. By now, Grier's knee had become a liability. Art Spinney had just manhandled him. Which brings us to a second feud. It was bad enough that Rosie was lame. It was worse that Spinney had it in for him. "After the game we'd played in midseason, Spinney put out in the paper that Grier was the worst tackle he'd ever played against, in high school, college, or pro," Huff remembers. "The next time Spinney played him, Rosie picked that guy up and threw him backwards on his ass."

So maybe Spinney had some extra motivation that day. But it was a one-sided matchup: without Grier at one hundred percent, we weren't the league's leading defense. Not even close. Would it have made a difference if Grier had been healthy? No doubt. But back then you didn't take yourself out unless you were near death, and for two reasons: With only thirty-five men on the roster, you didn't ask out of a game if you felt a twinge in your hamstring. You didn't even ask out if you'd been dinged so hard you didn't know what play had been called.

Second, you didn't ask out because you might lose your job. It was sort of an honor thing, a matter of pride. You have to wonder if the outcome on this day might have been different if Rosie had admitted how badly he was hurt going into the game. Instead, he started. And the last time I talked to him about it, his voice was cracking at the memories of what happened that day. This game has stayed with him for a long, long time. And he's still kind of broken up about it—not that he let himself start; today, he still beats himself up about asking to come out of the game.

"But I couldn't move," he told me, "and I thought I was hurting the team. The game before, I was chasing the quarterback to the sideline, and somebody cut me from behind. It was the same knee I'd hurt in college. It was a mess. It *felt* a mess. I left the dressing room after that game with a cast on.

"So I kind of beat myself up many, many days after that title game was over. Maybe I should have stayed out there and played that game, even if I couldn't move that well. In retrospect, I should have stayed in there. But no one told me not to come out.

"See, I thought we were going to win that game. Later it just dawned on me so badly that we lost that game, and I felt that, had I been able to go just a little bit longer, maybe we'd have won. But if I stayed in, I didn't know how to get my leg ready to take the punishment. See, today you can put heat on your knee, get whatever you need to loosen it up. I didn't know all that stuff.

"But I'm just so sorry. I didn't understand a lot of things I understand today. It was an incredible game, and there I am, just sitting. You can't do nothing. I could keep moving my knee, but it was not going to get better."

Would we have been better off with Rosie admitting to Tom that he wouldn't be able to make it, so that Frank Youso would have had a little time to prepare, instead of being thrown into the fire? Just one of the many things about the game we'll never know. I do think I understand where Rosie is coming from. I'd have never gone to Vince the week before a game and told him we'd be better off without me, no matter how badly I was hurt.

I do know that when Rosie Grier was healthy, he was a star, even with his less-than-diligent practice habits. Who knows how great he would have been if he'd been a little more in shape?

"If he'd have had, let's say, Katcavage's go-go heart, they would never have been able to handle him," Sam says now. "When we were in two-a-days at Fairfield, Rosie never worked very hard in practice. He worked at his guitar. He couldn't carry a tune, but his real love was still music. He had these loudspeakers, and in between practices, every afternoon, he'd be playing his guitar. We were all trying to nap. Someone stole the tubes out of his guitar so he couldn't amplify it. So one day at lunch, Rosie stood up at lunchtime and made a speech: 'All right, you guys. Someone stole the tubes out of my guitar. They better put them back, or I'll kick every one of your asses, one at a time.' He got his tubes back."

I don't think Rosie would have kicked anyone's ass; in truth, he was just a kind, loving, gentle guy, and as good as he was, he could have been a real superstar if he'd had the inner toughness the great ones have.

"We loved Rosie," Mo says now, "but we had to kick him around once in a while: 'Come *on*, Rosie, let's get going!' One time we played an exhibition game on a hot day in New Haven against the Colts, and me, I'm figuring, 'I can't take this anymore. I gotta go down.' So I dropped down on one play and grabbed my knee, like I'm hurt. I looked over and, so help me God, Rosie had the same damned idea on the same play. I said, 'Ro, get up.' Rosie said, 'But I was here first.'

"But I ended up coaching defensive line for twenty-two years, and he was one of the best tackles I ever saw."

"Yeah, we used to make fun of Rosie," Webster remembers. "He was supposed to come to camp in Winooski under 300, but when he came in, he just about broke the scale. We didn't have a scale that went over 300. They took him down to the meat factory, in downtown Burlington, and put him on the scale. He weighed 340 pounds.

"We used to always try and get him to quit eating. One time, we thought we were doing really good, keeping him from eating too much at dinner. But we got held up a little after a long, late practice. We had a meeting. We used to all go out in Burlington, but we were running out of time and couldn't get down to our favorite bar. We ran across the street from the campus, where there was a deli. We bought a case of beer, went around to the back—and there's Rosie back there with a big submarine sandwich."

...

**N**ow we'd lost the lead. Rosie was hurting, and we were losing the battle on both the offensive and defensive lines. Unitas was getting too much time. All of it meant that the offense had to produce, and we had to get something happening, and quickly.

Maybe Mel Triplett felt the pressure to break one on the ensuing kickoff. Or maybe Mel was just having a bad day. Incredibly, as he gathered in Rechichar's bouncing kick, he fumbled again. Fortunately, Rosey Brown was composed enough to not only recover the ball, but to pick it up and hand it back to Mel, who managed to hold on to *this* handoff, and plow his way out to the 33.

We had good field position, and Charlie decided to open things up a little. On second down, finally enjoying some protection, he hit Kyle with a perfect 15-yard curl-in, between the corner, Milt Brown, playing on that broken foot, and the safety, Andy Nelson.

As we huddled back up, I thought, *Okay. Here we go, finally.* I felt good for my friend, Kyle, and I felt good for the team. A Rote reception always seemed to give us a lift; for the Giants to have any chance on this day, we had to have Kyle Rote be a part of the offense, as he'd been for the last eight years. Playing on one good knee.

**T**he first time I remember hearing about Kyle Rote, I was at USC, and I was hitchhiking from L.A. up to Bakersfield, where my parents still had a house, even though they were living in Alaska. I was coming home to be with my sister for Thanksgiving. A guy picked me up, and together we listened to the broadcast of the SMU–Notre Dame national championship game on the car radio. As we drove over the mountain and down into the San Joaquin

Valley, it seemed like every time the announcer said anything, it was about Kyle. I remember thinking, *It must be great to be Kyle Rote.* He ran for 115 yards and threw for 146 that day—and scored all three of SMU's touchdowns. Notre Dame had been a 27½-point favorite in that game; the Irish barely won, 27–20—and named Kyle an honorary member of their championship team. The next year, as a senior, he made the cover of *Life* magazine. The Giants took Kyle with the bonus pick in the 1951 draft. Back then, one team got a bonus pick ahead of the actual draft, and then–Giant coach Steve Owen was awarded the pick by pulling a ticket out of a hat. Kyle signed the contract at Toots's.

But Kyle tore up his knee during training camp, in 1951, stepping in a gopher hole on a practice in Jonesboro, Arkansas. He must have had a terrible operation; someone must have botched it, and big-time. It was the ugliest-looking knee I'd ever seen. In later years, after a few beers, we used to ask him to show it to us, if you can believe how sick that might be. Such was the gallows humor in our locker room.

But in a strange way, that was our way of letting Kyle know how good we all knew he could have been. He pretty much limped through his first season; he played only five games. As a matter of fact, the Giants drafted me as insurance for Kyle. They figured I could fill in for him on offense, or, if he did play, I could play defense—which is exactly what happened.

My first two years, whenever Kyle was hurting, they put me in on offense. Then, in 1954, under our new offensive coach, Lombardi moved Kyle permanently to wide receiver and me to left halfback. I finally had a home, and so did Kyle. Today I'll leave it to another great receiver to assess Kyle's football abilities.

"As I've watched the NFL over the years," Raymond Berry told me, "I have a category in my mind for the elite receivers: Elroy Hirsch. Bobby Mitchell. Kyle Rote."

• • •

**K**yle was destined to make another more important catch in the third quarter, but this drive was doomed to stall. For the first time that day, on the next play, first and ten from our own 48, the Colts came on a blitz, sending Bill Pellington. Charlie had no chance, and Pellington wrapped him up at the 40. It was a clean hit; Pellington didn't have to pile on this time.

Bill Pellington is a guy you seldom hear about when people are talking about the glory days of the Colts, because their front four was always so dominant. But to hear the Colts tell it, he was the single most intense player to ever wear a Colt uniform. Or, as Milt Davis put it so eloquently, "He'd play with snot and blood coming all out of his nose, mad at everybody, his eyes deep-set in their sockets. He was always stirring us up, stirring us up."

He was a New Jersey native, a Navy vet who had done steel-girder work on New York bridges during the off-season. As the guy who called the signals in the defensive huddle—the defensive quarterback—Bill was one of the two real leaders on that unit, along with Marchetti. Gino led by example, and Pellington led by verbal intimidation. "He was intense in the huddle," Andy Nelson told me. "Someone catches a pass on you, he'd be in your face about it. I guess if you're winning, that's all right, but I didn't like it. I didn't particularly want anyone in my face after I'd given up a pass. Our huddle was a little rough at that time. It wasn't always pleasant."

**F**or the most part, though, the Colts put up with Pellington's abuse, because he backed it all up on the field, and led by ex-ample—even if the example was often borderline dirty. "He was as tough an individual as I've ever been around, tough mentally and tough physically," the Colts' linebacker Leo Sanford told me. "You didn't want to get too close to him. He had a knack for using his forearm like a clothesline. Teams tended to run their plays away from wherever Bill was."

That went for me, too. Most guys were satisfied just to bring you down. Pellington wasn't satisfied unless he'd made you pay—and he had several ways of inflicting his peculiar brand of punishment, which more often than not involved throwing that forearm.

"He wore a pad he'd tape around his arm," Ray Brown recalls. "After we won that championship, I'll never forget—we were playing the College All-Star Game, and there was a college kid coming into my coverage. He's a few yards away from me, I'm looking to pick him up—and all of a sudden Pellington's arm goes up, and it catches this kid right in the throat. The back of his head is the first thing to hit the ground. The doctors come out—I thought he was dying—and they did a tracheotomy right on the field. He'd swallowed his tongue. I thought Bill had killed the kid."

The forearm wasn't the only weapon in Pellington's arsenal, but the clothesline technique was his trademark, and at least once, it came back to bite him. "I'll tell you how tough he was," says Ordell Braase, the Colts' backup defensive lineman.: "After one clothesline, he came out after the series was over rubbing his arm. 'My damned arm doesn't feel right,' he said. Then he went back in and played a couple of series. Then after that the doctor says, 'Let me look at it,' and it's broken. Pellington was just intense."

Pellington's early play mirrored all of the Colts' performances so far; it felt as if the Colts were playing at a different speed. As we punted the ball back once again, more than halfway though the quarter, I wrapped myself in a jacket, took a seat on the bench, and wondered how we were going to turn this thing around. I didn't have long to wait for the answer. Our special teams gave us a gift, and put us right back in the game.

The Colts' punt returner, a rookie out of Florida named Jackie Simpson, thought about making a fair catch. Then he thought about making a big play. He didn't think enough about Buzz Guy, one of our backup linemen, and Billy Lott, our rookie backup full-back, bearing down on him. Simpson caught the ball just as both of our guys slammed into him, and the ball popped loose. Lying on his stomach, Simpson groped for the ball, and was gathering it back in—and then Rosey Brown landed on him. The ball popped loose again, and Rosey pulled it in.

Simpson loped off the field, trying to keep his head up. "I'm thinking, *If we lose this ball game I don't know what I'm going to do,*" Jackie told me. "Weeb didn't give me another chance on punts that day—Lenny was back there. So all I could think about during that game was *If we do lose, all the guys are going to be mad at me. The people back in Baltimore—what are they going to do to me?*"

He didn't have to worry. After our defense had held, after our special teams had risen to the occasion, with our team poised ten yards from the Colt end zone, I was about to give it right back. Again.

The truth is, in my career, I fumbled a lot, a problem that stemmed from the way I carried the ball my entire career—high school, college, pro. I used the ball for balance, as a lot of backs did, and do, and for a back to change his running style is really tough—

for some, impossible. Ironically, after fumbling nine times in the '57 season, I'd fumbled only three times the entire '58.

Do the fumbles haunt me? Not really. I recognized from day one that if you were going to play the game, and you were going to give it as much as you possibly could on every play, you were going to fumble it. Everyone fumbles. Even Jimmy Brown, who rarely fumbled, had given up the ball in our play-off game.

In any event, I fumbled the ball enough for both of us that day.

We had the ball on the Colt 10. The special teams had done their job. The defense was doing their job; they'd given up just seven points in the first twenty-five minutes.

We could take the lead back with one play. Charlie came right back with me. Maybe he wanted to give me a chance to make up for my first fumble. More likely, he knew that a pitchout, with me sweeping left, could get the whole ten yards if we blocked it well. He also knew that, with Sanford out and Myhra playing outside linebacker, this was a point we should attack.

This time we didn't line up in our usual sweep formation. Instead of putting Kyle split out left, in what we called a "strong left" formation, we put Alex out there, to occupy Milt Davis. We had Kyle in tight on left end, on Rosey's outside shoulder, as an extra blocker.

Great field position. A good play called. A good formation. The crowd going crazy. And number 16 about to give it all back.

This time, the speed of the Colt defense didn't force the turn-over; their smarts did. At the snap, Rote blocked in on Joyce, and Rosey pulled around him, coming out to clear me a lane. But out at the sideline, where Milt Davis was lined up opposite Webster, something about the formation told Milt we weren't going to pass. Something told Milt what was coming.

"Milt was kind of like a professor," Braase says now. "He'd like to sit there and think out loud. He knew the offenses. He studied them. He knew everyone's capabilities."

"They tipped it off," Milt told me. "I can't exactly say why, but to me, the lineup was not showing pass. So I had to make a choice. Do I cash in and bet on the run, or stay back with Webster? I knew that Nelson would be back there to protect me if it was a pass—he was a smart guy. So I took a step in, toward the line, and another. You know what's funny—I remember this like it was yesterday—just at that moment, the sun comes out. I remember the sun."

After that, he didn't have time to think—"the professor" relied on instinct. At the snap, Milt ignored Webster and slipped into the backfield before Rosey could swing out and get in front of me. As soon as I turned upfield, still a few yards behind the line of scrimmage, Milt met me. Just as I was trying to cradle the ball into my left hand, he lowered his left shoulder and hit my arm. The ball popped loose.

Just like the last time, Don Joyce showed up, this time just in time to recover the fumble.

The Colts had it back, with nearly five minutes left in the half—more than enough time to put a drive together. I walked off the field, trying to bury the anger. Sam was probably restraining the impulse to rip me a new one. The crowd was quieted, stunned. No one was booing, of course—not back in 1958. I wouldn't have heard them anyway: I was too caught up in my own thoughts.

Knowing that the Colts had terrible field position wasn't any sort of consolation. We'd been ten yards away from retaking the lead.

• • •

The defense trotted back on, to save our butts once again—a role most of them were accustomed to. Most of them, but not our new defensive tackle. Frank Youso just hoped he could remember where a defensive tackle was supposed to line up. Youso, the big second-round pick out of Minnesota, was scared to death.

"We knew Rosie was hurting," Huff says now. "But we had no one to take his place—we had no backup tackle on defense. But they had to make a change. They brought in Youso. And Youso was no Roosevelt Grier."

Youso told me he had endured an interesting baptism under fire: On his first day as a Giant back in early August, he'd flown into San Francisco for an exhibition game the day after he'd played in the college all-star game, and showed up at the stadium without any cleats. Jim Lee put him in anyway. He had to block the legendarily tough and intense 49er tackle Leo Nomellini—in street shoes. ("How ya doin', Leo?" Youso greeted Nomellini at the line. Leo threw him to the ground. End of conversation.) After that, you'd think nothing would surprise Youso. But Frank was as shocked as anyone when Jim Lee started looking up and down the bench for someone to replace Grier.

"He didn't have any other defensive tackles," Youso told me. "Apparently he liked my size, so he saw this big offensive tackle— me—and said, 'You're in on defense.' I said, 'I don't know *how* to play defense.' Jim Lee said, 'I can't help it. I got no one else. Do what Sam says.' So I go over to Sam and say, 'What do I do?' Sam said, 'I'll pat you on the right cheek if you're going right, your left cheek if you're going left, and if I don't pat you, hang on, 'cause they're coming right at us, and you're on your own.'

"I got tired of Sam patting my ass," Frank told me with his

characteristic laugh. "But I got *real* worried when after a while it started to feel good."

Powerless to do anything, I stood next to Charlie and Kyle on the sidelines, hoping that my second fumble wouldn't turn into a 14-point turnaround. The Colts turned in some impressive— well, some *immortal*—long drives that day. Including the one that came next—an 86-yard march drive, and pure Unitas.

Our pass rush had been weak enough, and now we had a rookie in. So Johnny went long to the running back Dupre—a real surprise call, considering that no one thought of L. G. as a deep threat; the longest of his thirteen receptions that year was twenty-two yards out of the backfield. Johnny had all the time in the world on this one, but Lindon was all over Dupre. Johnny smartly overthrew it to avoid the interception. On third down, Johnny faked a handoff to Dupre over the left side. Youso bit, Mo bit, the TV cameras bit—and Johnny turned to his right, flipping a screen to Ameche. It was good for ten.

Now, away from the shadows of the end zone, the Colts went to work on Youso. Johnny called four straight running plays to the left side: to Lenny for nine, to Ameche for five, to Lenny for three, to Ameche for three, bringing the ball up to midfield. On each play, they were running right at Youso.

By now, Frank wasn't just confused, he was bleeding: "My left hand was butchered. See, I was used to always getting my hands off the ground right away on offense," Youso recalled. "That first play, I figured I want to stay low, so I still have my hands on the ground. Before I could get up, someone stepped on my right hand. Two fingers were crushed. My middle finger was torn wide open, upper knuckle to the bottom; the blood is squirting out of my hand.

"I go off, Doc Sweeny put a tongue depressor on it, and

wrapped it up, and sent me back in." A rookie defensive lineman was bad enough. With one hand, it was worse.

Still, we had a shot at stopping them; we had them third and seven when Unitas pulled another one out of his high-tops. He had all the time in the world. He pumped to Lenny, brought the ball back in, and took off to the left side, facing nothing but daylight. By the time Huff and Youso nailed him down, Unitas had gained sixteen, down to our 30.

A penalty pushed them back, but they got 13 of it back on a square-out to Berry: a sign of things to come. On this one, Youso had finally beaten his man, and had a hand in Johnny's face. Johnny didn't even flinch.

"Johnny's single greatest asset was his ability to concentrate when people were in his face," Jim Mutscheller, the Colts' tight end, told me from his insurance office in Baltimore. "It just never affected him. He never worried a bit about who was about to knock him on his ass."

Now it was third and one, on our 21: a huge play. The two-minute warning was called. They came back out in short-yardage formation. We had to be figuring on Ameche up the middle. We lined up in short yardage: seven down linemen, and all four defensive backs playing like linebackers.

Johnny surveyed our formation. He must have seen that the play he called was dead. So he changed it at the line. He handed off to his right halfback, Ameche—but going wide left. Everyone was caught inside. Berry had been lined up tight on the left, and blocked in on linebacker Harland Svare, completely sealing the lane. The only man who could have stopped him was the cornerback Karilivacz—and L. G. Dupre took Carl completely out of the play with a terrific block.

The Horse went for six before Jimmy Patton dragged him

down at our 15. Now the Colts were knocking on the door again, and honestly, it seemed as if we had no idea what to expect.

Looking back, I think every play Johnny called on that drive was put in because of something they'd picked up on our defense. With the extra week to study, they'd studied Tom's defense, and knew it well. Like I said, Landry didn't change a thing from the first time we'd played them. But he didn't believe in changing things. He believed in his 4–3 defense, in his keys, in his percentages. And he wasn't about to leave them. Those beliefs may have hurt us that day, but those same beliefs, refined in later years, would earn him a Hall of Fame career as the coach of the Dallas Cowboys.

Right now, it looked like they'd put in a whole new offense, stuff we hadn't seen. The last play of the drive was the most brilliantly called and executed play of the half.

It was first and 10 from the 15. Berry lined up tight again, on the left side, signaling a run. At the snap, Raymond blocked down on Svare. Karilivacz read that as a run, and came up on the outside, just as John put the ball in Ameche's belly—and then took it back out. Great fake.

In the meantime, Berry dove *under* Svare, with his hands on the ground, as if he were going to block, then got up again and took off downfield. It's the kind of play you can call only if you know you'll have plenty of time in the pocket, and Johnny had plenty of time. Carl had bitten on the run. Neither safety had a chance. Johnny, with the play-fake, then the drop-back, faced no pressure.

Raymond was wide open in the end zone between Em and Patton. Fifteen yards, six points, and a 14–3 lead. Thirteen plays, eighty-six yards. Four passes and seven runs—and just about everything had worked. The whole thing had been painful to watch—especially for me. They'd exploited our weaknesses. They'd exploited our predictable tendencies. They'd outsmarted us. They'd outhustled us. They'd taken advantage of the breaks—two big ones provided by me.

About the only good news was the time remaining: less than a minute and a half remained before halftime, certainly not enough time for us to unravel any further. But believe it or not, Mel botched another kickoff. It was another low bouncer, and it clanked off his hands—but thankfully, the ball ricocheted backward, over Maynard's head, and out of the end zone.

The first half ended, mercifully for is, in typically ugly fashion. Charlie faded back on first—and slipped to the hardening turf. On the last play of the half, Alex was pulled down on a sweep—and the ball popped loose. But the whistle had blown, and time ran out on the worst half of football we'd played all year.

## CHAPTER 5

# HALFTIME

No one threw helmets in the locker room. No one cast blame. No one felt like arguing. No one had to say anything. And other than the coaches, no one did.

The idea that a team can turn itself around during the halftime break—with a fiery speech, with an intense session of strategy, with a coach who can dissect the previous thirty minutes of football, revise the game plan, and send a team out with a new, improved attitude—that's a myth. For a professional team playing its twentieth game in twenty weeks, the halftime is a chance to rest, to regroup, and to stay calm. And that's what we did.

Not that we had much time to get lectured anyway—the break lasted about twenty minutes. Back then the NFL didn't ask the Rolling Stones to play a concert in the middle of a fireworks show. The telecast that day was about football, from start to finish—although I imagine that, at halftime, the NBC execs were hoping for a more professionally played and competitive second half of football; otherwise, their product wasn't going to win too many new viewers.

Counting the time it took to slog off the field, then to come back on after our break, you could whittle our halftime down to fifteen minutes. That gave a quarter hour for the trainers to patch us up and for Jim Lee Howell to check his watch a couple of times. I didn't need any equipment repair. I probably could have used some sticky stuff on my hands, though.

Out on the field, the bands and baton twirlers did their best to keep our disappointed fans happy. In the locker room, we couldn't hear the Colt fight song, or the noisy, oh-so-confident Baltimore fans.

Our offensive stats? If they handed them out back then, the way they do now, I'd have read them and wept. Thankfully, I didn't get to see the numbers. Giant first downs? Two. Total yardage? Eighty-six. Total rushing yards—including my 38-yard run? Forty-seven yards. Don and Charlie had completed six passes in ten attempts for 39 yards. I didn't need statistics to tell me what had happened. Both of the fumbles had killed us. It hurt, but I had to get them out of my mind, and I did.

We could console ourselves with the knowledge that we'd played terribly—and yet were still in it. Everyone knew that if I hadn't fumbled twice, this would be a whole different ball game. "We knew we were beating ourselves with mistakes," Webster says now. "Fumbles. Me falling down. Linemen missing a block. Charlie overthrowing it to Kyle on that first series. And we still weren't out of it."

Their defensive front four was completely controlling our offensive line by overshifting to the strength of our offensive formation, into gaps we hadn't anticipated. Artie was sliding over to go head-up over Wietecha, like a modern-day nose tackle, which gave the Colt defense what amounted to a five-man line to the strong side of our formation.

We'd also wasted three series with Heinrich. Even our home field had conspired against us, pulling Alex's feet out from under him, dragging Charlie down on a sackless sack. More significantly, we hadn't shown the Colts anything on offense they hadn't seen. We'd never used a lot of trick plays as a team, but we always had my option pass at the ready; two weeks earlier, I'd thrown that TD to Bob Schnelker off the option against Cleveland, in the snow.

We'd ignored the trick play we'd unveiled in the play-off game a week earlier, where I'd taken a reverse handoff from Alex, then pitched the ball to Charlie, trailing the play out on my right flank. He'd rambled in for the game's only touchdown, carrying a safety. ("Don't ever pitch me the ball again," Charlie told me afterward. He was half smiling.)

We hadn't gone to the option today. In fact, we hadn't even thrown to Schnelker yet. We hadn't drawn on anything other than the catalogue of running plays that had always worked. And that was the trouble: the Colts were seeing everything they expected to see—our 49 and 28 power sweeps, right and left, our 47 and 26 power plays off tackle, and our 41 and 20 quick traps up the middle.

Nothing had worked with our passing game. The Colts had simply put too much pressure on Charlie.

On the other side, our defense had played most of the half with ten men; because of his injured knee, Grier had been a complete nonfactor, and Youso had picked a tough game to make his debut at defensive tackle. As always, Landry was sticking with his basic 4–3, trusting the cornerbacks to cover two of the league's best receivers—which was next to impossible with no pressure on Unitas, and very little help from our safeties and linebackers.

But the hard truth was that it felt as if the Colts wanted this game more than we did. Now we had fifteen minutes to turn this thing around. This wasn't going to happen with someone telling us how to do it, and neither coach tried. Every one of us knew what we had to do, and talking about it wasn't going to help.

We spent the first few minutes of halftime doing what we always did, especially near the end of a season: trying to lessen the pain in knees and assorted other joints, fixing and adjusting special equipment, checking the tape jobs on wrists and ankles. Grier tested the knee, and knew he was done. Johnny patched up Youso's torn finger again.

Of course, for Youso, blood was the least of his worries. He had to figure out a way to play defensive tackle, and quickly, against one of the best offensive lines in the game. You'd think a rookie offensive lineman who'd been thrown onto the defensive line would be getting some pointers, but you'd be wrong. "They never said a thing to me at half," Frank says now. "Never said a word to me. No one did. Not Landry, not Huff, not nobody. I guess they figured I was a pro, I could do the job. Besides, they wanted to give us a rest. We were working our buns off."

Instead, Landry addressed his whole unit, over in the training room—calmly, firmly, and quickly: "If you keep doing what I'm telling you to do," he said, "we'll be all right." That was Tom, and that was his system: studying tendencies, teaching keys and execution. As far as he was concerned, we knew the Colts' tendencies. "Now it's up to you."

Normally, Sam would have been the vocal one, if he felt it was needed. But he didn't rant or rave that day. It wasn't as if this wasn't a position we hadn't been in before. Sam knew that if the defense could shut them out, then even *our* offense could come back from eleven points. Basically, in the entire first thirty minutes, the defense had given up one long drive. Not a bad half-day's work. All they had to do was shut the Colts out the rest of the day.

I remember what Lombardi was saying to the offense, in the locker room. It's kind of hard to forget. "Frank," Vince said, calmly, "you've got to hang on to the football." As if he had to tell me. Then he addressed the unit—again, calmly: "What we have works. We *know* it does. What we're doing is working—we're just not executing it properly. We know we have to execute. Just execute. We have to stay with it, work with it, make our reads a little quicker. If we execute, we will win this ball game. So settle down; pick it up a notch."

He wasn't screaming. He wasn't ranting. He wasn't even raising his voice. Vince wasn't into the legendary yelling yet. His voice was measured. His restraint had nothing to do with the fact that he wasn't the head coach; to us, he was. His calm demeanor reflected nothing more than his confidence in a system he'd drummed into us in countless hours in front of a chalkboard, through countless practices—never like a drill sergeant, but like a teacher who respected his students, like a friend who trusted us to believe in our talents, and his system.

Vince would take that football philosophy of simplicity and execution to forge an amazing Hall of Fame career. As for me, I feel blessed and honored to have been there when it all began with the man I came to first respect and then love—and finally, dearly miss.

Where to start, when remembering my friend Vince Lombardi? With the man we called Vinnie, and liked to joke with—and play jokes on? The grinning guy with thirty-nine white, pearly teeth—all of them seemingly on top? With the guy who liked nothing more than to huddle in front of a projector in his living room, with his friends from the offense, while Marie cooked up something delicious over in the kitchen in his small house in Oradell, New Jersey?

The most effective motivational tactics of the Vince who

coached me always showed a soft side, and a love of the guys. Let's flash back to the beginning of that season. After we'd lost our fifth of six preseason games, he called a meeting after practice up at Bear Mountain, at 7:30 that night. We all bitched and moaned as we filed into the meeting room—until we found out that the meeting would be downstairs, at a basement rathskeller on the campus, and would include a keg of beer. We stayed on with Vince until after midnight. That was the Vince Lombardi I knew: the sometimes excitable, always emotional guy, but a *good* guy, who cared about each and every one of the men on his offense.

I know where I *won't* start when I describe Vince Lombardi: with this idea that Vince was some sort of dictator. I knew him well, first for five years on the field, and then for many years after that. I really came to know him after he'd left us and gone to the Packers, when our relationship could grow free of the player-coach constraints. But on the field, off the field, in our homes, at Toots's and Manuche's, I never saw the man the Packers talk about, or the journalists wrote about once he got to Green Bay. Vince Lombardi was no screaming madman. He was a man who loved football, yes, but it was far from the only thing in his life. He was a deeply religious guy who cared about his family, his friends, and his Catholic faith.

But the Vince who, according to a national magazine profile in the early sixties and cited in David Maraniss's biography of the man, *When Pride Still Mattered*, hit one of his own linemen in Green Bay, yelling at him, "Hate me enough to take it out on the opposition!" The guy who supposedly made most of the Packers, at one point or another, want to take a swing at him? Not the Vince I ever knew—and would know until the day he died.

Now, I think the former Packer lineman Jerry Kramer is a really smart guy. Don't get me wrong. Jerry made a fortune on the banquet circuit because of Vince and all of those championships rings. A good guy, a hell of a football player. But did Vince act the way Jerry said he did—with the "my way or the highway" attitude? Not with us, not back then; not with a veteran team that had been through the wars already—all kinds of wars.

Sure, he yelled. But all those clichés ("He treats us all the same—like dogs"): that wasn't Vince when he was with the Giants. It couldn't have been. It wouldn't have worked. And the man I knew would never have acted that way. I'm not saying he wasn't volatile with the Packers. Fuzzy Thurston, the offensive lineman whose later career in Green Bay would earn him well-deserved accolades, assured me that he most definitely was. Fuzzy was a rookie on the Colt roster that day, playing special teams, and when we talked about Vince recently, Fuzzy laughed and said: "You guys got to know him when he wasn't such an asshole yet. You guys got to know him when he was young and wasn't the boss. Oh, man, he never ever socialized with us at all. I never knew him as a person at Green Bay. He was never friendly at all. Very, very tough."

Bill Curry, the great center, played for Lombardi in Green Bay before coming to Baltimore. Bill tells me that he found Vince to be a complex, brilliant man who had a method to most of that madness in Green Bay: "He could exert great force, and get your attention. When the boiling point of the team got to where we were ready to mutiny, he'd back off. He knew when to be gentle. It would last a few weeks. Then there'd be a moment when he'd march into the room and put the hammer back down—especially after a game we'd won when we'd played poorly. Then he'd try and motivate you by putting you down. He'd come by my locker and say, in a real low voice, 'Butkus owns you, doesn't he?' He knew I couldn't respond. He knew I couldn't hit him. You know what I think? That in his heart of hearts, he really wanted to be one of the guys. But, of course, he couldn't be."

With the Giants, as an assistant coach, and relatively new to the game, Vince would listen to what we had to say. He even did calisthenics with us, in his classic rubber jacket and baseball cap. If I had to make a judgment call, I'd agree with Curry: I think Vince would have loved to have been one of us—and in many ways, he was. With the Giants, his popping off was innocent and fun; it was the give-and-take of a relationship where the respect was mutual.

We'd get all over him about some of his sillier rules. When we were practicing in training camp, if we weren't in the play that was being run, he'd make us stand ten yards behind him. But we'd get right up behind him, just to irritate him. One really hot day we were right on top of him; it was so freaking hot we didn't want to walk any farther than we had to for our next turn in the offensive drill. Finally, he turned around and bumped right into us. He lost it: "Get back! Move back!" As practice grew longer and hotter, and the day warmer and warmer, we refused to have to slog ten yards to get back to the huddle. We loved to get under his skin. On this day he picked up this little Band-Aid, and walked back ten yards, and put it on the ground. "Stay behind the Band-Aid!" he screamed. So, of course, we just kept moving the band-aid closer to him, as soon as he turned his back. Finally, he just began to laugh, that big rolling laugh.

We loved hiding his blackboard chalk, too. Drove him crazy. He'd be ranting and raving, "Where's my chalk? WHERE'S MY CHALK?"—and then he'd eventually figure it out, and give us that wonderful laugh again. With us, Vince never took himself that seriously, and that's the mark of a man who knows how to gain the respect of a team. When Vince pushed someone too far, he knew it. Sure, he swore a lot, but he always knew when to stop. He absolutely did not behave like a dictator with a megalomaniacal ego. He behaved like a man who knew how to motivate professionals.

I'm not saying Vince didn't overstep the boundaries every now and then, particularly with rookies. He'd lose it sometimes. The brunt of his temper often turned toward Youso. Frank may have been a rookie, but he didn't act like one. From the day he showed up that summer (in street shoes), with a big smile and a lot of confidence, Frank was his own man. You couldn't intimidate Frank Youso. Vince would try, but it never worked.

"One day," Don Maynard recalls, "Youso did something that got Vince angry, and Lombardi said to him, 'You big, blind, dumb tackle.' Youso answers, 'Well, Coach, I may be blind, but I'm not dumb.'" Our backup lineman Buzz Guy remembers another day when Vince was riding Frank pretty hard, and Youso forgot to bring his sense of humor to practice: "Frank finally told him, 'Shut your goddamned mouth, or I'm going to come rap you.' Vince shut up."

If that had happened in Green Bay, I imagine that Frank would have been on the next Greyhound out of town. But back then, Vince knew that each guy needs a different kind of motivation. Vince's style wasn't to treat everyone in lockstep; he was always willing to learn with us, to adjust.

Maynard has another memory that puts Vince in a much better perspective, during another film session. Vince didn't want to pick on Triplett that day; he'd learned his lesson about riding Mel. So he put the spotlight on our rookie kick returner. "On one of the games I'd gotten in as a backup safety, on defense. On Tuesday, about nine-thirty in the morning, Lombardi is running the film. He shows some play where some guy broke through the middle of the line, and I came up as a safety, and I didn't hit the guy. Hell, he was being tackled already, I figured, 'Why pile on?'

"So Lombardi runs it back a few times. Then, in the dark, he says, 'Aintcha *hungry*, Maynard?' I said, 'No sir, I had breakfast right before I came over.' The projector goes off. There's a little giggle. Then he starts laughing."

Pat Summerall's recollection of his first meeting with the man says it all very well: "Coming from the Cardinals and the staff we had, it was a real eye-opener. The first meeting I went to at our training camp in Oregon, nobody had seen each other for a period of time; we'd been out drinking beer, everyone welcoming each other back. The line coach, John Dell Isola, couldn't get the room quiet. I'm sitting next to Heinrich. Suddenly this guys walks into the room and clears his throat and the whole room falls into a hush.

"I say, 'Who the hell is that?' Heinrich says, 'That's Lombardi. You'll know soon enough.' Before long, he was 'Vinnie.' The Packers never called him Vinnie. That's not to say he wasn't without ego. He never made a comment [like], 'You're playing well,' or 'You're playing terribly.' He just said, 'You didn't do what I told you,' and that was his simple way of correcting and praising. 'You did what I said, so we won.'"

We always did it Vince's way. And that meant acting not only like a pro, but like a man. Celebrating was never tolerated on our offense—partly because, as I've said, your teammates wouldn't put up with any showmanship, but partly because of Vince's insistence that sportsmanship was part of our repertoire.

"I'll never forget one time," Alex says now, "when I ran a screen pass of about sixty yards, down the right part of the field, and when I went into the end zone, I turned to run under the goalpost, and put in an extra little high stride. On the sideline, he grabbed me and said, 'We don't do any of that here.' I hadn't even realized I'd done it, either.

"He made me into what I was," Alex says now, matter-of-factly. "Period. I was a lazy sonofogun when I come in. I just was never focused. Once, we were doing our calisthenics, and I was in the back, and he caught me goofing off, he made me come up front, and stood right over me from then on. That taught me something.

"Vince and I became close friends—in the off-season; but that's where it'd stop. He lived down in Rumson, New Jersey, and I was in Sea Girt, so we'd go out to dinner on Saturday nights. Strictly social. He never talked football when he was away, with his wife around. She ran him. As tough as he was, his wife could handle him.

"But he knew how to separate the social stuff and the football stuff. One year we went out on a Saturday night, and training camp was starting Monday. The end of the night, we're all saying good night. I say, 'See you Monday.' He says, 'What do you mean? We're parting friends, but when you come to camp, I don't know you.'

"See, come Monday, he wanted me to be like the rest of the ballplayers. He said, 'You'll see me next year—at the end of the season.'"

The Lombardi the Giants knew was a New York guy, a Brooklyn guy, finally coaching back in his hometown after his years coaching at the high-school level and at West Point. With the Giants, Vince was more or less in heaven: coaching with the team that, as a teenager, he used to take a ninety-minute subway ride up from Sheepshead Bay to watch in the Polo Grounds. The team whose head-coaching position, he'd told a friend when he was coaching at Army, was something he wanted "worse than anything in the world."

Vince definitely had the Giant pedigree. As a key member of the "Seven Blocks of Granite" at Fordham, the Maras' alma mater—a team that the greatest of the old sportswriters, Grantland Rice and Damon Runyon, glorified with all the power of their lyrical pens—he was working for his old Fordham classmate, Wellington.

After graduating from Fordham, Lombardi briefly played

minor-league football, spent five years turning a small parochial school in northern New Jersey called St. Cecilia—just across the George Washington Bridge—into a football powerhouse, then joined the staff of the legendary coach Red Blaik at West Point. Under Blaik, Vince helped turn Army into a powerhouse. In fact, when the Maras fired Steve Owen after the '53 season, after a run of twenty-two years, they actually wanted Blaik to replace Owen, but settled on our part-time assistant, old Jim Lee: a former end with the Giants, from 1937 to 1947.

Vince got the Giants' backfield-coaching job, but in one of Jim Lee's rare strokes of genius, he told Lombardi that he was completely free to run the offense. And Vince quickly dove in to the task: studying film of all our games, studying the techniques of other coaches—with an eye, in particular, to what Paul Brown was doing in Cleveland. Brown was the pro game's guru, ever since his AAFC Browns had joined the league in 1950—and had won the NFL championship in their first year.

Vince realized from the start that he had to put a flanker system into our offense to beef up the passing game. And he knew that we needed a stronger running game. As one of those "blocks of granite" on Fordham's offensive line, Vince always saw things through a lineman's eyes. He also knew that the key to everything was a possession running game that could control the clock. The first set of running backs to go with our revamped offensive line were Alex and me. (In Vince's dominant years in Green Bay, Paul Hornung and Jim Taylor would play those roles.)

Vince knew that shortcuts, in this league, would never work; the key to winning in the NFL would always be the brilliant simplicity of his schemes, and the repetitions. You'd never find your attention wandering during a Vince Lombardi lecture. Between the man's command, demeanor, and presence, he could be riveting. The message would always get through.

"I've been in quarterback meetings with Sid Gillman, with Buddy Parker, with Lou Saban," Jack Kemp told me. "I have never seen a quarterback meeting as precise, and as strategic, as Lombardi's. He had a mind that could see beyond the first two or three plays. He was the Garry Kasparov of football minds. I learned more in the first hour-long quarterback meeting with Lombardi than I learned in all my years before."

More simply, Alex puts it this way: "He was a real professor."

On the field, Vince had this energy inside him, an enthusiasm that just rolled right out of him, in the way he walked, in the way he rocked back on his heels, and in the way he talked. This wasn't a coach whose voice you'd tune out as he corrected you, as he implored you to get it right. You'd listen to every word.

As innovative as Vince was, as many hours as he spent watching film, he possessed an indefinable quality of being able to command immediate respect. For me, that respect was established very early on in our relationship, when he first came on board in 1954 and I found myself surprised and delighted to meet a brand of coach I'd never known: a man who was willing to listen to what the players had to say.

For my first few years, I had been used in just about any and every way a man can be used on a football field: as a wide receiver, as a defensive back, as a running back, as a field-goal kicker, as a kick returner, and as anything else that Steve Owen, and then Jim Lee, could think of (Landry took care of the punting). The arrangement exhausted me, and frustrated me. Where did I belong? When were they going to let me do the one thing I knew, instinctively, how to do?

In Salem, Oregon, in August of 1954, during his first training camp, at Willamette University, the first thing Vince Lombardi ever said to me, rocking back and forth, was "Frank Gifford, you're my halfback." Man, that was great to hear. (He'd say the same thing to Paul Hornung, who had struggled at quarterback, a few years later in Green Bay, which worked out pretty well for both of us. Hornung would go on to have a tremendous career. In fact, most of the plays that Hornung grew famous for up there had originally been designed for me by Vince in New York.)

But my respect for the man really grew on the night he visited the dorm room Charlie and I shared in Salem, that first August. Vince had come looking for advice—and he listened to what we had to tell him. What he'd been doing so far hadn't worked. In training camp, Vince had put in the option offense he had used at Army that was so popular at the college level in the fifties. But Charlie obviously was not an option quarterback, nor, at the age of thirty-four, was he going to become one. He was not about to start making a living attempting to do what three other teammates in his huddle were paid to do, and could do infinitely better.

Vince hadn't yet learned how quick, strong, and mean NFL pros were, compared with the kinds of players he'd coached in college. In college, a lot of the linemen filled up space. Up here, they were big, often huge, and really quick. A steady diet of running the ball would have ended Charlie's career, and quickly. And Charlie wasn't buying any of it.

But Vince ran Charlie's option in no-contact practice, over and over again. Charlie went along with Vince's calls—without so much as a word of protest. Then, in our first exhibition game,

Charlie just called our old plays. On the sideline, Vince would say to Charlie, 'Okay, let's go to that option, all right?' Charlie would give an affirmative grunt—and never once call it.

Vince wasn't afraid of Charlie, and he knew that the team had universal respect for him: a war veteran, with a lot of cool, and a superb arm. We knew we could win with him. But Vince didn't know how to treat him. To his credit, a lot of coaches would have put themselves in a deep hole. But Vince came to see us in our dorm room to work things out.

The problem with that, though, was that he was on bed check. He came in and sat down in our room. We were in two-a-day work-outs, and Charlie and I had planned to slip out for a couple of cold ones. That was the routine, no matter where we were training— Salem, Oregon; Winooski, Vermont; Bear Mountain, New York— first the meetings, then practice, then waiting for the after-curfew check, then going out for a few beers. That last step in the routine mattered as much to us as all of the rest of it, giving us a reason to get through the days. In every town a cheap bar would beckon, a place with some privacy, a jukebox, a couple of those locals hanging out. A few after-curfew beers gave us some downtime when we could just be *guys* again. Those late nights in those dark, jukeboxed bars provided many a highlight to those endless summers.

That night, in our dorm room, Vince knew perfectly well that we were about to slip out. But he wanted our advice, and as usual, he didn't beat around the bush: "What am I doing wrong?" he asked. Right away we recognized that this was a different kind of coach, a pretty big coach: This was a guy who could sit on your bed and ask you to tell him where he was messing up. This was a guy who would become arguably the greatest coach in history—and this was just one reason he would become great.

Charlie had very little to say, as usual. That night, I did the talking. The first thing I told this guy from West Point was that Charlie would be crazy to call that play—he'd get himself killed. "It worked for you at Army," I said, "but it won't work here. In this league, the difference is that the defensive tackles and ends can put an end to a career with one shot—and a lot of them are trying to do just that."

But my main message didn't concern strategy or personnel. I spoke of the way he was treating my roommate. Vince had ridden all of us, in his way, throughout that camp, and that was okay with the rest of us, as far as I could tell. But Charlie wasn't happy with it—and I told Vince so. "You don't yell at guys like Charlie," I told him. "This is a guy who watched guys die in the South Pacific. Treating him like some junior at West Point is ridiculous, and it's stupid. Give up the shouting. Give up the stomping. Give Charlie the offense he can run."

We lost the option from the playbook that night. Vince took a long intelligent look at the talent around him—and its most serious limitation: a real lack of speed. He began to assemble the offense based on what we could realistically do. I could throw the ball, and I could catch the ball, as well as run the ball, so he built the offense around me. He put in plays that Kyle could live with—not a lot of slant-ins where he'd get creamed, but square-outs and timing patterns. In other words, he devised a simple, pound-it-out offense that would set up the occasional big play.

The big plays, Vince would come to understand, would be Charlie's department.

The quiet leadership, that would be Charlie's department too. By the time Vince Lombardi left New York, he had as much respect for Charlie Conerly as the rest of us did. I think Vince Lombardi learned a lot about leadership from Charlie. It comes by example, not noise.

• • •

harlie's service in the war earned incredible respect on our team. He served as a corporal in the Third Marine Division as it worked its way up through the South Pacific toward Japan—all the way to Iwo Jima: just another leatherneck. He seldom talked about the war to me, unless he'd had a few beers, and even then, he wouldn't say much. The old marine axiom about that war says that the only people who talked about it afterward were the men who didn't have a rough war. Charlie epitomized that saying. Charlie had a rough one. His survival relied on luck—and a matter of a few inches.

"It was tough fighting, for Charlie," Perian Conerly tells me now. "One time, on Guam, on patrol, he was a lead man. He had a rifle shot out of his hands. I still have the rifle clip with the bullet hole in it. I also have the telegram that the Navy Department sent home to tell his parents about the incident. On the outside it said 'News Material,' so they wouldn't think it was a death notice."

Andy Robustelli, our other quiet leader, on defense, had been in the thick of the fighting in the Pacific too. Andy never talked about it either. He served as a 20-millimeter antiaircraft gunner and a water-tender on a destroyer escort—a very fragile little ship—off the coast of Okinawa. He'd be belowdecks, manning pumps in the fire room, when the general-quarters alarm would blare, and up he'd hustle to his station to shoot at Japanese dive-bombers.

When I asked him about his war experience over lunch at his restaurant in Stamford recently, Andy—graying; a little slower in gait; philosophical, as always, in conversation—just shrugged: "You don't think much about it—you just do it. We all did it."

In his own book, *Once a Giant, Always . . .* , Andy devotes exactly one paragraph to his war service.

As I researched this book, I discovered that, on the other side of the line, the Colts' own two true leaders, Marchetti and Donovan, had done their own tough time, Gino as a machine gunner with the Army in the Battle of the Bulge, and Artie as a marine—in the same battalion as Charlie.

"Yeah, I ended up on Okinawa," Artie says now, "but all I did was handle the ammunition. In twenty-three months in the Pacific, I never fired a gun. Conerly was in the same outfit, but I never knew it until years after [a battalion was a thousand marines, divided into companies]. We were playing in a golf tournament, and I said to him, 'Charlie, you're the oldest guy in the league. He says, 'I'm a month younger than you.' We trade stories—and it turned out we were in the same battalion in the Third Division."

Tom Landry flew B-17s. In fact, he flew thirty missions—five more than he had to. Charlie Winner, the Colts' assistant coach, was a POW.

In the younger generation, we had a lot of guys who'd served in every branch of the services in Korea, although most of them played football during their service time. Livingston and Heinrich played for a legendary team, with Ollie Matson, at Fort Ord. That team often scrimmaged against the pros— the 49ers and the Rams—and more than held its own.

Looking back now, through the shadows of so many wars, I think we lose sight of how much the Second World War was still part of our country that day of December 28, 1958—and part of the National Football League. The war had ended only thirteen years earlier. There was a visceral tie between the 1958 NFL and the postwar United States and its values. Average guys playing in a multiethnic league mirrored the makeup of the nation, where the philosophy of "team first" had roots, perhaps, in the foxhole ethic.

• • •

ive minutes. Let's be ready." That was the head coach, giving his halftime talk as if we were little kids in grade school, instead of professionals who'd been doing it for years. ("He had to be the last person ever to carry a pocket watch," Pat says now. "No matter what happened, on the field or off it, he'd go to the pocket watch.")

Most of my teammates didn't find Jim Lee as annoying as I did, just kind of laughable. But then, I felt I had a reason to dislike him. He'd singled me out in '57, embarrassing me in front of my team. And I never forgave him.

It was preseason, 1957. I'd just come off my MVP year, and we'd won the title. We were having a mediocre preseason, as we often did. I wasn't playing all that well, but I never saw much point in leaving it out on the field in August. So one day we were practicing at Fordham, and Jim Lee took off on me. After yelling at everyone else, he turned to me: "And then there's Mister Hollywood, Number Sixteen, the Most Valuable Player in the National Football League. Right now he is the worst player on this football team. He hunkers up when he's supposed to be running with the ball." . . . and on and on he went.

I didn't say anything. Sam swears now that he saw tears in my eyes. "I was so embarrassed for you. How in the hell could a football coach say this about Frank Gifford? That might have been the last time I spoke to him."

There was no reason for Jim Lee to speak those words. I'd already lived through the Hollywood thing with my teammates, and earned their respect by now. No one had given me grief about USC or California or movies for years. They'd seen me leave it all on the field, game after game.

After that, I never considered Jim Lee Howell to be my coach again.

In the long run, Howell's profile in NFL history is remarkably low. In his years in New York, he won a championship, and took us to another title game. That's a pretty fair record. But he suffered by comparison when put next to Landry and Lombardi, both of whom were able to immediately command respect without insisting we give it.

Jim Lee's way of trying to get us to take him seriously is epitomized by the way our backup lineman M. L. Brackett remembers Howell now: "He'd try and stand tall, throw his shoulders back, speak like some sort of senator. He went on to the Arkansas State Legislature later on, you know, and maybe that worked down there, in politics. But it didn't with us. He just wasn't very impressive."

When I asked the rest of my teammates about the man with the pants pulled up above his stomach, most of their answers made it sound as if I were asking for remembrances of a distant uncle of whom they hadn't thought in years.

"I think Jim Lee was a CEO, you know what I mean?" Al Barry says now. "He was head guy, and he said, 'You handle this, you handle that.' He never had a meeting. All I remember was him sticking his head into the locker room and saying, 'Five minutes, five minutes. Be ready.' What I remember about being coached on the Giants was pretty much just sitting next to Pat Summerall on the bench. Pat would analyze every play, tell me, 'Watch this guy do this, do that,' and that was how I was coached."

Cliff Livingston's memories of the man are limited to a booming voice saying nothing but "All right—settle down." Lindon Crow laughs about Howell's role as the travel agent: "He'd drill us, but not about football. 'Okay, what time does the bus leave? What time does the train leave?' And everybody had to repeat it."

Harland Svare recalls Howell's chief responsibility as making sure the balls were pumped up.

O n the other hand, Jim Lee's counterpart, right down the hall-way, evoked enough memories and anecdotes for the Colts to fill their own book. One thing that no student of professional football history can ever dispute is that Wilbur "Weeb" Ewbank must stand as one of the best coaches the game has ever seen, or ever will. If one figure on the field that day—a field crowded with greats: future Hall of Famers, immortal coaches—has been slighted by history, it's Weeb Ewbank.

Weeb won three championships—'58, '59, and Super Bowl III in January 1969—and two of those games are universally considered to be the two most memorable games in league history. Or, as Weeb himself put it in an interview many years later, "I won a world championship every six and two-thirds years, and that's not a bad average." Not that he was doing the math or anything.

But Ewbank's name is seldom, if ever, mentioned alongside the names of Halas, Brown, Lombardi, Landry, and Shula. Unlike his peers, he wasn't imposing enough—physically, verbally. His strengths were more mental than emotional: "My crew-cut IBM machine," Carroll Rosenbloom once called him. His personality could be abrasive, to some; "Weeb was a weasel," Artie says now, with a laugh. "If he told you something—if he told you that black was white—you'd better believe him."

The true voice of reason on that team has nothing but praise for his coach; and when Raymond Berry talks, you have to listen: "See, you can ask me if Weeb belongs up there with the likes of the greats, even if he isn't widely known that way—with Lombardi, Landry, Shula. Me, I'd put it differently. I'd say, 'Maybe you have to get those other guys up there with Weeb.' Weeb Ewbank had the ability to bring in a system that was totally sound, and keep it simple. And he could recognize talent. You can't always find someone who can bring both of those things together."

To my way of thinking, recognizing talent—seeing a man's strengths and weaknesses, and playing to them, as Lombardi learned to—makes a good coach into a great coach. Weeb took a quarterback off a Pittsburgh sandlot; a lot of people took credit for that pickup, but Lenny Moore, among others, swears that it was Weeb's tutelage that turned a castoff into a king. Then again, Weeb always knew quarterbacks; he'd been one himself, at Miami of Ohio.

Weeb's draft picks built the heart of the team, from Parker and Sandusky on the offensive line to Moore and Dupre in the backfield. And he took Big Daddy off the waiver wire.

"Believe it, man—Weeb had an ability to see our capabilities; he really could recognize talent," Moore told me. "He could see down the road. I'll give you a great example: We had Fuzzy Thurston that year. The season after this game, we went into the meeting room at training camp, and Fuzzy's seat is empty. Weeb said, 'Fellas, I got bad news for you. Fuzzy isn't here. Someday, Fuzzy is going to be an all-pro. But we couldn't wait on him.' Turned out to be true." (Maybe Lombardi had something to do with that, because Fuzzy became a key figure and leader on Green Bay's offensive line during the Packers' championship years.)

"And Jim Parker? Listen to this; here's where Weeb comes in again. He had films of Rosey Brown. He sat Parker down, and said, 'Watch Rosey Brown. Rosey Brown is the best offensive tackle in the game. Parker, you learn from Rosey Brown.'

"And Johnny? George Shaw was our quarterback in '56. Weeb picked him in the first round in '55, and he was good. George was a running and passing quarterback, and there were very few of those guys in the league. George Shaw was the man. Nobody paid Johnny any attention. Weeb took a shot. It paid off. But you know what Weeb told us about that? 'I could see down the road,' he said. 'I knew it would take time. I knew it all along.'"

Even Artie gives Weeb credit for his football savvy. "I thought he was a terrific coach, I really did—when he wasn't screaming or yelling. Whatever success I had was due to him. He made me into a defensive tackle. He taught me how to use my peripheral vision: 'Get a yard and a half off the line,' he said to me, 'and you can see everything right and left.' It's true. Then he taught me to use my instincts—that most of the time, the way the blocking went, the blocking pressure would almost always take you right to the ball. He had a saying: 'Take a stance, deliver a blow, find the ball, and get in the flow.' That was his theory in a nutshell, and it worked." (Once again, I disagree with Artie: that's a good way to get your ass knocked off with trap-blocking.)

"He didn't have much of a sense of humor, though," Artie continues. "We used to kid around, older guys, we had a lot of fun— we'd throw cold water on each other. So Lenny Lyles is a number-one draft pick, he's in a whirlpool, he never played much . . . they threw a bucket of water on him, he jumped out, broke his ankle on a radiator. So Weeb sends our defensive line coach, John Sandusky, to talk to us. He says, 'Weeb says it's a thousand-dollar fine if he catches anyone throwing water.' So Gino says to Gaucho (Carl Taseff), 'When Alan the Horse comes around the corner, you throw the water on him. I'll nod to you to let you know he's coming.' Gaucho says, 'Okay.' Here comes Weeb out of his office, all dressed up for his TV show. Gino nods. Gaucho throws. Soon as he sees what he's done, he tries to put the water back in the bucket. Too late. Two weeks later, Gaucho was gone, to Philadelphia. No sense of humor."

Well, Weeb had to have a sense of humor to put up with Artie. Anytime anyone new came to camp, Weeb had a rule: If you can't beat Artie in the 40, you're gone—just keep running, out of the stadium. As far as Artie can recall, he never beat anyone.

Weeb's motivational style did not earn every Colt's admiration; he could use the needle, and not gently. "Weeb and I didn't get along too well," Jack Call, the backup Colt running back, remembers. "I'm going to tell you something: This team won in spite of, and not because of, Weeb. He was the boss, but that's about it. I looked up to Unitas more than to Weeb."

Artie wasn't the only Colt who didn't trust Ewbank. "Ray Berry gave me some good advice," safety Ray Brown told me. "He said, 'Ray, never let Weeb get you to comment upon a player, because if he cuts him, and someone criticizes him, he'll blame it on you.' He'd tell you things, but never follow through on them. That was part of his image with the guys."

Ewbank seems to have been a football version of a Billy Martin–type guy. He could take a losing team to the top, but never keep it there for long. "I think his problem was that he was too easy," Gino told me. "In the long run a team would die on him. We did. Same thing with the Jets. He took a team up—and then the team dies. Basically, he was a guy who, the longer you stay with him, the longer you take advantage of him. Everyone could pretty much do what they wanted."

On that day, they'd been doing exactly what Weeb wanted. And they seemed to want it more than we did. That's not coaching; it's desire, on the part of the players.

It's funny to look back at the two coaches who led their respective teams in what is called the greatest game ever played. Was it us, or them, who just didn't get it? Did these two teams pull off their great seasons in spite of the coaches, or because of them? It's hard to say. In my many years as a player and as a broadcaster, I've often seen teams win big with a coach the players downright detest. And I've seen teams lose big for a coach with a great-guy label.

**B**y now, the Colt band had taken its bass drums and trombones back into the stands. The dancing girls in leotards with the reindeer horns on their heads had vacated the dusty, fast-chilling field. The defensive line had slapped new tape around bent thumbs and bruised forearms.

We had thirty minutes of football left to get this thing right.

In retrospect, the trouble to that point stemmed from the rigidity of both of our coaches' simple schemes and strategies, the philosophies that had gotten us here. On defense, Landry's cornerbacks were getting no help, and our pass rush had been nonexistent. On offense, after the first quarter, they were all over me. We weren't the type of team to feature one player, but toward the end of the '58 season, as injuries began to take their toll, I'd become more and more of a key in terms of rushing and receiving. This was obviously not lost on Ewbank and the Colts. Except for my 38-yard run, they'd been all over me in the first half.

**I**n the last few minutes of the break, Kyle approached Charlie and suggested that, just maybe, they could exploit something Kyle had seen: every time I ran wide, the Colt safeties were crowding to the line. Maybe we could take advantage of their eagerness.

During halftime, one of the things we talked over was the

problem we had had with the running game. Kyle and Charlie discussed the possibility of using more play action in the passing game. Charlie soaked it all up, cracked his ankles a few more times, and prepared to go out and play thirty of the best minutes of his career.

"Time to go, men."

That was Jim Lee, at the door. Then, it was back down the tunnel, up the dugout steps—no introductions this time, no ceremony, no Bob Sheppard from On High. As we came up from the dugout gloom, I noticed that even though it wasn't yet three o'clock, the temperature had dropped considerably, and there weren't any shadows crossing the field now. It was *all* shadow.

No one spoke on the way back onto the field. Just the sounds of cleats. Everyone knew what he had to do, and we had two quarters—or so we thought—to do it. If before the game I'd sensed how beat up we were, how maybe we weren't primed to take on the sky-high Colts, as we came out for the second half the fatigue was gone.

We had one last half of football to help prove that the first-half Giants weren't the real Giants, that the Giants were not just a defensive team. And that I could hold on to the football.

We weren't going to have to go through any Heinrich warm-up. We weren't going to be hampered by a helpless Grier.

This was still our title to take.

## CHAPTER 6

# THIRD QUARTER

It figured that, sooner or later, Sam would get in a fight that day. I'm surprised he didn't lay me out during halftime. But if he wasn't going to square off against me, you had to figure it would be against someone in a Colt uniform. Who could have predicted that the guy who threw the punch at Sam would have been a short man in an overcoat, wearing a fedora on top of his crew cut?

During the first few minutes of the third quarter, the Colts had started to march again. Unitas had picked up right where he'd left off, mixing up the plays and throwing in some new stuff, including an 8-yard completion to Mutscheller. Now the Colts had the ball on their 32. Funny that Joe Boland would choose that moment to tell his radio audience, *"Just getting the third period under way, and we're anticipating fireworks."* He was more than right on.

Johnny had just completed another perfect square-out to Berry to their 25-yard line, right on the Colt sideline, in front of the coaches. By now Sam had seen enough of the Johnny-to-Raymond pitch-and-catch. He'd had a half hour to stew about how easily the Colts had sliced through the defense at the end of the first half. He took it personally. And he took it out on Raymond. Karilivacz had Ray by the ankle, and Berry had already gone down, just in bounds—and here comes Sam, full speed, piling on.

"Berry was dragging someone, and I hit him with everything I had," Sam told me, his voice rising. "That's football. What, you think I'm going to run thirty yards to get there and not hit anybody? I hit him legal. I didn't get a flag, right? Anytime you don't get a flag, you're legal. That's what officials are for."

Now here came Weeb, all five-foot-six of him, running right onto the field—and he swung his left fist at old number 70. "That little asshole, he hit me right in the jaw," Sam said. "It surprised me. I think I called him a sonofabitch."

Artie remembers that when Weeb turned around, after the officials had stepped in, none of the Colts were behind him to back their coach up. End of confrontation. Weeb's temper dropped dramatically when he realized he was about to go on-on-one with a man who once knocked out Jimmy Brown.

Play resumed, and Sam hadn't calmed down any. On third down, Dupre took a short pass, got by Harland—and then here came Sam, who nailed him, on the 35, short of the first down. We'd stopped them. No, Sam had held them.

I remember seeing a sign on a locker room wall somewhere once. It read: "Expect Nothing. Blame No One. Do Something." That was Sam Huff on that series. He'd done something. He'd made Weeb lose his cool. Advantage, Giants. It wasn't much, but it was something.

**M**aynard fielded Ray Brown's punt, and we took over on the 21. There's no question Sam had pumped up the defense, and the crowd. Unfortunately, he didn't play offense. We were now playing with a completely makeshift offensive line. Stroud was playing right tackle, replacing Youso, and a rookie, Bob Mischak, a West Point guy who hadn't played a great deal that season, was in at right guard.

I had no doubt that Stroud could handle the shift. Jack was the consummate pro, and then some. He was a physical-fitness freak, with not an ounce of fat on him, and way ahead of his time in that regard—lifting weights when the rest of us had never even *seen* a weight. Jack was also a pioneer in another way: he supplemented his diet with something other than beer.

"He was always drinking these mixes with bananas and protein and all this crap," Youso told me. Frank had been Jack's roommate in training camp that year. "Jack would talk real slow—a real manly man. And he was real strong. He always had these big springs he'd pull on to get stronger. He was always pulling on these springs. Me, I couldn't stretch them four inches.

"He was also a great guy to have by your side. I'll never forget the exhibition game in Los Angeles that year. They had a line-backer (and a friend of mine) named Les Richter. One play, after the play was over, Richter came in late and really whacked me. Jack went over to him, looks at him, and says, 'It's over for you, Richter.' Richter says, 'Come on, let's just play football.' Jack hit him anyway."

**B**ut with our makeshift line, we went nowhere on this drive. I gained nothing on a run, and lost three on a flare pass out in the left flat. On third down, Artie came through the right side of our line and sacked Charlie. Chandler had to punt from our end zone, and while he got off a good kick—Don always did—the Colts took over on their 41.

It was now put-up-or-shut-up time: The Colts had a short

field, and one more touchdown would more or less seal the out-come. If the defense was ever going to save us, this had to be the time.

On first down, Johnny, with plenty of time, found his big, quiet tight end Mutscheller in the middle—wide open. Mutscheller was primarily the safety's responsibility. But Patton, the strong safety, was playing up short, thinking, *Stop the run.*

Mutscheller found the seam, and made a terrific 31-yard catch on a pass that Johnny had thrown a little too high. And Patton made Mutscheller pay. To this day, Mutscheller, the unassuming insurance broker, recalls the play vividly—well, the first half of it, anyway; after that, Jim's memory became a little foggy: "The way the play was designed," Jim told me, "we hoped the action in the backfield would pull Patton way over to the right side. I went down and did a 'Z-in,' a slant. The pass was high. As I caught it, I had both feet off the ground, and Patton caught me just right. I landed right on my head. I stood up in the middle of Yankee Stadium, and said, 'Where am I?' I just walked off the field—I was kind of goofy."

On the next play, a running play that Katcavage and Huff stuffed at the line, Mutscheller, wandering around the sideline, heard Ewbank say, 'Who's in there for Mutscheller?' The answer came from somewhere on the bench: "Rechichar"—Weeb's favorite whipping boy. "Get him out of there!" yelled Weeb. And Jim went back, trying to clear the cobwebs.

In the meantime, Unitas got another first down with yet an-other hook to Berry, who once again took advantage of the cushion Karilivacz was giving him. Now they had it on the 15, and we were in deep trouble. Or, as Boland put it, *"Unitas has hit on thirteen of eighteen forward passes, and the boy is very definitely on the beam."*

A meeting of the minds before a practice prior to the '56 title game against Chicago: Alex Webster, Charlie Conerly, Head Coach Jim Lee Howell, Mel Triplett, and me.

*(Kidwiler Collection/Diamond Images/ Getty Images)*

With Charlie *(right)*: my best friend, our quarterback, our leader.

*(United Press International)*

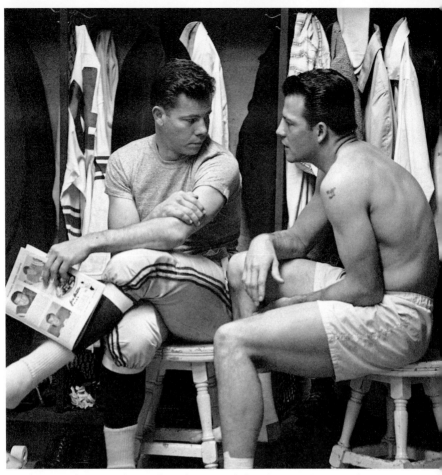

Receiver Kyle Rote and me, talking things over before the 1958 championship game.

*(Robert Riger/Getty Images)*

The Colts' Raymond Berry makes one of his twelve receptions of the day as Giants cornerback Carl Karilivacz tries his best to defend.

*(Hy Peskin/Sports Illustrated/Getty Images)*

Mel Triplett (33) running left, about to meet up with a leaping Gino Marchetti (89).

*(Hy Peskin/Sports Illustrated/Getty Images)*

Rosey Brown (79) leads the way for me, as he always did so well, on our 48 sweep.

*(Hy Peskin/Sports Illustrated/Getty Images)*

Colts defensive tackle Artie Donovan in a rare moment of reflection.

*(Darryl Norenberg/NFL)*

Colts quarterback Johnny Unitas and Raymond Berry coolly take in all the action from the sidelines.

*(NFL/NFL)*

My second fumble, in the second quarter: The Colts' Milt Davis (47) has just knocked the ball loose, and my teammate Al Barry is trying to recover it. Unfortunately, the Colts came up with the ball.

*(Hy Peskin/Sports Illustrated/Getty Images)*

Giants offensive coach Vince Lombardi and me, calmly discussing the finer points of our offensive strategy.

*(Robert Riger/Getty Images)*

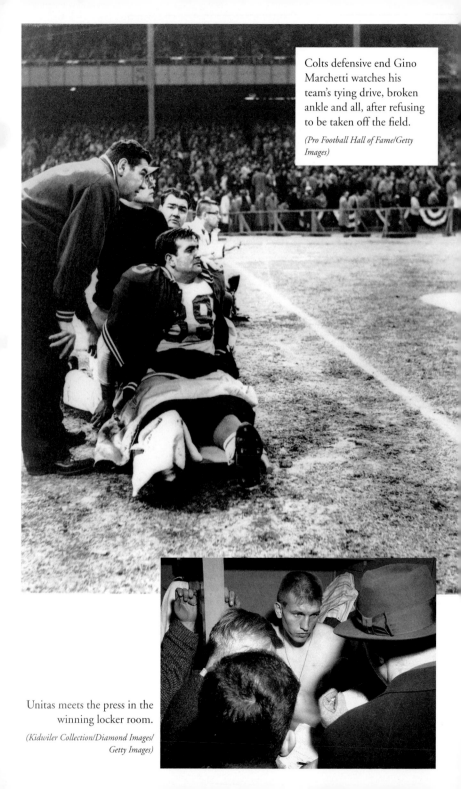

Colts defensive end Gino Marchetti watches his team's tying drive, broken ankle and all, after refusing to be taken off the field.

*(Pro Football Hall of Fame/Getty Images)*

Unitas meets the press in the winning locker room.

*(Kidwiler Collection/Diamond Images/Getty Images)*

OFFICE OF THE VICE PRESIDENT

WASHINGTON

December 29, 1958

<u>Personal</u>

Dear Frank:

I have just turned off the television after seeing the fabulous playoff game. While I am not supposed to take sides in such a contest, I must admit that I was pulling for the Giants probably because of my friendship and admiration for you and Don Heinrich.

I know you must be disappointed as to the result. But certainly you can be proud of the superb performance you gave. I also saw the game last week with the Browns and I will have to agree with George Marshall when he rates you the best all-around back in pro-football.

In any event, it was a great season for the Giants, for football and for you personally.

My wife, Pat (USC '37), joins me in sending our best wishes for the New Year.

Sincerely,

Richard Nixon

Mr. Frank Gifford
New York Football Giants
100 West 42nd Street
New York, New York

Apparently, our vice president, like millions of other fans, put aside all pressing business for three and a half hours on December 28, 1958.

*(Courtesy of the author)*

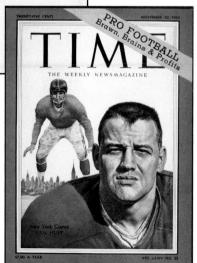

Sam Huff, national magazine cover boy, 1959.

*(Time Life Pictures/Time Magazine, Copyright Time Inc./Time Life Pictures/Getty Images)*

At the 1978 touch-football reunion in Central Park, when the Colts beat us again. *Back row, left to right*: Dick Modzelewski, Ray Weitecha, me, Charlie Conerly, referee Sonny Jurgenson. *Left to right*: Gino Marchetti, Artie Donovan, Johnny Unitas.

*(Courtesy of the author)*

1986--- 30 years after this backfield won the NFL World Championship (Giants, 1956)
Alex Webster, Kyle Rote, Charlie Conerly, Frank Gifford.

An aging foursome gathers for a mini-reunion in 1986. *Left to right*: Alex Webster, Kyle Rote, Charlie Conerly, and me.

*(Courtesy of the author)*

Well, he didn't look much like a "boy" to any of us at this point. Right now he looked like a ten-year veteran, engineering a picture-perfect drive. We had to hold them. We didn't have the offense to recover from a 21–3 deficit. The Colt offensive line was simply manhandling our front four. And *if* John was going to pass, it figured that he'd go outside to Berry, as poor Carl tried desperately to figure out how to cover him.

Johnny passed, all right—not to Berry, but to Moore. Lenny had been hanging out there on the right, split wide, all day. Ewbank had figured that if Lenny was hurt, the best role he could serve would be to take Lindon out wide, stretching the defense, and assuring that he would be man for man with Crow.

Now it was time. Johnny took a quick three-step drop. Lenny broke from the line of scrimmage on a slant into the middle. They hadn't used it before, and they'd never use it again. This time it worked perfectly, with Lindon's tackle saving a touchdown at the four-yard line. No way you can blame Lindon. He had to respect Moore's speed. He was close to his man, but Johnny's pass was right on. Had we known that Lenny was hurt, Lindon could have played him closer, but as it was, it was hard to fault Crow. He was man for man with one of the game's greatest on this play, and he lost the duel.

When the next series of downs was over, Joe Boland would compare our guys to "the Greeks at Thermopylae." Having been pushed around for what seemed the whole afternoon, we stood tall—and wide. We went into a goal-line defense: Rosey Brown came in, replacing Svare. Rosey, of course, was our best offensive lineman. But he was also our finest athlete, and this was our version of a big-body goal-line defense—nothing like today's short-yardage goal-line defenses, but then again, neither could you compare our paltry 35-man roster with today's 53.

Exactly seven and a half minutes remained in the third quarter. By now, the temperature had fallen drastically. Even from my vantage point thirty-five yards away on the sideline, you could see the breath of the linemen as they lowered into their stances. When the temperature drops below freezing, subtle changes occur: the ball feels harder, and the field gets trickier. "It had become crusty," Ray Brown recalls. "Not icy in the sense of slipping down, but crusty. Your cleats would break through the turf, where there was turf, and if you fell, it was hard."

Looking back, at this point we did have one advantage: from this close in, Johnny's arm was somewhat neutralized. His receivers couldn't make quick cuts. It was our line against their line, with everything on the line—literally. If we'd won the game, these four plays would have gone down in history. Yet another what-if.

**R**obustelli was having a tough day against big Jim Parker, to say the least. So on first down Andy lined up out a little farther outside than usual at right end. As our lightest defensive lineman, he was quick enough to cut off a sweep, and strong enough to help inside. Youso was lined up where Andy usually played, and Rosey Brown took his place at the tackle spot, with Sam in the middle.

The ball had been spotted somewhere between the 3 and the 4, at the right hash, with the wide side to the left—and that's where they went. The give was to Ameche, going left—right at Youso. At the snap, Parker blocked down on Rosey, pushing him inside. Dupre came out of the backfield, laying such a hard block on Youso that Frank's head snapped back. Berry pulled a brilliant move: instead of trying to block Robustelli up high, he hit the turf and rolled, sideways, right at Andy's feet, forcing him back far enough so that all Andy could do was grab at thin air as Ameche ran past.

Now Ameche had a hole. Karilivacz was coming in, but too late. It looked like a sure touchdown, until, out of nowhere, Emlen Tunnell, our safety, sliced through the chaos from the other side of the field and wrapped Ameche up around the waist, slowing him long enough for Sam to make his way through the traffic to finish the tackle, just outside the 11-yard line.

It's high time we talked about Emlen Tunnell. In a well-thought-out game plan, Baltimore, like most teams, always factored in Emlen on any and all pass patterns. He needed to be isolated and out of the play; he was a constant danger to break it up or pick it off. Before his career was over, Em had an incredible seventy-nine interceptions, second highest total in league history. He had multiple concussions during his career, and he gave out more than his share. After some plays in which he'd make a great hit, Em would take a long time getting up, but he always did. Even in scrimmages in training camp, if you were a receiver, or potential receiver, you wanted to know where Em was—to stay away from him.

"He was a great, great, *great* ballplayer," Rosie Grier says now, lest there be any mistaking it. The Hall of Fame agreed, inducting Tunnell in 1967, his first year of eligibility.

Em was the first friend I ever had on the Giants. How could you not like a guy who walked into the Giant offices on Columbus Circle one day in 1948, right off the street, and asked for a job? He was given a tryout, and then a contract. From the very first day, the Maras loved Em. Tim, the patriarch, was particularly fond of him. While his career began as almost an afterthought,

Emlen Tunnell became a Giant legend, one of the greatest to play the game.

So how come, when people talk about the greatest defenders of all time—like Sam, who got the credit he deserved—so few people mention Em? Chalk it up to the Tom Landry system—a system that called for team play, rather than freelancing. And, in retrospect, Tom's system worked: How many great names do you remember from Tom's Dallas defense? Very few. Tom wasn't looking for stars—only players who could play his defense.

Off the field, Grier remembers, "Em was as wild as you can get. Not wild fighting. Never yelling and drinking, but always looking for a good time. He was never out there picking on people—he just enjoyed life, and having fun."

Em was a great philosopher. And an even better storyteller. No matter what the theme of our conversation, he'd come up with some story to relate to it, some philosophical ramble. Most of the time, you could nod off for a while, come back—and he'd still be telling the story. It would always make you laugh—like his conversation with our old coach, Steve Owen, during a game against the Rams in Los Angeles. Elroy Hirsch had beaten Em on a pass from Norm Van Brocklin for a long touchdown. As Em left the field, Steve Owen hounded him: "Why did you let that man get behind you?"

Em stayed quiet. Owen persisted, with his usual dip of snuff cascading down his chin: "Why? Answer me!"

"Listen, Coach," Em said. "How much you think they pay Van Brocklin? Maybe $25,000, hunh?"

"What's that got to do with it?"

"And how much you think they pay Hirsch? Maybe $15,000, right? Or more?"

By now Owen was angry, eyes bulging, spraying the snuff. *"Why didn't you stop that touchdown?"*

"Listen, Coach," said Em. "Van Brocklin gets $25,000. Hirsch gets $15,000. You pay me $8,000. And you expect an $8,000 man to stop a $40,000 forward pass?"

How can I be sure that that's the way it went? Because that's the way Em told it on my radio show. And I always believed Em's stories. Well, I believed they made for good radio, anyway.

On the first great play on this goal-line stand, Emlen had set the tone: if the Colts weren't going to let him near the ball, he was going to go find it. Now the ball was on the left hash, second and goal, a yard and a half to go. This time, Johnny decided to take matters into his own hands. So did Sam. On Unitas's sneak, Art Spinney, the all-pro guard, tried to plow the way for Unitas—the man Spinney once referred to, simply, as "the meal ticket."

At the snap, the center Nutter fired out at Sam, and Spinney went straight at Rosey. Nutter managed to turn Sam around backward, but Sam shoved himself into the pile, just long enough to turn the play back, and long enough for Modzelewski and Katcavage to collapse inside—Mo managing to grab Johnny's ankles, Kat reaching over his man and grabbing Johnny up high.

From the sideline, all we saw was a mass of humanity—but no signal. No touchdown. When referee Ron Gibbs unpiled everyone, he put the ball on the 1-foot line.

Third and goal. The Stadium on its feet.

On both plays, they'd gone left, toward Youso—and on third down, Unitas went right back at Youso again, handing off to Ameche. Frank was a quick learner. On this play, Berry, the wide receiver, would stay in to block down on Youso. On paper, Frank outweighed Raymond by about eighty pounds, but Raymond had already shown himself to be a lot better blocker than he should have been. At the snap, Berry went low on Frank—and Youso went down to meet him, closing the hole. Frank was getting the hang of things.

Meanwhile, inside, two all-pros were waging the rarest of battles: offensive tackle Jim Parker was trying to block offensive tackle Rosey Brown. Our guy won. Rosey stood Parker up, and pushed him right back into the hole, just as Ameche was trying to run over Parker's broad back.

Again, the whole thing could have gone either way, until Jimmy Patton slammed into the pile from behind. Jimmy may have been small, but he was one tough guy. Ameche, trying to get through the pile, was spinning his wheels. As Alan tried to get a last bit of traction, Carl finally came in and wrapped him up on the 1.

On fourth down, no one even looked at the sideline to see if Myhra was coming in to try a field goal. I suspect that even if Weeb had tried to trot Myhra out there, Johnny would have pushed him right back to the sideline. But Weeb didn't want three points. Years later, Ewbank said, "I wanted to bury them right there with a touchdown."

Johnny had tested the inside of the line three times, and failed. He didn't have the room for a Berry square-out, or a slant to Moore. Now he'd finally go to the right—but not with a conventional play.

On paper, his call looked risky. And it was. The call was "428." The "28" meant Ameche would be going wide around the right side. The "4" designation in front of the 28 meant that Ameche would then be passing the ball, to Mutscheller, who was supposed to slide off his block of Livingston and drift into the end zone.

"It was supposed to work," Mutscheller told me, "because

Ameche hadn't thrown the ball all year, and it would surprise the heck out of them." They'd never used the 428 during the season. But according to Mutscheller, they'd worked on it at practice.

In the radio booth, Boland set the stage: "*This New York defense has been tremendous, but can they do it once more? They've had to dig deep into the emotional well . . .*"

There comes a point in any game when, no matter what you might say later to the press, you know it's over. And a touchdown here meant it was over.

**T**he din was really deafening; the two different sides' cheers mixed into one roar. The Stadium was on its feet, as we were on the sidelines. From this point on, no one would sit on the bench the rest of the day.

Berry split left. Moore split wide to the right. Johnny took the snap, and pitched it to Ameche, going wide right.

A great play by one man—Cliff Livingston—blew the whole thing up. Our high-living bachelor, the guy who played as hard on the field as off it, made the play of his career.

Mutscheller was obviously thinking about getting open, and his swipe-fake block didn't slow Cliff down a hair. Livingston completely ignored Mutscheller's block, designed to slow Cliff down for an Ameche pass attempt, and nailed Ameche from behind, dragging him down at the 5.

"John, in his most inventive way, called a pass," Ameche would say years later. "Not having heard that play before, I completely blew it, and I thought it was a sweep."

Ameche said it was the first time they'd called the 428 in six years, which is a little curious—Alan was only in his fourth year with the Colts. That's probably why he didn't hear the "4" part.

"I'm standing in the end zone by myself," Mutscheller told me. "And Alan doesn't realize he's supposed to throw the ball. I still remember it very distinctly. I'm standing there wide open. He just didn't even look at me. I went down three or four yards, turned out, and I'm right in the end zone. As I remember it, I was pretty much open."

Even if Ameche had known what he was supposed to do, he'd never have been able to get the pass off: Cliff was right on him. At the snap, Unitas's pitch was a quick, hard line drive of a toss, but Cliff was just as quick in getting out there. I've never known a quicker linebacker than Cliff, and he proved it on this play.

If Mutscheller could have stuck with his block on Cliff a millisecond longer, Livingston wouldn't have been able to get to Ameche—but neither could Mutscheller have gotten open in the end zone. And Mutscheller would have had to be wide open. "Alan," Mutscheller says now, "was absolutely the worst passer in the whole world."

Bottom line: We had their trick play stuffed from the moment Cliff made his move.

"Why I was there, I have no idea," Cliff told me. "I have no idea. Then, as soon as Ameche had the ball, I made the tackle." He was being modest. It was a classic Livingston move. His instincts were perfect. He beat his block and made a super play on the ball.

The stadium went crazy—but the defense was completely cool. The entire unit just trotted off the field. Not a single fist thrust in the air, not a single yell or taunt or chest-thump.

"It was a different time," says Cliff now, matter-of-factly. When I told him, fifty years later, how impressive his reaction was, he answered with six simple words, and they spoke worlds: "We didn't win the football game." That's all he said about it.

And did anyone give Ameche grief, on the Colt sideline?

"Of course not," Mutscheller says. "We were too gentlemanly. He was a heck of a guy. Alan had a heck of a game."

Neither Jim's nor Alan's days were done.

**C**harlie, Kyle, and I took off our jackets, pulled on our helmets, and headed for the field. We took over on our own 5. And I remember feeling at that point that we could take it all the way. I just didn't know how quickly we'd get there.

In the next five minutes, we completely turned the game around.

On first down, I got off a good one—not a long one, but a good one. I made something out of nothing on the 41 trap, and Marchetti came in untouched and swung a big right forearm straight at my head. Somehow, I ducked under it and slid ahead for five yards. I was already on the ground when Pellington came in *way* late, lowered his shoulder, and nailed me in the back. There was an official standing right there. No flag.

Another run and Phil King got three yards; our rookie from Vanderbilt was spelling Webster. Now it was third and two. We couldn't give it up this deep again. The defense was exhausted. It was time for Charlie to shake it up a little. He went to the play Kyle had suggested during halftime.

"We'd worked on that earlier in the week," Kyle said years later. "I'd told Charlie that I noticed how every time he pitched out, the safety came flying up to stop the run and it was giving us trouble. So I suggested we fake the pitchout, and when the safety came up, I could get behind him."

Kyle had no idea how big it was going to work this time.

"Give me some time, guys," Charlie said in the huddle. "Brown right, L-split [Kyle], fake 48. L-down and in. *Break*." That put Webster split to the right, and Kyle at the left end, split to the left.

At the snap, Charlie faked the pitch to me, then faked another handoff to King going up the middle. The fakes froze everyone—except Marchetti. As soon as Charlie turned to look up the field for Kyle, there was Gino, leaping, both arms in the air to block the pass. Charlie didn't have time to do anything—set his feet, or even completely cock his arm. He just let it rip downfield, off his back foot.

Charlie's pass hit Rote perfectly, in stride, at the 35. Kyle had beaten Milt Davis by a step; Milt just couldn't cut on the broken foot. Kyle, the old running back, tucked the ball under his right arm and turned upfield.

Now Taseff, their cornerback, had the angle, and met Kyle in full stride at our 45. Taseff lowered his shoulder, but Kyle gave him a super move, and Taseff missed a sure tackle. As Kyle headed for midfield, he looked back to his right—and here came Andy Nelson, gaining fast; Kyle could have used some of the speed he left back in that gopher hole, when he tore up his knee as a rookie. At the Colt 45, Nelson corralled him, and started to drag Kyle down—and here came little Ray Brown to finish the job. The lawyer from Charlie's hometown popped them both.

The famous Clarksdale, Mississippi, guy had thrown the pass. Now Clarksdale's other native had forced the fumble.

"All I remember," Nelson says now, "is that I hit Rote. I didn't know he had fumbled, though. I'd have tried to get it. As it is, I was flying in the air, then I hit the ground and did a backward somersault."

"Andy and I both knocked it loose," Ray Brown says now. "I saw it bounce, and I thought, *I'll be damned.* Man, I was gonna get that ball—until it bounced right into Webster's hands."

Webster? What was Alex doing down there?

"I think it's the only play in my whole career I ever happened to get downfield on," Alex told me. "I wasn't in the pattern. I'd run a circle route, and when Kyle made the catch, I just started running upfield, and then Kyle got hit pretty good, and the ball just sort of bounced into my hands. Looking back, I didn't realize I was that slow."

Running full speed—such as it was—Red scooped the ball up perfectly, and took off toward the goal line. Well, maybe "took off" is a slight exaggeration; "rumbled" is a lot more like it. It was Taseff, who'd missed the tackle on Kyle at midfield, who got up and chased Alex down. No surprise there. Artie considered Taseff to be the best athlete on the team. (A few years later, Taseff would be called into duty as a running back when all the other Colt running backs were hurt—and gained 100 yards in the game.)

Alex headed for the corner of the end zone, but Taseff dove at his knees, and took him out at the 1.

"I was happy to get out of bounds," Alex told me, laughing. "I ran out of gas completely."

Alex slowly rose to his feet—as a group of fans vaulted from the stands toward him. One of them actually put his arms around Alex to help him up, giving him a friendly pat on the backside as he walked back onto the field.

The play had covered 86 yards, by way of a 27-yard pass, a 20-yard run, a 15-yard fumble, and Alex's 24-yard sprint.

For all the fluky things that had happened on the play—Taseff missing a wide-open tackle, Alex pursuing, then making the perfect scoop—this play belonged to Charlie. It had been one hell of a pass.

Now we had the ball first and goal on the Colt 1. "We're in the huddle," Alex remembers, "and Charlie says, 'You got it here—take it in.' So I got the handoff, straight ahead, a 20 quick-trap, and I got clobbered in the line. And I got hit hard in the head. Hard." Donovan had Alex low, and as Webster went down, a trio of Colts fell on him.

Now the Colts were bracing for their own goal-line miracle. Second and goal from the 1.

In the huddle, Charlie offered to let Alex try again. Alex was having none of it: "I'd never run over forty yards in my life. I was beat. And the tackle on the play before . . . I swear, that was the hardest I was hit in my whole career. So I said to Charlie, 'Give it to Mel.' What the hell. I don't have to score a touchdown. That was the way we were. No one could care less who scored. We just wanted to score."

So Charlie gave it to Triplett. Mel ran straight—and up. He vaulted over the line, landing in a huge pile of bodies, with Artie somewhere in the middle. Both teams had collapsed inside, and the crowd was so big that the goalpost was shaking.

To this day, Artie refuses to give us that touchdown: "I hit him, and he hit the goalpost, but the ball never crossed the line. The ball never got over. I swear it."

As usual, Artie's version of things is wrong. We had our first touchdown of the day. It was 14–10, Baltimore.

**B**ack on the sideline, none of the Giants celebrated. Charlie didn't say a thing. He never did. He was a man without artifice, attitude, or ego. In execution, in cool under fire, that pass to Rote epitomized Charlie Conerly. It wasn't a laser pass; it wasn't a 60-yard bomb. It was the perfect touch pass, at the one moment in the whole game when we needed it most. If we punted from our end zone, maybe they would have come back and put it away. Instead, Charlie had pulled one out of his hat. It was the best pass of the day, Unitas's included. No one remembers it—as, to my way of thinking, not enough people remember Charlie Conerly.

Charlie was really a straight shooter." Perian Conerly says now. "What you saw is what you got. He had a quiet dignity about him. They didn't have any money when he was a child. Well, no one had any money. His daddy was a policeman in Clarksdale. At one point, his daddy was the jailer. They all lived in an apartment in the county jail. Charlie once said to me, 'I'll tell you one thing: I never wanted to be a criminal after I saw what those poor slobs had to go through in jail.'

"With his first contract, Charlie bought his daddy a little farm between Duncan and Alligator, Mississippi."

Charlie and I started rooming together in 1954, out in Salem, Oregon. We were the most unlikely pair you could imagine: a kid from USC, by way of the oil fields and Hollywood, and a former marine from Mississippi. Charlie had a lingering distrust of Northerners. In my first year, I said to him, "Charlie, I'm not a northerner . . . I'm from California.'

"I know," he said, "but y'all are fruitcakes out there."

Iwo Jima, Tarawa, Kwajelein. Places I'd only heard of from newsreels. I guess being in the war made it easier for him to endure all the grief he took, year after year after year. Charlie played with a terrible football team at the start, in the lowly Polo Grounds, in a town that was very unsophisticated about football. The fans would boo Charlie for things he couldn't help, or had nothing to do with. He didn't have an offensive line. He had poor receivers, and the crowd was brutal.

"I remember one game where Charlie completed nine in a row," Perian remembers. "The tenth fell incomplete, and they booed."

That first season I saw my first "Conerly Must Go" signs. It shocked me. The boos shocked me; the signs shocked me. He never said one word about it. It never seemed to affect him one way or the other. But I'm sure it did. Years later, I tried to get Charlie on the veterans' ballot for the Hall of Fame. But you just can't overcome some of the Hall's criteria. You just can't say, "If only he'd had an offensive line, better receivers . . . " He lost four years at the beginning of his career, playing for bad teams. A career that had already been postponed by a little thing called World War II. For what it's worth, Charlie's been in my hall of fame since the day I met him.

We hadn't given the defense much time to rest. We'd gone 87 yards in four plays. But they didn't need any more rest. Charlie's completion had pumped everyone back up; it no longer felt like a one-sided game anymore. And the defense was as fired up as we were.

And three plays later, it was the Giants who had the momentum: Kat stuffed a Dupre run; Mo sacked Unitas; and though Johnny was able to scramble for a few, Svare brought him down well short of the first down. The Colts punted it right back. It had been a textbook defensive series and, more important, we had brought some pressure on Unitas. Youso was getting his sea legs, and Mo's motor was really running.

When we returned to the field this time, we were a completely different unit—literally. Phil King, the rookie, had replaced Webster. Rote had been replaced by our reserve wide receiver, Ken MacAfee. With his bad knee, Kyle wouldn't play the rest of the game. On paper, it was a big loss. But Kyle's absence now gave a shot to our underused tight end, Bob Schnelker.

Bob was a big, talented receiver with excellent speed and sure hands. He had been a clutch receiver for us, in the last two seasons making forty catches for an astounding 21-yard-per-catch average. He was a quiet guy, a substitute teacher whose passion was mathematics.

The Colts seemed to have forgotten about him. Charlie hadn't. Charlie was ready to take over this game. On second down from the 22, Charlie called Bob's number. We lined up Brown left, R-split, R down and in. That split Schnelker to the right, where he would run the down and in. He ran it, as always, with precision.

Charlie had his best protection of the day as Bob curled in front of Taseff at the 40, and gathered the pass into his stomach, just as Taseff wrapped him up. Taseff's coverage was good, but Charlie's pass was better.

The pass had been good for 17.

"Charlie had seen something," Bob told me, not long ago, as we sat together in the stands for a high-school football game between my son Cody's Greenwich (Connecticut) High School team and a local Florida powerhouse. "He was good at that. Saw something in the coverage. Or maybe it was the first time I was that open."

Bob hadn't suggested the play; Bob *rarely* suggested plays. Bob never said much of anything. He was simply a really savvy football guy you could always count on to execute. "I never asked to get the ball, that's for sure," he told me. "If Charlie called your play, then that's the way it happened, and your job was to get to the place he expected you to be."

We had it first and ten on the Colt 40. The quarter ended, and we felt good for the first time that day.

## CHAPTER 7

# FOURTH QUARTER

**F**ull shadow blanketed the field, which was dotted with bits of paper and debris that had floated down through the gathering dusk like a strange, man-made snowfall. On the sideline, some of our guys were wrapped in full-length capes, huddling against the chill. We had a hamburger cooker near the bench to keep warm.

In the huddle, before the first play of what we thought would be the final quarter, Charlie pulled out all the stops: he was going to go right back to Schnelker again—but this time he was going deeper. Vince and Charlie had been talking on the sideline. They knew the Colts would still be playing run.

Charlie stepped into the huddle: "Listen up now: Brown right, fake 47, R down and in. Give me a little time, now. On three—*break.*"

Our formation gave nothing away: both backs in, both ends tight. At the snap, Charlie faked a handoff to Phil going up the middle, then faked another into my belly. I gave it the full Oscar, pretending to tuck the ball in and head upfield. Taseff bought the whole thing. Meanwhile Schnelker broke off the line and headed straight downfield—surprising Ray Brown, the safety, with his speed. Schnelker was wide open, and Charlie put it in his hands, 35 yards downfield.

"They always said about me on all the bubble gum cards that I had 'great hands,'" Bob told me, a little reluctantly, because Bob has never liked to blow his own horn. "And I wasn't particularly fast, but I was faster than everyone thought, because I had a real long stride."

By the time Brown could recover, Schnelker's long stride had gotten us 46 yards.

Now, with a first down on the Colt 15, Charlie wanted to finish the job right then. The call was for me to circle out of the backfield: an A-flare. But we lined up in a running formation: both ends tight, three backs in the backfield. And the line gave Charlie all the time he needed.

MacAfee broke for the end zone, and Milt Davis had to stay with him. That left Myhra covering me. Charlie looked right, freezing Myhra. The rest was easy. I circled around Myhra, who was caught flat-footed. Charlie lofted the ball in perfectly. I caught it at the 6, and as Davis closed in, I put the ball away, lowered my shoulder, stayed in bounds, and got it into the end zone.

We had taken the lead for the first time since the first quarter. If ever a moment called for some celebration, this was it. In today's world I imagine I would be all over the field, high-fiving anyone I could find, looking for a camera and making sure it knew what number to focus on. I didn't do that, because *we* didn't do that.

I have nothing against all the celebration that goes on today, at every level of the game: high school, college, or professional. Sometimes, when it really gets wild—and players start strutting around, banging on their chests, and bumping each other—I actually get a little embarrassed for them. I mean, let's face it: it's still a team game, and if Charlie didn't have the time provided by all those big guys in the trenches, and Schnelker didn't make a move that helped me to get open, and right on down the line, I wouldn't have scored. Given all that, why doesn't everyone just jump up and down—"Hey look at me?" Come to think of it, sometimes they do. We just didn't.

But the real truth is that it literally never crossed my mind. Honestly. You're just not conditioned that way. You never thought of doing it in high school, you never thought of doing it in college, and you never thought of doing it in the pros. Not in my time. What's changed? Maybe television's made the difference, but that's too easy an answer; we were on national television that day, too. I'd just scored the go-ahead touchdown in the NFL championship game, and it had just been watched by 45 million people. It was the biggest stage a football player had ever had. I knew the cameras were on me. I handed the ball to Ron Gibbs and jogged to the bench.

We'd gone 81 yards in four plays. Combine this drive with the one before it, and Charlie's statistics for our last two series were four for four, for 140 yards. Not bad for the "other quarterback," the thirty-seven-year-old who wasn't good enough to start.

Unitas went right back to work from the Colt 20. He went to the pass on the first five plays, starting with a slant to Moore for 11, beating Lindon by a step. Now Johnny gave us a taste of things to come: with Karilivacz playing way off Berry, Johnny hit Raymond for 14 down the left sideline. Landry had decided to take away anything deep, if he could, and Carl was playing Raymond deep. Carl was so out of the play that Patton had to make the tackle.

We began to stiffen. The defensive line was getting a good surge, led by, of all people, big Frank Youso. And now the noise became a factor. Johnny stepped to the line, and realizing that his players couldn't hear the signals, motioned for the crowd to quiet down. Only Johnny would think he could quiet Yankee Stadium. Of course, the roar just grew louder. Johnny had to burn a time-out.

But after an incompletion and a 1-yard scramble—during which Youso recovered to chase Johnny down—Unitas faked a pitch to Moore, then found Mutscheller open over the middle. Johnny led him perfectly. Lindon was close to Moore—too close. He broke up the pass, but drew the interference call. It was worth 17 key yards.

Now the Colts had it on our 38, and Johnny went for it all: He sent Dupre deep out of the backfield. Our safeties flanking him closely, L. G. reached for Johnny's pass. The pass was just about perfect, just inches long, off Dupre's fingertips. On third down, Johnny threw a look-in to Moore, split far to the right, but this time Tunnell, with help from Crow, was all over him, and broke it up.

The Colts sent out Rechichar for the tying field goal, from the 46. Maybe all the bad karma between Weeb and Bert now came into play. Maybe Bert's having warmed the bench all day figured into this kick. More likely, it was the distance: In 1958, 46 yards was a long shot for the straightaway kickers of the fifties.

Bert missed, way short. The ball crossed the goal line—on the ground. A touchback, and we had the ball on our 20. (In '58, after a missed field goal into the end zone, they put the ball on the 20.)

We came out on offense with three guys who hadn't started the game: Mischak was at guard. MacAfee had replaced Rote. More significantly, Vince had King spelling Alex in the backfield. Phil had been our number one draft pick that year, out of Vanderbilt;

we had a solid backfield already, but Wellington loved to draft for offense. Phil had had a good year for a rookie: 83 carries, averaging almost 4 yards per.

Phil was a funny guy. He always had an opinion. He was part Indian, so we called him "Chief," when we could get a word in. I liked him a lot. Charlie never liked anyone who talked a lot. He did, however, cut Phil some slack, because Phil was yet another southerner on a team full of them.

Phil also had a hidden talent, as Youso remembers it—a key skill that the rookie revealed in training camp. "In Winooski one night, the rookies got together and had a little beer party, and we found out that Phil could drink a mug of beer in three and a half seconds," Frank remembers. "Well, we thought it would be great if we could sucker in the vets with a contest. We threw in fifty dollars. The old guys matched it, and you were the vets' guy. We all thought, *How the hell could Frank Gifford drink any faster than Phil?* So we're all set to pick up our money. Phil drinks his in four seconds. Frank, you grab your mug—and suck it all down in a second and a half. You just opened up your throat and didn't even swallow. We got suckered in by the old-timer."

I remember it well, but I tried that recently, and damned near choked.

**B**y now, the offense had a rhythm. I could feel it. We began to move toward the touchdown that would clinch this game. Charlie picked up where he'd left off—throwing the ball. This one was a hitch to MacAfee split to the left, the first time Ken's number had been called. Ken was a solid receiver, nothing flashy, who'd been a starter a few years back until Schnelker took over the position. Milt Davis was giving him a huge cushion, and Charlie picked up on it right away, and hit Ken with a turn-in that picked up 15. Charlie was now seven of eight for the half.

The clock was now another player, as we started to move the ball on the ground. Charlie called a draw to Mel, behind my block, and we gained 7 as I made a good block on Myhra. Now it was my turn: a 49 sweep, with both guards pulling. Vince used to drool over this play, because if everyone did his job, it was a guaranteed big gainer. Schnelker blocked in on the linebacker, Triplett led the way and blocked down on Big Daddy, and Stroud bounced outside, looking for the cornerback. It wasn't a wide sweep. It looked as if I were running straight into a swarm of blue and white—but I slipped through a sliver of daylight. Taseff came up to drag me down, but I'd gained 10 yards, into Colt territory, and picked up another first down.

We had it on their 46, with less than eight minutes to go. The Colts were dragging. Everything Charlie called was working, and now he called my play again: a 41 slant, right up the middle. I gained 4. We were on their 42, second and six.

And then it all came apart. In a game full of key plays, none was bigger than this. It was a 28 sweep out of a strong left formation, with King getting the handoff. Both guards would pull to set up a wall. Daddy was lined up right over Barry, the left guard. At the snap, as Barry pulled to the outside, it was Rosey's job to block in on Daddy.

But Daddy was so quick off the ball that Rosey never had a chance. Lipscomb blew in untouched. King took the handoff deep in the backfield, and as he was trying to put the ball away, Daddy hit him high. The ball flew out and bounced backward. Joyce pounced on it, and it bounced out again. Ray Krouse recovered for the Colts.

I don't care what you say about the football game that Johnny Unitas and Raymond Berry played on December 28, 1958. For my money, Eugene Lipscomb played as good a football game as anyone on that field that day.

You know what they say about hindsight, of course, but this play can't help but beg a "what-if": What if we'd kept Alex in the game? He wasn't hurt. I guess Vince (or maybe Jim Lee) had a hunch. But I know this: Alex never fumbled. Mel fumbled. Kyle fumbled. I fumbled. Everyone fumbled. Alex Webster never fumbled. And his replacement had.

Today, Alex still doesn't know why they'd made the switch: "I wasn't hurt. Maybe they figured Phil was fresher than I was, younger and stronger. I just don't know."

You could feel the collective sigh as we trotted back to the sideline. We'd played smart football, our kind of football. For the entire second half, we'd put the sloppy play behind us. With our backs to the wall, we'd come back to take the lead, and we hadn't let up. But one bad play, one fumble, and the whole thing began to unravel.

The Colts had it on our 42. And again, Johnny went for it all on the first play. And for a second it looked as if he'd gotten it. Moore ran a fly pattern down the right sideline, with Crow beside him step for step. Lenny managed, somehow, to gather it in through the forest of Lindon's waving arms, inside the 5-yard line. To this day Lenny swears he had both feet in. The official ruled he had a foot out of bounds.

The next play could have sealed it for us: Karilivacz anticipated the hook to Berry, jumped the pattern, and almost picked it off; he had both hands on the ball. But he couldn't gather it in. If he'd intercepted, that interception would have been the Johnny Unitas pass that everyone remembered. It was not to be.

On third and ten, John came right back to Berry. Raymond drove straight upfield at Carl, and turned out to the sideline. Unitas's pass was right there. Eleven yards, and a first. John and Raymond were just getting warmed up.

But now, as they had so many times that year, our defensive line came up big. They seemed to be getting stronger—or maybe the Colt line was starting to weaken. Robustelli and Modzelewski sacked Johnny twice in a row. On the first sack, Johnny faked a run and bootlegged right to get some time, but Robustelli was all over him. "Andy'd had a long game." Sam says. "Parker was one of the best that ever played the game, and he had Andy frustrated all day. He tried every move he had. He'd spin, but Parker would still block him." On the second sack, Mo just bulled his way over Spinney.

On fourth and twenty-seven, they punted. Patton returned it 16 yards up the sideline, to the 19.

At this point, on the sideline, the Colts' two defensive stars shared a brief dialogue—well, brief on the part of one of them, anyway—as Donovan shook his head and turned to Marchetti. "I said to Gino, 'You know, this is the first championship we've ever been in,'" Artie says he told his linemate. "'"We're so much better than these guys. We should be up by three or four touchdowns on these assholes, and here we are fighting for our lives.'"

Gino remembers the conversation. He nodded, and replied, "You're right, Fatso."

The consecutive sacks had the Stadium rocking. The defense had come up big, and it was our game to win. There were five minutes remaining. All we had to do was control the ball one more time.

On third down, Charlie got the first down, rolling right and hitting Webster out of the backfield. Alex had put a move on Ray Brown, the safety, and stepped out of bounds on our 34. The clock was running, and Charlie wanted to keep it that way. One first down—just *one first down*; ten yards of dirt—and we would win the title.

Alex was stopped after a yard on a first-down slant. But on second, I got the call: "47 power off tackle, right"—and found a hole. Stroud and Mischak did their work, and I picked up 5.

Four more yards, and we'd have it locked up.

We huddled. And I changed the play in the huddle. And Charlie called my sweep: "Brown right, over, 49 sweep. Okay? On three. *Break*."

The play came off as well as could be expected. It was designed for me to take it wide around the right side or, depending on what we needed for the first, cut it hard back upfield. This time, I took it outside, until I saw a gap, planted my right foot, and turned it up, knowing exactly what I needed for the game-winning first down.

I'd gained about three yards when Marchetti shed Stroud's block, lowered his head, and hit me waist-high. "I hadn't had a lot of people running right at me during that game," Gino remembers. "So I kind of figured you'd cut in. A back was coming at me, and I was able to elude him, and when you cut back in I was in real good position with my feet, and I was able to hit you solid."

But I had momentum, and I fell forward as Marchetti was pulling me down. Now Donovan came in, over Barry's block, and threw a big right arm at me. I ducked under it. Then Lipscomb came in, and landed on Gino—and Marchetti started screaming. His ankle was broken.

Everyone started to yell, "Get off him! Get off him!" It was chaos. Marchetti remembers those next few seconds, as he reached for his leg: "Some Giant said to me, 'You can get up now, Gino—the play is over.' I could have cared less. I was in so much pain, if I wasn't a grown man, I'd have cried."

They carried Marchetti off on a stretcher, but he insisted the trainers put him down so he could watch the outcome. So there he sat, on the ground, near the end zone, his lower leg wrapped in ice, a Colt jacket draping his shoulders.

Ordell Braase, Marchetti's backup, watching from the sideline, remembers the play well: "Why would you want to run at Marchetti?" he asked me. The answer, to me, is obvious: you go with what you got there, with the sweep and all its options.

I'll say it again for the last time: I still feel to this day, and will always feel, that I got the first down that would have let us run out the clock. And given us the title.

Gibbs had picked the ball up at the end of my run. He held on to it, and didn't put it back down until all the chaos had subsided and Gino had been removed from the field.

Then they brought out the chains. And it was a couple of inches short.

It turned out that the best play Big Daddy made that day, on a day when he made the biggest plays of his career, was on a late hit on his own man. I know he didn't plan it that way, but breaking his teammate's leg won his team a championship.

I wasn't happy about the spot. And I told Gibbs about it. As Artie recalls it now, "You were shouting, 'I made it, I made it!' I told you, 'Shut up, and get back to the huddle.'" I don't remember ever shouting in any game, but I do recall being dead certain that I'd made the first down.

• • •

Decades later, soon after Ron Gibbs passed away, I would get a letter from his son, which included this passage: "Dad told me a few days before he died, 'You know, Joe, maybe Frank was right . . . maybe he did make that first down . . . We shouldn't have ever picked up that ball before the measurement.'"

On the sideline, I tried to make our case, forcefully: We had to go for it on fourth down. We had it on our own 40. We needed a couple of inches.

"I was standing right next to Lombardi," Jack Kemp told me, "and he was talking to Howell. You came over and said, 'We have to go for it!' Any coach in his right mind would have gone for it. But Jim Lee Howell was not in his right mind."

M. L. Brackett told me he can still picture the scene on our sideline: "You, Kyle, Charlie, and Stroud were all ranting and raving." I wasn't ranting or raving. But I wasn't happy. Even Don Chandler, the best punter in the league, says now that he thought we should have gone for it. Under three minutes left, with a three-point lead? With our offense in control for the last quarter and a half? And their best defensive player, the best defensive end in football, now lying on a stretcher on the sideline? With our home-field fans screaming their lungs out?

Jim Lee didn't check his watch. He didn't have to. No one was going to change Jim Lee's mind. The huge scoreboard clock in front of the big Bronx courthouse looming over the bleachers said it all: less than three minutes left. We had the best defense in the league. So he sent out the punting team.

Chandler got off a great punt. The Colts took possession on their 14. The defense took the field.

Now the clock showed two minutes and twenty seconds to go. The Colts had only one timeout left. Their field-goal kicker was just about the worst in the league. They were playing against a hostile crowd. Sam's unit was rested.

Sure, the Colts had Unitas. But could the comical-looking guy I'd first seen in an exhibition game in Maine two years before, fresh off a sandlot, with his jersey sleeves held up by rubber bands, his pants flapping around his pencil-thin legs, actually cover eighty-six yards against the best defense in the league? With just one timeout left?

He was facing a defense that hadn't given up a point in the whole second half—a defense that had turned in the goal-line stand of all time in the third quarter, and consecutive sacks to stop his team's last drive.

I'd like to say we felt confident on the sideline, but if I did, I'd be lying. Up until now, Unitas had sold me big-time. I had watched him mature over the past few years, and watched him on film for hours. He was special in so many ways. And his stage for football history was set.


Johnny talked about that final drive in regulation a lot over the years. He said he knew we'd protect the sidelines because passes down the middle would eat up the clock. Berry confirmed it: "We knew you'd try to concentrate on keeping us from going outside," Raymond told me, "therefore giving us that middle. Once you go in the middle, if a defender makes a mistake, you could take it all the way. But if you take too long to get the next play off, the clock can kill you."

Johnny wanted most of it on the first play: with all the time in the world, he lofted a long arcing pass to Mutscheller—but Tunnell and Patton had him blanketed, and Johnny, wisely, threw it too long. On second, Johnny surprised us by going to Dupre on a 12-yard circle route, but this time his pass was underthrown.

Third and long. And while history keeps talking about Unitas to Berry, without Lenny Moore, this game would have been over. None of our defensive line was within yards of Johnny as he faded back. Moore broke toward Crow, stopped at the 25, and turned around to catch the ball. Johnny put it low, and Lenny reached down, cradled the ball, and fell to the 25-yard line as Crow scrambled to make the tackle. Too late. They had the first down by inches. And they were out of the shadow of their goalposts.

They still had seventy-five yards to go. With time running out.

At this point, I could just say, "Unitas to Berry, for twenty-five yards. Unitas to Berry, for fifteen yards. Unites to Berry, for twenty-two yards." And that would pretty much cover it. I heard the words then, and I hear them now. That we had to hear them then, echoing from the Stadium speakers, spoken in our home announcer's dulcet tones, somehow made it even more painful.

The next few minutes—arguably the greatest few minutes any receiver has ever had in professional football—were the logical result of the hours, and hours, and hours of preparation Raymond Berry routinely put in: for any situation, in any game. The more I talked to his teammates, the more I became convinced that the key to Raymond Berry's amazing performance that day was that he never left anything to chance. There was no situation he hadn't envisioned in his head—no coverage, no turf condition, and no pass—because he'd prepared for it all beforehand, and practiced for it endlessly.

"I have never seen a man so dedicated to his work," Ray Brown, the safety, told me. "In our practices at Memorial Stadium, Raymond had this net set up on the sideline, a big square frame with a net in it. John would throw to him, in front of this net. Then John would finally go into the locker room, but Raymond wouldn't be done. He'd ask me to stick around and throw to him.

"So I'd throw balls to him, toward that net. And Raymond would come from the left. He'd come from the right. He'd jump. He'd get me to throw all the different patterns. He'd dive. He'd tumble. He'd practice every possible pass, preparing for any situation."

They were on their 25, first down. From here on in, Johnny knew he wouldn't have time to call huddles after every play, so he told the offense to expect the calls at the line of scrimmage: one of the first no-huddle offenses. The Colts hadn't planned on it.

I'll let Raymond set up that drive from here.

"It took me years to figure this out," he told me. "Then I finally got it: The factor that no one could possibly account for was this no-huddle concept that happened quite by accident in that final drive in regulation. Your defense, at this very critical time, had to play against a no-huddle. I think it threw their rhythm off. That's why they weren't able to make adjustments. We had to go to a hurry-up type offense. John would call two, even three in the huddle, then we'd go to the line, and we'd go with a 'check-with-me' system. John would call the numbers, and it all happened very quickly. It was all pretty simple at that point, but, really, it had been simple for the whole game. That was Weeb. We hardly had but a handful of plays."

On first down, Johnny followed his game plan: we were defending the outside, and he threw to Raymond inside.

"It was a formation we used during that game a lot," Raymond remembers. "Lenny, split right, ran a ten-yard square-out to the right, Mutscheller ran a twelve-yard hook. I had come open late on the sideline. I was the third option. When he faded back, he was looking for Moore. Then he went to Jim. Then he finally went to me. In all the years we had it, I think that was the only time he ever went to me on that play."

That Unitas had that much time tells you how little pass pressure he was getting from our wiped-out defensive line. By the time he got to Raymond, it seemed like about five seconds had already passed.

Dupre, the halfback, was the key to this play. He circled out of the backfield to the left and turned it upfield. Carl tried to stay with Dupre, which left Harland, coming over from his linebacker position, man-to-man on Berry.

Berry had beaten Harland. He took Johnny's pass, and then, with everyone figuring he'd step out of bounds, he cut right up the middle of the field, getting a block from Dupre on Huff. Raymond looked just like his old hero Elroy Hirsch back in that movie theater in Paris, Texas, as a half-dozen Giants tried to chase him down. First it was Livingston; Raymond juked him, and broke the tackle. Now Patton came in for the tackle; Raymond slowed, and Jimmy overran him. Finally, Crow and Emlen converged on Raymond at midfield.

They'd gained 25 yards. The play had taken ten seconds. The Colts called their final timeout with a minute and five to go.

During the timeout, Joe Boland's color commentator, Bill McCoglan, made the first mention of what none of us had thought about: the prospect of an overtime. *I* sure hadn't thought about it, anyway.

*"You're quite familiar with what a minute and five seconds means*

*in the NFL, Joe. You can do plenty in that time. Right now I know*
*what John Unitas and Weeb Ewbank would like to do: if not go all*
*the way, they'd like to pick up another ten or twenty yards, and get in*
*position for a field goal, and if that did happen, and they came through*
*on the field goal, for the first time in the history of the NFL we would*
*witness a sudden-death play-off."*

First and ten at midfield. And with no timeouts left, we knew
Johnny had to keep passing, but somehow his play-fake to Dupre froze Harland, which left Karilivacz alone on Berry. Raymond
ran a simple curl-in. Carl was still giving Raymond a deep cushion,
and Johnny put it right where he had to: low and catchable. Carl
missed the tackle. Livingston had to come across from the other
side of the field to bring Berry down.

Now they were on our 35, with the clock still running. They
had time for one more play, and they needed yardage to give Myhra
any chance at all to tie the game. By the time Johnny got the snap,
the clock was down to forty seconds. Everyone knew what was
coming, of course. I knew it. Sam knew it. Sixty-five thousand fans
knew it. The ushers knew it. Sheppard knew it. Forty-five million
people watching on TV knew it.

Karilivacz knew it, too; he was ready this time. Berry broke from
the line of scrimmage, ran 12 yards, and turned. Ray gathered the ball
in and turned back outside. Carl came in late, and missed the tackle.
By the time Harland brought Raymond down, he was on the 13.

Three plays, 62 yards. Unitas to Berry, Unitas to Berry, Unitas
to Berry.

On the sideline, Myhra was getting nervous. The Colts had
the kicking drill down to about twelve seconds for the field-goal
team to get onto the field, line up, and kick it. Myhra turned to

his holder, George Shaw, and told him to be careful not to slip if they had to go out there. Years later, Myhra remembered his actual words as "Don't fall on your derriere, or there won't be nothing." I'm guessing his words that day weren't quite so innocent.

On the sideline, Milt Davis was smiling: "All the preparation I'd seen Johnny put in—now it was coming to fruition."

Andy Nelson was just shaking his head at the drive that had put them here: "That was the best pitch-and-catch I'd ever seen."

As the Colt kicking team ran onto the field, the clock was winding down to twenty seconds—but the scoreboard clock wasn't official; Gibbs had the official time. The Colt kicking team lined up, and got set, with the ball on the left hash mark. The big second hand on the scoreboard clock swept under ten seconds.

The ball was on the 13. Myhra would kick the ball from the 20. Nutter snapped the ball.

The clock showed seven seconds to go as Weeb Ewbank's second-least-favorite kicker took three steps, kept his head down, and kicked it.

As our line went for the block, Mo put Artie right on his back.

"I'm lying there on my ass," Artie remembers, "thinking, *Oh, no. We didn't make it.*"

Gibbs threw his arms into the air: good.

Summerall, standing at a perfect angle from our sideline, swears it went right.

No one was as surprised as the man who had snapped the ball. "If he had to kick that field goal twenty more times he wouldn't have made it once," Nutter told me. "He was *a terrible* kicker."

"What helped Steve on that kick," Ordell Braase says now, "is that after the first series of the game, he was playing linebacker, after Sanford went out. I think the best thing for us was that he didn't have time to think about anything during that game. He played the whole game, and he knew he had to play a hell of a game, and he did. So he didn't have to wait around on the sideline the whole game. Hell, his father owned all the land in North Dakota—what was there to worry about?"

Buzz Nutter told me the exact same thing: that having Myhra pushed into action as a linebacker "was the luckiest thing that ever happened to us. Myhra didn't have all day to stand around."

Myhra would agree, several years later: "If you had time to think about it," he said, "we probably would have blown it."

On our sideline, no one said a thing. We just knew we'd have to go back to work.

Rechichar kicked off into the end zone. We took possession on the 20, and Charlie ran a sneak. The game was over. At least, that's what a lot of people thought. Actually, most of us didn't know *what* to think. In my entire life of football—from the Bakersfield Drillers to the USC Trojans to the New York Giants—the game had been played in four quarters: win, lose, or tie.

In the four decades that professional football had existed, no one had ever played an overtime game—not one that counted, anyway. There'd been an overtime for an exhibition game a few years earlier, but we hadn't been aware of it. The overtime rule had been instituted for this game by Bert Bell, the commissioner.

Ordell Braase told me that Weeb had told the Colts during the week that overtime was a possibility. (There's another example of Ewbank's preparation being more thorough than our guy's.) But on our sideline, confusion reigned.

"I was sitting next to Heinrich," Summerall told me. "I said, 'What do we do now?' No one knew how overtime went. Someone said, 'I think the captains toss a coin again.' But no one knew what was going on."

Sam was ready to call it a day. He figured a tie wasn't so bad. "I just said, 'Great. At least we get half the money.' Then the official came over and said, 'Three minutes.' I said, '*What?*' I wasn't quite sure what 'sudden death' meant."

Most of us didn't understand the logistics of an overtime period. Who kicks off? How long is the break? If one team scores, does the other team get another possession? I do know this: none of us could have possibly envisioned that this new change in the rules was going to have a long-lasting impact on the game of football. All we knew was that we had to keep playing this game.

"*Yes,*" Joe Boland told his radio audience, "*we've come to the end of regulation time, the end of the game, and we're going to see the first application in history of the sudden-death rule.*"

# CHAPTER 8

# OVERTIME

The next fourteen plays, the next thirteen minutes and twenty-five seconds, did more than change the face of professional football. They altered the cultural landscape. They turned our sport into national prime-time entertainment. They changed the viewing habits of millions of people.

They turned colleges into breeding grounds for football players. They turned professional football players into athletes who would earn more money in a single game than I'd earned in twelve years of hits to the head and hits to the heart. And they did it by marrying football to television, a medium that could fit its commercials neatly into the regular breaks of our game: timeouts, quarters, halftimes. With a sport TV could call its own, that medium could now turn to Madison Avenue and say, "We have hooked your customers. We can sell your product."

And believe me, our overtime made the difference. The overtime allowed West Coast viewers, Midwest viewers, living room latecomers all over the country to turn on their sets and stumble upon a football game that should have been over. Overtime represented a whole new kind of ball game, for a nation founded on the idea of new frontiers. For the first time ever, we had a game where the first team to score a point would be declared world champion—by knockout, if you will. One blow, and the title would be declared.

After the commercial, millions of people were drawn to their television sets—except, ironically, in New York, where the game was blacked out. In jacket, tie, and overcoat, collar turned up against the chill now turning to a freezing cold, his right hand wrapped around his binoculars, his left resting on a clipboard, speaking into a microphone, Baltimore announcer Chuck Thompson stared into the NBC camera with all the grim seriousness and urgency of a guy issuing a civil-defense alert:

*"This is Chuck Thompson, speaking to you from Yankee Stadium, where the Baltimore Colts are playing in the first overtime period in the history of professional football."* (Chuck seemed to have forgotten that he was addressing a nation, not just the city of Baltimore.)

In the radio booth, Joe Boland could barely contain his excitement: *"Never before in the history of the NFL or professional football has there been an extra period. A most historic moment in football history: a sudden-death play-off, with all the marbles on the line."*

It was history in the making—or so we'd just been told. For the Giants, it was just more football that had to be played. One more time to find some way to pump the adrenaline into bodies that had been thoroughly exhausted.

I'm not offering excuses: the Colts had to do the same thing. But I think there was a definite difference between the feelings on the two benches. No: I *know* there was.

Buzz Nutter told me he just couldn't wait to get out there. "Man, to me the feeling was unbelievable," he said. "Absolutely unbelievable. I was so pumped up, I could have played another whole game right then."

The Colt kickoff team was about to take the field when Jack Call, the backup running back, turned to Leo Sanford, the linebacker who'd torn up a knee in the first quarter. Sanford had insisted on staying in for special teams. He was going to limp his way out there. Call turned to Sanford: "Man," he said, "I'd hate to lose this."

Call remembers Sanford looking at him and saying, "Don't worry about a thing. We're going to win it. We're going to take it."

"And I thought of all the times Johnny had done it before," Call told me. "I thought of the confidence we'd always had in John. And I thought, *Hey, maybe he's right.*"

No one had more confidence, of course, than Raymond. Berry felt that Johnny, given the chance, would no doubt have something up those sleeves that were always somehow too long for that strange-looking body. And if, somehow, we could find a way to shut Raymond down, Johnny would no doubt have something else in mind.

"At that point," Raymond told me, "after we'd tied the game, our confidence level was off the board."

On the Giants' side of the field? No rah-rahs from anyone. No extra incentive, it seemed, to dig deep and grind it out one more time. Just going back to work.


The captains gathered at midfield. It was just after 4:30, Eastern Standard Time; exactly seven days after the shortest day of the year, it was completely dark inside the Stadium now. The lights lit

the field like a night game. The white haze of our breath accentu-
ated the drastic drop in the temperature.

Johnny was alone at midfield; Gino had finally been taken
from the field: "All of a sudden the police come up and say to the
trainers, 'You better get him off—there'll be fans all over the field
when this is over,'" Gino told me. "So they took me into the locker
room. It drove me crazy down there. I could hear the crowd, but I
had no idea what was going on."

Our captains, Rote and Svoboda, stood swathed in our
full-length dark blue capes, shelter against the cold. Johnny
wasn't wearing a coat. Maybe the Colts weren't feeling the cold like
we were.

Johnny called the coin flip, and lost. The Colts would kick
to the north end of the Stadium, the outfield. Gibbs brought the
captains together to give instructions no one had ever given before:
"The first team to score, field goal or safety or touchdown, uh, will
win the game now, and the game will be over," he said.

We'd get the ball first. We had the whole things in our hands—
very briefly.

This time Rechichar's kick was high, and short, and as Don
Maynard watched it from the end zone, he figured he could take it
in full stride. He had terrific speed. He could bust it right up the
middle. As the ball began to fall from the dark sky, here came Don,
like a sprinter bursting from the starters' block, looking up—into
the lights. In front of him, our wedge was clearing out a serious
lane. There were no Colts within fifteen yards of Don as he caught
the ball on the 10-yard line, in full stride—and had it slip right
through his hands.

The four-man wall in front of him would last only a heartbeat.

Maynard had to stop, rooting around on the ground to retrieve the ball. By the time he had it back in his hands, he was swarmed under at the 20.

It was a rookie mistake. Don had never before looked for a kickoff in brilliant lights etched against a night sky, at least not in the pros. And not in Yankee Stadium in front of 64,185 fans—and 45 million other fans, from coast to coast.

"Hey, at least I didn't give it to them" is what laid-back Don said recently when I tracked him down in El Paso. Of course, he can laugh. His own Hall of Fame career was just beginning. For a lot of us, the clock was winding down.

On our last series of the season—on our last three-and-out of a long, lost year—we didn't play badly. We just didn't play crisply. We played tired.

My 49 sweep on first down worked well enough—I picked up four yards. Hell, it was just as good as the fourth-quarter sweep for the first down they didn't give us. And it was a good call: Braase was now in for Marchetti at left defensive end, and we thought we could exploit that. At the snap, both guards pulled, and I headed right. But Braase beat two blocks and turned the play inside, and Joyce, coming over from the right side, made the tackle.

On second down, Charlie went to the man who got us here: Schnelker. Bob went down fifteen yards, and slanted in. He was open at the 45, the cornerback behind him and the safety coming in. But Charlie's pass led him just a little too much, and it was a little too low. It would have taken a near-spectacular catch by Bob. In the end, Charlie's last pass of that season and that game goes into the scorebooks as just another incompletion.

On our final offensive play of the game, knowing they'd be

coming with everything they had, Charlie rolled to the right, buying time, looking again for Schnelker, fifteen yards down the right sideline. But Bob was covered. Charlie had his arm already cocked when he decided not to risk the interception He had some room, and in a split second made the decision to run the ball. Pellington slowed Charlie down, and linebacker Don Shinnick moved in to finish him off, corralling Charlie up high, and pushing him back. Charlie went down a yard short of the first down—another almost-forgotten play that would shape and mold this first-ever sudden-death play-off into a historic happening.

"Don never played the play the way it was drawn up," Andy Nelson told me. "He played his own defense." Shinnick had led the pregame prayer for his team; maybe it had taken five quarters for it to be answered.

Charlie had made the right decision when he tucked it in. Vince didn't have to tell him, "Don't turn it over down there." In the back of his mind I'm sure he was thinking that giving it back to the defense wouldn't be the worst thing in the world. After all—giving up two consecutive long drives? That didn't happen to our defense.

At that point, Berry says, he knew that Johnny was just getting warmed up. "You see, Unitas was not necessarily a normal quarterback," Berry told me. "He did not have a fatigue problem with his arm. He thrived on work. To Johnny, pressure was just a fuel for a fire that burned inside. He could throw and throw and throw after practice, and it never bothered him. This was a big factor at this point. He just never got tired. I think maybe Charlie, being much older, got tired. Johnny just got stronger."

Today, Raymond swears he was feeling no pressure: "It was business as usual. I guess one of my unusual characteristics was my ability to focus. I had the mental gift of being able to tune out the entire world."

The radio announcers wondered whether we'd go for it. We never considered going for it. We couldn't risk giving it up down here, on our 29. Chandler got off a tremendous, soaring punt—62 yards. Taseff returned it one yard, to the 20.

The Colts had eighty yards to cover. But this time, with no pressure from the clock, Johnny could take the time to do what he did best: study the defense as he got to the line, and change the play if he saw the defense giving him something. He would do that a whole lot in the next few minutes.

In the huddle, Ameche said years later, the first thing Unitas said was "'We're going to go right down and score.' You could just feel the confidence."

The second thing he did, of course, was call the perfect play. Tom had made a defensive change, lining Sam up outside right, to give Carl some help on Berry, and why not? Raymond had ten receptions—so far; we had to stop him. That gave us two linebackers out on Johnny's left, but it also took Sam out of anything up the middle. And when Dupre broke off tackle, and cut back in, he had nothing but daylight. By the time Youso and Sam wrestled L. G. down, he'd gained 11.

On the next play, Johnny pumped to Berry, turned, and threw a 60-yard bomb to Moore, sprinting down the right sideline. Hours earlier, Lenny may have told Johnny that he thought he could handle Lindon all day, but while Lindon had given up some receptions, he had always been close. This time, Lindon was with him every step of the way, and knocked the ball away. To my way of thinking, that day Lindon Crow played one of the best games at cornerback I've ever seen.

A draw to Dupre got 2. Now, third down and eight. If we held them, we'd get the ball back with pretty good field position.

We all have a play that haunts us. This one is Harland's. Johnny faded back and looked left toward Raymond, and Johnny's read showed him that both of the linebackers were staying with Berry, Svare, and Huff trying to help Carl. Johnny turned and flipped a flare to Ameche, circling out of the backfield. Harland recovered just a little too late, and came back to dive at Alan's feet at the 39. He grabbed Ameche by the ankles. But Ameche stretched it out as he fell, and landed on the 41. First down.

"It's been fifty years," Harland told me, "and that's the thing I remember most about that game: that I was back too far when he dumped it off to Alan. I've never forgotten it."

They now had good field position. John called a run to Dupre off right tackle, and Huff held it to 3. And on second, Johnny never had time to look downfield: Mo blew past Spinney and sacked Johnny back at the 37. Mo had saved his best for last.

It was third and fourteen. Everyone knew what was coming—and we were seemingly powerless to stop it. Maybe it was too much to expect a great effort from a defense that had put in a heroic effort for three weeks, back to back to back.

Maybe our line was just beat, and now playing with personnel out of position. Whatever it was, Johnny had far too much time. He looked right, but Lindon had Lenny covered. So now Johnny looked now where he always looked when he was in trouble—for Berry. "By now," Raymond told me, "we'd been together three years. We knew what each other would do in any situation."

Johnny scrambled to his left, as Robustelli had tried to spin inside on Parker, and Parker, using Andy's own momentum, had driven him deep inside. As Johnny ran left, he broke into the clear. With all the time in the world, he motioned with his left hand for Berry to go deep. But, as Raymond later admitted, he didn't have the gas *left* to go deep. He came back toward Johnny. Carl stopped, tried to come back—and slipped on the frozen turf, just long enough for Ray to look the ball right into his hands.

How many times in that game had our guys slipped on our own home turf? Too many to count. Today, Raymond swears that his customary and precise pregame survey of the field had nothing to do with the fact that one of his biggest catches of the day took advantage of the frozen spot he'd checked out three hours earlier.

Berry had picked up 21 yards.

Now they were on our 42. And the next play was arguably the greatest Unitas audible of all time. He'd called a pass in the huddle. But Sam, anticipating another pass, had dropped off just a little, to help out in the coverage. John also knew that our line— Modzelewski in particular—would be letting it rip; that Mo would be looking for his third sack.

Johnny added it up, and changed the play with an audible, sending Ameche behind a trap block, right up the middle.

"It was his best call of the game," Braase says now. Modzelewski remembers the play all too well. At the snap, he flew in, looking for that third sack. "*Never* did I expect him to have a running play, a trap on me," Mo told me. "Never. I got trapped, and Ameche broke it up the gut. If I was still coaching," Mo added. "I'd still tell my linemen to rush. But Johnny made a great call."

With Sam out of position, Ameche ran untouched for 15 yards before Carl grasped a piece of Raymond's jersey to slow him down. Patton brought Berry down at the 19. The play had gained 23 yards.

Years later, Unitas was asked about that trap play—the last play anyone had ever expected.

"It was nothing magical," he said. "I didn't pull it out of a hat. The defense told me what to do."

The Colts were in field-goal range at the 19, but with Myhra always a concern as a kicker, they weren't about to try and win it with a field goal now. On first down, Johnny handed off to Dupre, but Sam nailed him at the line of scrimmage.

But on second down, however, they broke our backs, and made the final outcome inevitable.

It was Unitas to Berry again, and this time, with Berry split to the left, they came with a quick slant-in. At the snap, Ameche and Dupre flooded out left, taking the linebacker Svare with them. Sam stayed in the middle, dropping back, trying to read Johnny, sliding to his right, looking for pass. Meanwhile, on the line, Parker rolled up Andy Robustelli, who was taking his pass rush inside.

Robustelli went down, clearing a lane of sight for Johnny, and Johnny, reading it all in a fraction of a second, nailed Berry crossing across the middle. Berry took it to the 8 before Patton could drag him down. The play had taken great timing; Johnny had only a fraction of a second to sneak it in. This was to be Raymond's last catch—a remarkable twelfth reception.

You could feel the wind come out of the crowd. On the sideline, I just felt helpless. I can remember feeling, 'It's over.' Strangely, I also felt almost a feeling of relief. We had given everything we had, not only in this game, but also in the must-win final weeks, and now, simply, that was it.

Even Steve Myhra doesn't miss from the 8.

• • •

Now, in a game full of unpredictable plays and unpredictable events, an even weirder thing happened. The television signal was focusing on a couple of guys on the field hoisting a big "Let's Win Colts" banner—when it suddenly faded to fuzz.. The rocking and stomping of the crowd had apparently unplugged a cable, and America went dark.

All we saw was a guy running on the field, chased by five cops. Pat Summerall says that the broadcaster Lindsay Nelson once told him the guy was an NBC employee, a business exec, who'd been told to delay the game until they could get the signal back. I have my doubts. But it's a good story in a day of great stories.

I do know that the delay gave Unitas time to talk to Ewbank on the sideline. Years later, Ewbank would say that his instructions to Johnny were clear: Keep running the ball, to get it between the hash marks and make Myhra's kick easier. I don't think John was listening to a word Weeb said.

They lined up on the 8. The crowd had started to come out of the stands, ringing the field, setting the stage for what by now seemed an inevitability. On first down: Johnny called an off tackle over the right side for Ameche, but Lenny Moore completely missed his block on Katcavage, and Kat, with deep penetration, tripped Alan up. Sam finished him off after a one-yard gain. They'd put the ball between the hash marks.

Myhra stayed put on the sideline.

Analysts, players, and modern-day coaches are still talking about the next play. All Johnny had to do was run it once more on second down. Then Myhra could kick it on third, and if something went wrong—a bobbled snap, a penalty—they'd get another shot.

As the Colts lined up, Johnny, once again, came with a surprise. Livingston, on John's right side, was lined up inside tight end Mutscheller's inside shoulder. Unitas would look for Mutscheller to get wide open on the outside, and as he faded back, he had plenty of time.

Maybe no one thought he'd take a chance with a pass. Maybe we should have learned by then. When Cliff, after checking Mutscheller, came on the pass rush, he was too late.

Unitas pumped to Moore in the end zone, but that was just to freeze Lindon. He never intended to throw to Moore. Then he went back to Mutscheller, who was completely alone out at the sideline. Jim caught it at the 1, for a six-yard gain just inside the sideline, slipped on the turf, and fell out of bounds. Finally, the home-field turf had given the Giants a break—too little, too late.

"I nearly fainted," Ewbank said. "When the television cable went out, and they were fixing it, John came over and said, 'What do you think?' I said, 'Let's keep it on the ground.' I told him to give the ball to Alan, who was sure-handed, and keep it as much in front of the goalpost as we could. Myhra wasn't the most consistent kicker around, and if we had to go for the field goal, I wanted to give him every edge.

"Well, dammit, John lobs it over a linebacker and right to Mutscheller. After the game John said that if Jim had been covered he would have thrown it out of bounds. That's one of the reasons why Johnny was so great: he believed in himself. But a coach doesn't think that way. You think, *What if the rush gets him? What if he fumbles? What if it's picked off?*"

Again, what if? But as Landry always said about his defense, there are no what-ifs—and not when Unitas made a call. Johnny had a defense he liked, he had an open receiver, and he had a good chance at a touchdown. To his way of thinking, going for the touchdown would be far safer than going with a chancy field-goal kicker.

"Yeah, I was surprised he threw the ball," Buzz Nutter told me, "but I never expected us to kick the field goal there. We'd have kicked on fourth. I do know we've all been giving Mutscheller grief for fifty years now. He could have been the hero. Instead he falls out of bounds."

Berry wasn't surprised about the play at all. Nothing John did surprised Raymond. "And don't forget that we'd had that field goal blocked early," Berry says now. "We knew we were going to win that game. We knew that Johnny was going to get it into the end zone. It may have been stupid thinking—driving eighty yards against the best defense in football? But we had such a confidence level right then that I don't think a field goal ever entered my mind."

The pass to Mutscheller was hardly a gamble: As far as I'm concerned, Johnny throwing the ball to his wide-open tight end in the flat was as sure a thing as a run. Is that gambling? It's not gambling when you believe in yourself.

No one said it better than Johnny, in the locker room a few minutes later, when reporters asked him why he'd taken such a risk. He answered their question with a question of his own: "Why shouldn't I have passed then? After all, you don't have to risk anything when you know where you're passing."

*Journal-American* reporter Dave Anderson remembers it slightly differently. He remembers standing in front of Johnny's locker and asking Johnny about the pass, and watching Johnny pause as he considered the question. "Then he turned to me, with that cool expression on his face," Dave told me, "and just said, 'When you know what you're doing, you don't get intercepted.'"

...

The final play in this game has been replayed so often that half of America knows it in their sleep. Third and goal from the 1. No sign of Myhra, of course. As long as the Colts had a chance to control the outcome of the game, without Myhra's erratic foot, there was no reason to try one on third; even if there's a fumbled snap or a penalty, it was still going to come down to Myhra's foot again.

Johnny had a play left to burn.

Our entire defensive line was set. It had been damaged by injuries, particularly the loss of Grier. But there was still the pride, still the leaders who had gotten us here—Andy, Mo, Sam, Cliff, Harland. They had made spectacular goal-line stands all season, and they were not just going to roll over.

In the Colt huddle, Johnny, of course, was as cool as could be. He set the formation, gave the call—a 16 slant. Our defense was probably expecting the Colts to run left, where they'd had success all afternoon; Unitas sent Ameche right.

It would have been fitting for this game to end with a moment of high drama: a head-butting pile at the goal line, the goalposts shaking, Ameche fighting and churning for an extra inch, Huff flying in, maybe a controversial spot. Instead, the final play of the longest game in NFL history was completely one-sided. If a single play can be a rout, this play was a rout.

At the snap, the tight end Mutscheller blocked in on Cliff Livingston, and sealed off not just Livingston, but the whole left side of our line; Mutscheller drove Cliff sideways into Katcavage and Modzelewski, taking them out of the play.

"That was the biggest satisfaction in my life, that block," Mutscheller says now.

That left one Giant defender, Emlen Tunnell, facing one Colt,

Lenny Moore. Lenny wasn't known as much of a blocker, and Emlen played free safety like a linebacker, but this was the block of Lenny's career: he barreled into Emlen and stood him up, driving him back.

Ameche lowered his shoulder and ran through the wide-open hole—"so big," Alan would say years later, "that Artie could have run through it." Ameche had expected to meet a defensive surge. He met none. He tumbled into the end zone. No Giant had laid a finger on him.

*he Baltimore Colts, coached by Weeb Ewbank, are champions of the professional football world."*

**B**y the time Ameche hit the turf, the fans were already swarming the field. I was already heading for the locker room. But the drama was far from over.

Andy Nelson stood watching, half in fear and half in awe, as fans shimmied up the goalpost, then tore it down. "If I'd know how much a splinter would have been worth," he says now, "I'd have stuck around and gotten one."

The ball itself took a roundabout journey. Ameche, probably out of fear of the mob, had just left it on the ground. Buzz Nutter scooped it up and carried it inside, and gave it to the guard at the Colts' dressing room. Later, of course, he, too, had second thoughts about that ball: "Man, that would have been like a Babe Ruth home run ball. Of course, back then I guess maybe you'd have gotten twenty-five dollars for it."

Marchetti remembers how agonizing it was to be lying on a gurney in the empty locker room and trying to figure out what the cheering meant: "Finally, Pellington opened the door, and lets out a shout: 'We're the world champs!' Then my leg felt better."

One newspaper account called the Colt locker room "raucous." Andy Nelson remembers it very differently: "The locker room was quiet. Shinnick led the prayer. We were all pretty emotionally drained. There wasn't a whole lot of jumping around."

All Artie recalls is that there wasn't any beer.

Johnny, Dave Anderson has told me, was as cool as ever as he fielded questions from the reporters. It was just about then that word came down about the game MVP award: a Corvette. Near the end of regulation, goes the story now, the award—and the car—had been voted to Charlie. After the overtime, the decision was reversed: Johnny was named the MVP. There's no record of Johnny's response, but my guess is that Johnny had about as much use for a Corvette as Charlie would have. They were not Corvette guys. They were team guys. (When a representative of *The Ed Sullivan Show* offered Unitas $700 to stay in town and appear on TV, Johnny declined. He wanted to go home. Ameche took his place on the show.)

No one was as drained as Raymond Berry, who told me he hadn't celebrated with his teammates. He'd sprinted off the field— "But I wasn't really sprinting. It was like I was floating. It's such a high, I really can't describe it any other way." When he got to the locker room, he was overcome by emotions that, even today, he has trouble describing. He looked around, and suddenly felt the need to be alone.

"I went into a toilet stall and shut the door. I don't have any memory of why I did, but there I was. I was just sort of overwhelmed. I sat down, in my uniform. I was not a religious person, I was not a person given to giving God any thought, but I was so aware . . . it was like I was enveloped in this awareness of God. In my little twenty-five-year-old mind, I knew there was some connection between God and what had happened on that field. I couldn't put it together, but it was just overwhelming, it was a very strong awareness. I had never had any experience like that; it was very unique and unusual.

"After that, the next thing I remember is standing out on the street by our bus after the game and seeing Bert Bell with tears in his eyes. I remember thinking, *What was that about?* As the years passed, I guess I realized what it was about—that Bert Bell knew what had just happened to football." (Up in the press box, Bert Bell had told Baltimore writer John Steadman, "I never thought I'd see a day like today.")

**O**ur locker room was quiet, of course. Guys peeled off bloody tape, headed for the showers. The longest season we'd ever played—the longest season ever played in the NFL—was over. It had been an emotional roller coaster, and now it left an unbelievably empty feeling. You'd done the best you could—we all had—and it hadn't been good enough. There was nothing more to be said. It was time to move on.

I was sitting in my locker stall, obviously feeling terrible about the loss. My father came in, with Toots, and I just felt so sad that my dad had come so far to see us lose, and to see my two fumbles, which had probably cost us the game.

But then something happened that I'll never forget. Vince came over, and I stood up, and he put his arm around me. He said, "Frank, don't feel bad, because we never would have been here without you." And that helped me get through one of the lowest points of my career.

The writers moved around the room, gathering the few quotes they could get. It was Emlen who probably summed it up best, when he spoke of Unitas's magic: "Everything we expected him to do, and what you absolutely believed he would do, he didn't do. He did exactly the opposite. Those of us who have been around knew we had been beaten by a better man."

M. L. Brackett, our backup lineman who'd seen duty only on special teams, was feeling as down as the rest of us, and recently told me that all he could think about right then was getting back home to Alabama. "I was just sitting there," M. L. was saying. "I'd taken most of my uniform off. I was looking at the floor, thinking what could have been. I'd been a Bear when we lost the title game in '56, to the Giants, and now I had another chance, and we'd lost again.

"So Chris Schenkel, our announcer, came in, and he was smiling. We'd become friends over the course of the season. He came up and shook my hand. Now, I knew he had something to do with United Airlines, because he would always make sure our baggage was okay, so right then I said, 'Hey, Chris, do me a favor: Give me direct clearance between Yankee Stadium and Alabama—I'm going home.'

"And Schenkel said to me, 'I want you to do something. One thing. I want you to remember this game. Because this is going to go down as the greatest game ever played.'

"I'd never thought of it. It never crossed my mind. But after that, I never forgot what he said: 'Don't let it get out of your mind: This is the greatest football game ever played. It's going to go down in history.'"

...

The Colts' plane was given clearance to Friendship Airport in Baltimore, where, several hours later, thirty thousand fans greeted their heroes. The plan had been to put the team on a flatbed truck, but with the huge crowd milling on the tarmac, the plane taxied to a hangar, and they put the players on two buses. "The plane couldn't even get near the airport," said Marchetti, who'd endured the plane ride, despite the broken bone.

The plane taxied to the other side of the runway, behind an elementary school, where the players got off and loaded the buses. As soon as they began to move, says Marchetti, "the next thing you know, the fans are jumping all over them."

"They were rocking the bus," Nelson remembers. "People stomping on top, beating on the windows. I thought they were gonna turn it over. The cops came and said they were going to arrest them, but Johnny and [GM] Don Kellett got out and talked them out of it."

Johnny's cool had won out again. In fact, Nelson remembers, his friend showed no emotion whatsoever, from the locker room to the plane ride to the final ride on the bus back to Memorial Stadium, where the players had left their cars.

Nelson and Unitas lived near each other, and they'd ridden over to Memorial Stadium in Andy's car on Saturday. Now Andy would give him a lift home.

"He didn't say a thing on the ride home," Andy told me. "Well, three words: 'See you tomorrow.' We had some celebration scheduled at The Belvedere. But that was it. Just three words: 'See you tomorrow.'"

Years later, Johnny's widow, Sandy, told me about the time one of their children asked Johnny, "'Dad, what did you do when [that game] was over?' He said, 'I got the hell out of there.' He'd done his job, and that was it."

**A**rtie, of course, went back to the neighborhood in the Bronx, to spend the night with his folks in the apartment on 202nd Street, where he could finally lift a celebratory beer. The next morning, Artie says, he was standing outside Goldberg's Candy Store when the proprietor came out and asked, "Hi, Artie. What, out of work again?"

**M**axine and I took my dad down to Toots's that night, with Charlie and Perian. My favorite saloon was quieter than usual, but it wasn't like a wake or anything. In fact, we said little, or nothing, about the game. What was to be said? We knew the season was over, and that we'd all be going our separate ways—some of us within a few hours, some in a few days. Life would go on.

Toots and my dad did their best to make me feel better about fumbling the ball. And Toots helped loosen up Dad a little. Dad was more of a beer drinker; he wasn't used to Toots's style of drinking brandy. Before the night was over, they stopped feeling sorry for me, and started feeling sorry for themselves, almost sobbing.

As bad as I felt about the game I had helped lose, that night I felt a warm, wonderful glow over being with my dad. Because of his work, or lack of it, in the oil fields of California, Texas, and Alaska, we hadn't shared much together while I was growing up. I can only recall one game he saw me play at USC or, for that matter, at Bakersfield High or Bakersfield Junior College.

As I shared that evening with him and Toots, and my other teammates, somehow, the love and respect I felt for this hardworking "oil field man" eased the pain of what had happened a few hours earlier.

## CHAPTER 9

# AFTERMATH

On the morning of December 29, 1958, the residents of the Bronx went back to work, walking streets emptied of crowds, opening the delis and bars, climbing the stairs to the subway platform next to the Stadium for the trip downtown to a typical Monday-morning workday. Normalcy had returned to New York: the newspaper deliverymen called off their strike that day, although it was one day too late for anyone in the city to read a next-day account of the game.

Outside of the city, though, readers got the news in the out-of-town editions. The accounts of our game left a couple of impressions: first, that it had been a hell of a football game, and second, that it had been played by athletes who still belonged to some other subclass of species. To read Arthur Daley in the *Times*, we were still one notch above wrestlers: "It was a wildly exciting and utterly mad affair. The final touch of insanity came when these massive meatballs couldn't settle supremacy after sixty minutes of bitterly bruising battling. They had to go into overtime. This sudden-death period was the first ever required in formal football warfare."

Adding to the outdated image of neolithic warriors laboring

in leather pads and helmets were the words of an un-bylined *Times* writer, who, in his story on Unitas, referred to Johnny as "that rarity in pro football—a player with all his teeth."

On the other hand, Daley, an old friend of the Maras, did conclude his piece with the simple, celebratory cry, "This was a football game. Wow!"

The tide had begun to turn. Obviously, we weren't aware of it. "No one knew the actual value of what had just taken place," Rosie Grier says now. "We didn't know we'd just seen the beginning of the future of the game. All I knew is that we'd lost some extra income."

A few weeks later, *Sports Illustrated* called our contest "The Best Football Game Ever." But the real momentum wouldn't really start gathering until the mass media caught up within the next few years to something that we, as players, had already started to feel: that, as Jack Kemp put it to me not long ago, "baseball may have been the national pastime, but football was the national passion."

That game began to convince sports editors to start assigning writers to football teams, instead of using off-season baseball and boxing scribes to moonlight at our training camps. Once we had actual beat writers, and extensive TV coverage, the true exposure began. But the real tipping point was the cover of *Time* the following fall. It featured a portrait of Sam. When the national general-interest magazines decided to announce that professional football was now a part of the cultural landscape, we knew we'd arrived. Not that it mattered much to us. Salaries didn't explode; they still crawled upward, by a thousand or so a season.

The *Time* cover illustration was significant in another way, though: It showed Sam's face, in an artist's portrait, unhidden by helmet and faceguard. Without his armor on. The artist's portrayal of Sam depicted not a football player, but a person. In a way, that cover announced that we'd come out from hiding: We were real people, real athletes. Not toothless meatballs.

The other media shoe fell in October of 1960, when the CBS newsmagazine show *The Twentieth Century* miked Sam up live for a segment entitled "The Violent World of Sam Huff." The CBS cameras followed Sam as he went through his daily routine at our training camp, tracking his every move during the days and nights of August in Vermont. Narrating the segment in a somber, serious voice, in keeping with the public impression of us as warriors, a bespectacled Walter Cronkite sounded as if he were narrating the preparations for a battle whose stakes were nothing less than the fate of the free world. (Walter could have used a better writer: speaking of a rookie's difficulty in gaining acceptance from the veterans, he intoned, "To break into this tight little aristocracy, a rookie needs the hide of a battleship, the sheer guts of a wounded water buffalo, and enormous talent.")

The size of the television viewership, of course, made the most obvious case of all that pro football could be lucrative for the networks. "I think our game was the day when television finally woke up," Ordell Braase says now. "I think after that, they said, 'This is pretty damned good. All we have to do is back up a trailer loaded with equipment to the stadiums.'"

I can only guess as to why the national media, when it introduced our game to the public at large, decided to feature the angle of our defense. Sam swears he had nothing to do with all the fuss, despite the suspicion of several of the players I talked to that Sam had a publicist, or that he purposely piled on late on his tackles so that "the late-to-get-up number 70" would be the number that the cameras always focused on.

Maybe it had something to do with the Cold War, and a political climate in which our national defense was in the daily news. Both the *Time* piece and the CBS show paid detailed attention to the strategies of our defense, each accenting all of the hours the players spent in classrooms, as if the media had made a world-shaking discovery: that these knuckle-draggers actually had brains.

**I**n the days following our game, the guys made their way back home, to Alabama and Mississippi, to Texas and Oklahoma, to Minnesota and Pennsylvania—most of them as quickly as possible, to get back to their off-season jobs. The three thousand and change we'd picked up as losers wasn't bad, but it wasn't enough for anyone to retire on. Maynard resumed his plumbing. Grier hit the road with a cavalcade of singers, emceeing a show that featured The Coasters, with Rosie insisting on doing a little singing himself at each show. Vince started a job doing public relations for a local bank—for a couple of weeks.

Charlie and Perian put the kitchenware back in storage at the Concourse Plaza Hotel and headed back to Clarksdale. He probably threatened to quit, but as always, he'd be back, at least for a few more years. Maxine and the kids went back to California while I stayed in town to do my radio show, subbing for Phil Rizzuto on CBS until Phil headed south for spring training and I could head back to California. Soon after that, the Yankees would move back into our stadium, and Mantle would move back into my locker. Or Sam's.

I made yet another visit to Toots's later that week, and accepted congratulations and condolences from my pal. It was one of my final visits to my old friend's saloon. Eighth months after the '58 game, Toots sold his business, and soon after, a wrecking ball brought down the greatest room on the island. He would open another version of Toots Shor's a few years later, but it never rivaled the old one. It was big, and fancy. It still had a circular bar, but that was about it. It wasn't a saloon. And a few years later, he lost that one. Toots's time had passed.

Much later on, I ran a dinner to try and save Toots and his restaurant when he was deeply in debt to the government. Everyone turned out. Talk about a star-studded dais: Jackie Gleason. Rocky Graziano. Mantle and Ford. Willie Mays and Bob Mathias. Wellington and Bowie Kuhn. Arnold Palmer and Bob Hope. It was a great evening—and the IRS enjoyed it so much, they attached the money from the dinner. We couldn't save Toots's place, and we couldn't save Toots. He didn't get much out of that night but a whole lot of love. He deserved it.

A few days after the game, I got a letter, dated December 28, the night of the game, sent to Giant management, from the Office of the Vice President. Not of the league. Of the country. "Dear Frank," it read. "I have just turned off the television after seeing the fabulous play-off game. While I am not supposed to take sides in such a contest, I must admit that I was pulling for the Giants . . . I know you must be disappointed as to the result. But certainly you can be proud of the superb performance you gave. In any event, it was a great season for the Giants, for football, and for you personally. My wife, Pat (USC '37), joins me in sending our best wishes for the new year. Sincerely, Richard Nixon."

It's no surprise that Nixon had been watching. We'd met six years earlier, when I'd looked over at the sideline before a game in Washington, and seen him waving—and waving, and waving. Finally, I realized it was me he was waving at, and I walked over. "Frank?" he said, in that unmistakable voice, "I'm Richard Nixon." I assured him I knew who he was. We became casual friends and we would see each other often when he was out of office and living in New York. To me, he was just a nice guy who loved the game. I could never get over how it always seemed as if Dick Nixon really did think that a pro football player was somehow more important than a politician.

But looking back, it's tempting to see that letter—and all of his subsequent letters to me, through the years—as a signal of what Raymond Berry called "the birth" of the NFL. Richard Nixon and football became synonymous. *Monday Night Football* debuted in 1970, the second year of Nixon's presidency. Nixon always seemed to identify with the ups and down of the life of a pro football player. Soon, the same could be said of the nation.

The years immediately following our game were tumultuous ones for the Giants players and its coaching staff. We'd play in four more title games in the next five years, but the team would undergo tremendous change. We were still winners, but the golden age had begun to fade for me already—specifically, in the first week of January 1959, when Vince took a call from the Green Bay Packers. Head coach Jim Lee figured to be going nowhere, so Vince took the job.

Allie Sherman, another Brooklyn kid, came in to coach the offense. Allie and Tom took us to the title game the next year, and again we played the Colts. This time they cleaned our clocks, by a score of 31–16, down in Memorial Stadium. Few football fans seem to remember that game outside of Baltimore, which is fine with me. We didn't score a touchdown until the final minutes, and Unitas, once again, picked us apart.

The most memorable day for me in 1959 in Yankee Stadium had nothing to do with a football game. They say that every dog has his day, right? Well, the old goat got his, literally—Charlie Conerly Day: Sunday, November 29, 1959. Before a game against the Redskins, in a ceremony on the field, Charlie and Perian were showered with a cornucopia of gifts: a trip to Europe; a vacation in Dauphin Island, Alabama; a portable television; a sewing machine; a knitting machine; a tape recorder; a transistor radio; an aluminum fishing boat; golf clubs; a set of encyclopedias; and, of course, the cottonseed and ton of fertilizer. They also gave Charlie a Corvette. Somehow, a Corvette still didn't seem to fit the man.

For Perian, the car took a little of the edge off being deprived of the one she hoped to get back in December of 1958. But the new Vette didn't last too long. "You know what happened?" she told me, laughing. "Three months later I went down to Jackson to see my mother, and Charlie lent it to a teenager who cracked it all to pieces."

In all, the package was worth $25,000—$5,000 more than his salary.

But it wasn't the loot that mattered. In some small way, the affection made up for all of the abuse Charlie had had to endure. "He was really excited," she told me. "Of course, he never could understand why anybody would do anything like that in the first place. Would even bother with something like that."

Charlie played for two more seasons after that, managing to boost his salary in the process: When Wellington asked him to come back for the 1961 season, Perian told me, Charlie asked Well how much money Jimmy Brown was making, and asked for one dollar more. Perian says he got his $30,001. A few years later, he started doing the Marlboro Man commercials.

But for my money, the greatest tribute my roommate ever got wasn't on the day he was showered with cottonseed. It was the night he was showered with love. The site, fittingly, was P.J. Clarke's. It was December 10, 1961, a Sunday night. The handwriting was on the wall for Charlie. He was on the bench; Y. A. Tittle was our starting quarterback. After years and years of telling Perian that he was going to hang it up, this time Charlie was finally going to make good on his promise.

I was on my one-year hiatus from the team after my concussion, and I'd been broadcasting a game that Sunday. I'd heard that Conerly had come off the bench to win the Giant game. He'd thrown three touchdown passes against Philadelphia, and the Giants had clinched a tie for the Eastern Division title. I couldn't wait to hook up with him.

I got to P.J.'s before Charlie did. Maybe he was celebrating up at the Concourse, or he'd been to a couple of other places. I was in the back room, and as usual on game night, it was jam-packed. All of a sudden, someone said, "Charlie's coming! Charlie's coming!" Charlie Conerly walked into that crowded room—and it was the loudest ovation he'd ever heard.

I'll never forget it. After all the criticism he'd taken in the bad years from fans and writers who didn't know how the game worked— after being sacked seventeen times in one game in '52—here was this all-American from Mississippi, finally getting the ovation he'd deserved all along. He'd gone off to fight the Japanese—leaving most of his good years on the battlefields—then come to our town to work his butt off, without complaint. And now the whole of P.J. Clarke's—representing, I'd like to think, the whole town—was on its feet, as if it was finally giving him his due. As if it was trying, in one moment, to make up for all the quiet suffering he'd endured.

I'm sure he never, ever forgot that night. I know that I never will. It was a moment unlike any other: a great friend, a great player, a great saloon. The beginning of the end of a great time.

After the 1959 season, Tom Landry was hired to be the head coach of the expansion Dallas Cowboys; no surprise there. What was surprising was Jim Lee then telling Wellington that 1960 would be his last year, even though his contract went through 1961. I can hardly blame him; without Vince and Tom flanking him on the sideline, no wonder Jim Lee wanted to go back to Arkansas. It was one of the few smart decisions he ever made.

But when Vince heard that Jim Lee was leaving early, he was devastated. He'd always wanted to coach our team, and if he'd known Jim Lee had designs on an early retirement, I'm sure he would have stayed. Vince, of course, turned things around immediately up in Wisconsin, but his heart was still with the Giants. After the 1960 season, Vince came to New York. I met him at Al Shack's when he was on his way to see Pete Rozelle—Rozelle confirmed these conversations for me—to see if he could get out of his contract in Green Bay to coach the Giants. The guy who threw a wrench into it was Dominic Olejniczak, then president of the Packers. Olejniczak felt he had no choice but to hold Vince to the Green Bay contract. It would have set a terrible precedent.

Any question about whether Vince truly wanted to coach the Giants was answered during one of my conversations with Mo. "We played Green Bay in a preseason game one year," he remembers. "Andy Robustelli and I were walking around downtown Green Bay, and a car pulls up. It's Lombardi. 'Get the hell in!' he says. He started talking about how he wished he was coaching the Giants, and he was in tears. 'I should have been there coaching you guys,' he said. He was crying in the car."

It does make you wonder, though: What would have happened if Olejniczak had let Vince come home? Would the NFL have kept growing so swiftly and dramatically if the Packers hadn't become the powerhouse Vince engineered? Would the public have become so quickly fascinated by our league?

The 1960 season is something I'd just as soon forget. And I probably did forget parts of it, because of what happened on November 20, 1960. It was one of the more memorable plays in NFL history, and one I still see more often than I'd like, every time another football season rolls around. I wish I could receive a royalty for every time I look at it. I was on the receiving end of a tackle from Eagle linebacker Chuck Bednarik. It wasn't the Eagle linebacker who hurt me. It was the hard, frozen Stadium dirt that did the damage.

We'd traded for the Colts' backup, George Shaw, and he was the one—not Charlie—who hit me on a slant, coming across the field on our own 30-yard line. I was wide open, and as I looked to cut upfield, I didn't see Bednarik coming full speed at me from the far side of the field. Bednarik, taking aim, actually turned his head away. There was no helmet-to-helmet collision. There was no clothesline; his arms weren't even raised. Bednarik's left shoulder pad hit my left shoulder pad. Period. Our helmets never even touched.

In a backward free-fall, with no time to cushion myself, my helmet slammed to the hard ground; that caused the concussion. So if history wants to think that I was somehow leveled by the hardest hit ever thrown, let it.

On my visit to Bob Sheppard's home fifty years later, Bob told me he remembered the play pretty well too—as well he should have. As soon as I'd been lifted off on the stretcher, one of the Maras—he can't remember if it was Well or Jack—immediately came up to the press box and asked him to make a very ominous announcement.

"They said, 'Bob, find out if there's a Catholic priest in the Stadium, and have him go down to the locker room.' So I got on the microphone and said, 'If there's a Catholic priest in the Stadium, will you go to the locker room.' Fifty people stood up. A hundred. [Well, it was the Giants, after all. We never lacked for fans of the Catholic faith.] I thought they were going to give you the last rites."

It turned out that a guard had suffered a heart attack and died. Things got really interesting back in the trainers' room. The guard's body was covered up. Then they wheeled me in.

"I'm taking off my shoulder pads," Sam remembers, "and here come the trainers rolling a body on a gurney covered by a white sheet. Mo was undressing right next to me. 'Uh-oh,' I said to Mo. 'He's dead.'" (I'm not sure Sam would have been all that displeased, either.) Even Sheppard felt he had to show up, after making his announcement: "I thought, *Well, I'll go in and look at Frank Gifford's remains.*"

I've never really had a chance to make my case about that play, and if I did, I might have taken Chuck off the banquet circuit. He needed the money. I've kidded him about it. He's even kind of a friend of mine. But his whole attitude just turned me off. No one did that back then. The shame is that Chuck is more remembered for making that play than for being the truly great player he was.

Many years later, I had been having trouble with my arms—things tingling. I went into Dr. Russell Warren's Hospital for Special Surgery. Russell had actually tried to make the team, in 1962.

He was a good football player. Instead, he went on to found a great hospital. I had an MRI on my head and neck, and the technician asked me, "Were you ever in a car accident? Your neck looks like a typical car accident injury. A fracture of a couple of vertebrae"— the Bednarik hit. That's how I know it wasn't even actually a head concussion, but probably a spinal concussion. Today, the back of my neck looks like a bad road map. Dr. Frank Camissa did a hell of a job—cleaned it all out—allowing the spinal cord to move back from the calcification that had taken place in the front of my neck. I was fine after six weeks. Well, almost.

**C**ontrary to popular thinking, the concussion wasn't the only factor in my temporary retirement. By then, my broadcasting career was taking off, and I was getting tired of everything but the games themselves: the practices, the travel, the time away from home. As always, I had a future to look toward, and a family to look after. But I was healthy enough to practice with the team as a visiting newsman that year, and I not only found that I still had the moves and speed, but I also found I missed the game.

In training camp of my comeback year of 1962, I was in for a rude awakening: Allie put me on the bench. I was a backup flanker, not the kingpin I had always been. I was sitting on the bench during an exhibition game against the Eagles in Princeton, thinking, *I'm not going to make it this time.* The Giants had picked up Aaron Thomas, a big, fast receiver out of Oregon State, and now I began to think again about quitting for good. I was too proud to talk about it to anyone—I couldn't tell my wife or my teammates. So I sought the advice of one of the wiser sports philosophers of our time: I went to see Toots.

Toots used to say that bartenders were psychologists, and

in this case, he was right. As I sat in his apartment that night—at his bar, of course—I said, "I can't take this anymore. I don't think this guy wants me. I don't know what to do." It was well into the night. Toots was drinking at least his third brandy, and by now he felt like *he* could take my place on the Giants. He said to me, "You never quit on anything in your life. No one wants to be around a quitter."

By midnight, I was ready to whip the world. I stayed on the team, and I had a good season: 39 receptions, 7 touchdowns. In fact, I made the Pro Bowl again, in 1963, at my third position. So I couldn't have lost too many brain cells at Bednarik's hands. I probably lost a whole lot more at Toots's.

S am stayed in a Giant uniform a few more years, then fell victim to Allie Sherman's bloodletting of the old roster. In the space of two years, Allie traded away—or chased away—the heart of our defense: first Cliff, then Rosie, then Mo, and finally Sam. Allie wanted to put his own stamp on the team—especially the defense, maybe because he'd always been an offensive coordinator.

On paper, Allie had some success: he took the Eastern Division title in '61, '62, and '63, but lost all three championship games—the first one big-time, 37–0, in Green Bay, to an angry and motivated Vince Lombardi. As the old song goes, breaking up was hard to do for that defense. "I'll never forget when Sam found out he'd been traded," Mo says now. "He was visiting me in Cleveland Heights, Ohio, and we were at my place—Mo and Junior's Cocktail Lounge and Restaurant. We're sitting around, the phone rings. It's for Sam. He goes white in the face. 'I've been traded to the Redskins,' he says. A month later, I get a call at the restaurant, and it's the same thing: 'We just traded you to Cleveland.' After that,

Sam used to say to players, 'Stay the hell out of Mo's restaurant, or you'll your ass traded.'

"The Giants are where my heart has always been," Mo says. "I wish someone had this picture of a moment I'll never forget, a moment that says it all about the Giants: I'm playing with the Browns, against the Redskins, and Sam and I are walking off the field together, and both of us are looking up at the scoreboard to see how the Giants did that day. Not because we wanted them to lose. Because we wanted them to win."

The day dawned cloudless and hot. I checked out the field personally: The north end was scuffed, worn down to the bald dirt in huge patches. It would be tough to cut in spots. As the captains met at midfield, the temperature was high enough to be a factor for the big guys; in fact, Artie would take himself out for just about every other series. The paramedics stood off to the side of the field in white scrubs, next to their gurney, and their ambulance, in case one of us collapsed, I guess. They must have known about how intense our rivalry had been.

The crowd was so eager to see us play that day, they ringed the field, pressing right up around the sideline—several hundred of them, at least, at game time. They were Giant fans, for the most part, but a smattering of Colt followers stood in the crowd too, eager for another chance to see Unitas throw to Berry. Some wore T-shirts. Some didn't wear shirts at all. Some had probably just wandered over from a day of sunbathing in Central Park to watch the curious show: a dozen men of various sizes and shapes, well into middle age, assembled for a reunion game of touch football, summer of 1978—twenty years after the glory game.

For the Giants: Kyle, looking young and spry. Pat—graying,

but slim. Alex, still with red hair, which might have even been real. Charlie looked every bit the gentleman farmer/cigarette model: white hair, deep tan, a few more wrinkles to his wrinkles, accentuating those classic features. Rosey Brown wore a porkpie hat. Mo had gained a little weight and lost some hair. Ray Wietecha still looked like the muscular, athletic center he'd always been.

Sam wasn't there. "I didn't play two-hand touch," he says now.

I was still in playing shape, but my hair had morphed into a strange seventies-style flop. We were all decked in slick new Giant jerseys made out of some synthetic material—a brighter, almost unnatural blue, much lighter than the old ones had been.

Wearing the Colt whites—gleaming jerseys that never got dirty that day—were all of their stars. Johnny was limping a little on those bad knees, but the smile on his face, framed by a shock of hair falling across his forehead, gave no hint of the tougher days to come for him. Raymond, of course, was slim, and seemingly hadn't aged a day.

Gino had grayed some, and a small pot spilled out over the top of his shorts. Artie didn't have a pot; he'd just widened by about ten sizes, in all directions, his midsection tapering up to that smiling crew cut (he kind of looked like a grinning artillery shell). Lenny Moore had an Afro, but that was the only weight he'd put on; he was in game shape. Parker was a little wider, Ameche a little grayer, and Myhra, one of the best athletes on their team two decades earlier, had gained some weight himself.

The referee was former quarterback Sonny Jurgensen. Calling the plays for CBS was an old friend, announcer and ex-player Tom Brookshier. It was all in fun, a game played for charity, and it's a good thing it was; this time, they didn't need an overtime to beat us. And we still couldn't cover Berry.

The beginning of the game took on the feel of an eerie flashback. After Lenny returned the kick past midfield (it was a 70-yard field), it took Johnny two passes to get them into the end zone; on the touchdown, I fell down trying to cover Lenny (and gained even more respect for the job Lindon had done on Lenny back in '58).

After Myhra kicked off—and, not surprisingly, flubbed a worm-burner that bounced twenty yards—Berry picked off a Conerly pass, and Johnny hit Raymond with a bomb for another touchdown. A few minutes later, Johnny hit Ameche with a bullet—I swear, he hadn't thrown a pass that hard twenty years earlier—then hit Moore with another bomb. Within five minutes, it was 21–0, Colts. The Colts looked as if they hadn't lost a thing. They even ran the 428—the pitchout to Ameche, who actually threw a completion.

Sure enough, in the second half, history repeated itself: just as in '58, we rallied. Charlie's elbow was hurting him, so I replaced him at quarterback, in time to throw two completely illegal touchdown passes. On the first, Kyle ran out of bounds, behind the crowd, then came back onto the field to catch my bomb. On the second one, I ran five yards past the line of scrimmage before I threw to Kyle for a score. ("Notice how they cheated on both touchdowns," Sonny observed.)

From there, though, it was downhill for the graying Giants. During the '59 preseason, I'd gotten a brief tryout at quarterback, until Vince called off the short-lived experiment, and on this day in 1978, I proved the wisdom of that decision: with a few minutes left, I threw into coverage—and Unitas, of all people, picked me off. If I was a little pissed off that I'd thrown a pick—the competitive fires never burn out—I got real joy from watching Johnny on that play, because it really was a sight to see. His knees were obviously hurting, but he wanted to run it in for a score.

He made a few cuts, went to the outside, and turned it on

as much as those legs would allow him to. In the end zone, he grinned, looked around—and emphatically spiked the ball. It was the widest smile I'd ever seen on his face.

When *CBS Sports Spectacular* aired the games later, accompanied by a cheesy disco sound track, Pat and Sonny's postgame interviews from that day were interspliced with clips of the '58 game. The *first* clip they showed? Not a Unitas pass, or Ameche's plunge. It was a replay of my first fumble.

Pat and Sonny asked us all to remember the '58 game, and our failing memories provided a few more highlights. Pressed by Jurgensen about the controversial decision to pass to Mutscheller, Artie replied, "The only thing controversial is the Giants. They still think they're better than we are."

Johnny revealed, astoundingly, that he hadn't known what had happened on Ameche's blown option pass on fourth down until they'd gotten together for our touch game: "He just told me last night," Johnny said, laughing. "He didn't hear the 400 number."

Kyle, laughing and smiling, was typically self-effacing when Pat asked him about his performance in the '58 game, and his speed (or lack of it) on the 86-yard bomb/fumble that temporarily turned the game around. "The guy that tackled me [Andy Nelson] had time to rush Charlie, turn around, and catch up with me," Kyle said with that almost-sad smile.

My favorite moment of the postgame interviews came when Pat interviewed Charlie, who had remained characteristically sparing with his words. Pat asked his old teammate a long question about how the game had become so legendary: Why did Charlie think that might have been? Was it perhaps the overtime that contributed to the legend? The question took about half a minute.

Charlie thought for a second, squinted, and said four words: "Ah'm sure it did."

Pat was left with a silent microphone. End of interview.

Afterward, at the Tavern on the Green, the Giants, for once, declared themselves the winners: we outdrank the Colts hands down, while we traded stories. Mo told Johnny, laughingly, that the draw to Ameche on the overtime drive—the one that had trapped Mo right out of the play—was "a stupid call." Johnny smiled at him and asked: "How many yards did I get?"

It was a hell of a day: a sunstruck, carefree afternoon of touch football with old friends who'd put on a few pounds, and put together a few good memories. We were still in our forties and fifties, all of us still feeling immortal. None of us thought about the significance of the occasion, that this would be the last time so many of the stars of that game would ever assemble as one. None of us yet knew how the legend of our '58 game would grow as we grew even older. None of yet knew that, as the NFL continued to grow, fans would seem to want to reach back to that December day for something that was, indefinably, disappearing.

None of us were really feeling time closing in on us yet. Most of us were in the middle of a new professional prime in the late seventies. Charlie was farming and running seven shoe stores down in Clarksdale. At that point, he still held all of the Giants' passing records; Phil Simms was still in his third year—enduring the Giants Stadium boos. Seven years later, Simms would hear the cheers, for a phenomenal Super Bowl performance. But I don't think he ever got a standing O in P.J.'s.

Charlie became the most famous of all of Jack Landry's Marlboro Men, doing print and television ads well into the seventies. "When the TV ads ran, we got residuals," Perian says now. "It was like finding money in the street. We'd go on location to Mexico, all over the place. They were looking for a lean, lank macho type, and Charlie fit the bill.

"The cowboy ones were good, but my favorite is the one where Charlie is wearing black tie and tails, leaning back in his chair." I myself never saw him in that particular uniform. After he sold the shoe stores, he and Perian did a lot of traveling, and enjoyed a daily golf game. He died in 1996, at the age of seventy-four. He's enshrined in the Mississippi Sports Hall of Fame. But he never did make it to Canton. "Charlie is the best football player who is not in the Hall of Fame," Wellington once told the *New York Times*, and I wholeheartedly agree.

**P**at was doing play-by-play for CBS, and, three years later, would pair up with John Madden for twenty-two years of some of the finest play-by-play and color work the medium ever saw. Alex Webster had succeeded Allie as the Giant head coach for four years, with limited success, and was replaced. But his two successors, Bill Arnsparger and John McVay, had even less success at the job than Alex. Red wasn't bitter about it. "Why complain—no one's going to listen anyhow" is Alex's philosophy now. He was just happy to be along for the ride, and his generosity of heart has always been an inspiration to all of us.

Andy took over as the Giants' director of operations for six years, and would stay until 1979. Now you can find him at a table in his restaurant in his hometown of Stamford, graying, but obviously content with a life well lived. Ro never wanted anyone to think of him as anything special, and still doesn't.

As for myself, in the summer of '78 I was in the eighth year of the Monday-night triumvirate with Howard Cosell and Don Meredith. Don remains a close friend, and he's the godfather of my son Cody.

Maynard didn't make it north for the touch game. But Don

did all right for himself after Jim Lee and Allie cut him following the 1959 training camp to keep a twenty-seventh-round draft pick named Joe Biscaha. After the season, Don called Landry in Dallas, but no one returned the call. (You can't help wondering how the early Cowboys' fate would have been different if they'd returned the future Hall of Famer's telephone call, can you? They could have had Don Maynard—for seventy-five cents.)

Don heard that there was going to be a new league in 1960, and that New York would get a franchise. One of the charter owners of that team was my old friend and longtime sports broadcaster Harry Wismer, who had once owned part of the Washington Redskins. Don had heard that Wismer had hired Sammy Baugh (the legendary Hall of Fame quarterback who had led the Redskins to two NFL titles during a sixteen-year career that spanned the thirties, forties, and fifties) to coach. Maynard made the call.

"I played against Sammy's teams three times in college, so I called him up and said, 'I want to play for you,'" Don told me. "I was the first New York Titan ever signed. This time, I was loose as a goose. I knew I was going to be around, so I demanded a no-cut contract." They gave it to him. The team labored in front of empty crowds in the Polo Grounds for a couple of years, but Don stuck in there. He became Namath's favorite receiver on the New York Jets. He now wears a Super Bowl ring. And his bust is in Canton, Ohio.

Al Barry played two more years, his last in the new AFL for the Los Angeles Chargers, in front of crowds "of about six thousand." He was blocking for a quarterback named Jack Kemp. In 1961, Al became an insurance broker and financial planner in California. When he sent out his first solicitations for clients, in 1961, Kyle wrote back, "Who's going to lead the way for Gifford?" Al has a son named for Kyle.

Harland Svare had two head-coaching stints, with the Rams and Chargers. Now he's in the health-supplement business out in Colorado. Dick Modzelewski enjoyed a twenty-two-year stint coaching defense for five different NFL teams, before retiring in 1990. After enduring three back operations, and having various other joints rebuilt, Mo is retired, still fun-loving and happy, and living near his children in Ohio.

Cliff Livingston, our handsome, high-living bachelor, did pretty well for himself. He landed a dozen television commercials, and had a brief but very lucrative run as a contestant for several weeks on the quiz show *Name That Tune*. "The money dwarfed my professional football salary," Cliff told me from Las Vegas, his new hometown. "But, hell, that wasn't hard to dwarf." One of the commercials featured Cliff as a Marlboro Man, one of many—but hardly the most famous: "The main guy was Charlie; the rest of us just smoked around him."

Don Chandler was traded to the Packers in 1965—where he picked up two Super Bowl rings with Vince Lombardi. When he retired from football, he returned to Tulsa and went into the construction business, building apartment and office buildings. He's enjoying the good life in Tulsa: the last time I talked to him, he'd just shot an 88 on the golf course—and won eight dollars.

M. L. Brackett played three years in the NFL, then made a wise choice. He quit the game that had ended up giving him twenty-two scars, for a safer world: steel mills. "I just didn't feel that pro football was a place for a married man, what with the nightlife on the road and the bars at home," he told me. He became the supervisor of a steel mill in Alabama.

Frank Youso played two more years with the Giants and then asked Wellington to trade him to the Vikings; he missed his hometown of International Falls, Minnesota, where he still lives, five blocks from the house he grew up in.

When Mel Triplett died in 2002, the Mississippi Legislature issued a special proclamation commemorating his life, his football exploits, and the glory and honor he'd brought to the state of Mississippi. For the record, it noted that Mel left fifty grandchildren. Like the man said, Mel really liked women.

We lost Emlen Tunnell way too early. "He always talked about dying young," Grier says now. He did, in 1975, of a heart attack at the age of fifty-three.

The Concourse Plaza Hotel is now the Concourse Plaza Senior Center, a redbrick home for the elderly, surrounded by the offices of bail bondsmen. But it still has the red awning—a little tired, but it's still there.

Rosie Grier has taken a remarkable journey down what he calls "Life's Highway," ever since, in one of Allie Sherman's worst trades, in July of 1963, we sent him to the Rams for a lineman named John LoVetere and a high draft choice. Rosie's arrival in Los Angeles was a key piece of the puzzle for what became one of the greatest defensive lines in football history: the "Fearsome Foursome"—Grier, Deacon Jones, Lamar Lundy, and Merlin Olsen.

Rosie went on to do some television acting, became an ordained minister, and wrote a couple of books—including *Rosie Grier's Needlepoint for Men*. He even did a little movie acting, although I don't think *The Thing with Two Heads* will go down in cinematic history. (But then, my *Darby's Rangers* didn't, either.)

But history will always remember Rosie for his heroism on June 5, 1968. He was a bodyguard for the Kennedys on Bobby's fateful campaign. Rosie was onstage with the candidate for his last speech, at the Ambassador Hotel in Los Angeles, and used his quickness and strength to disarm Sirhan Sirhan—a few seconds too late. The memory lives on, etched in Rosie's mind, because of the random sequence of events that changed a nation's history far more significantly than a football game ever could have.

"That particular night," he told me, "I was told to stay with Ethel. She was six months pregnant. When we went on the stage, we had cordoned off a space to the right-hand side to get him off-stage. He was supposed to come back to me. Unbeknownst to me, an assistant maître d' came up at the last second and told him there was a quicker way to the back, to the kitchen. So he jumped off the stage. Now we're helping Ethel off, and everyone is out of position.

"The shots rang out, and Ethel jumped, and I covered her. I heard the screaming. I came up, came around the back of a refrigerator, stepped over two people, grappling with him, gun waving. I went for his legs. George Plimpton, the writer, goes for the gun hand, and now people are starting to attack Sirhan Sirhan. I have his legs locked, and George couldn't get the gun away from him. So I grabbed his hand and stuck my finger behind the trigger, so he couldn't snap it on the firing pin, and I put the gun in my pocket. Now I'm fighting those people off. I said, 'There's been enough violence.'"

Years later, Rosie and Jackie Onassis became good friends: "I'd call her up and play her records I thought she should hear. Aretha, Ray Charles." He'd come a long way from that electric guitar in Winooski.

These days, Rosie serves as a community service director for the Milken Family Foundation, getting out into the Los Angeles community, speaking to schoolkids. He's still making a difference.

I saw him just the other day. Like all of us, he isn't moving quite as quickly: "It's the knees. I can get down, but I can't get up. I was at a school talking to some kids the other day, kneeling on the floor, and as I got to get up, my left knee said, 'Unh-unh.' Man, I fell over. People were trying to help me up and we were all laughing. I said we can laugh about that, because in life a lot of times you can fall down, and be embarrassed; the key is getting up. I got up."

Jack Kemp didn't make the touch football game, because I think he might have had more pressing business at the time: he was in the middle of an eighteen-year term as a congressman, representing a district in upstate New York, after he'd led the Bills to consecutive AFL titles in the mid-sixties. "I had eleven concussions in thirteen years," he told me. "There was nothing left to do other than run for Congress."

In 1988 Jack mounted a presidential bid, losing out to George Bush, who appointed him secretary of Housing and Urban Development. In 1996 Jack was the vice presidential nominee on the Dole-Kemp ticket. But whenever I talk to him now, it's always about football.

"I revere my time in the NFL of the fifties," Jack told me. "It really was a golden age. I felt I was a part of one of the greatest enterprises ever undertaken. It's a great memory. It was a life that I wouldn't have traded for anything. Today I've got seventeen grandchildren, ten grandsons, and five of them play football, from Pop Warner to high school. In fact, I wrote a poem for my family: 'Family, faith, football, and freedom are the values of the Kemp family; nothing can beat 'em.'"

The Colts had their own emissary to Capitol Hill: Ray Brown, the defensive back who was earning his law degree as a player, ended up clerking for the Supreme Court justice Tom Clark, who'd earlier been Harry Truman's attorney general. Ray is still practicing law down in Mississippi, litigating for the railroads. Milt Davis, the professor, finally got his PhD, after thirty-three years. When I finally tracked Milt down, he was farming in the Willamette Valley of Oregon.

Leo Sanford, the linebacker, bought a new house with the winners' share, and got into the class-ring and graduation-supply business. Jackie Simpson, the safety who fumbled that punt, played another year in Baltimore, then up in Montreal for a while, then opened up a bar, and eventually retired to Pensacola, Florida. Jackie still has his two rings: "Some people took a sterling silver dining set for the '59 win," he says. "I took the second ring. It was a good decision. I got a divorce, and she would have gotten the silver."

Fuzzy Thurston, of course, moved on to Green Bay. Fuzzy told me he was a day late in reporting to his first Packer training camp. "Lombardi asked me, 'Who the hell are you?' 'I'm Fuzzy Thurston.' 'You were due yesterday. Don't let it happen again.'"

The rest of that story is history. Fuzzy earned enough championship rings with the Packers—five—to open up his own ring-supply business.

The Giants of 1958, by the way, each got a commemorative tie clip.

Fast food was very, very good to Gino Marchetti and Alan Ameche. Four years after the touch game, they'd sell their restaurant business to Marriott. It's now known as Roy Rogers. "I wish I'd bought some of that stock," Andy Nelson says. But things worked out pretty well for Andy, too: drawing on his barbecuing heritage, learned at the knee of his dad in Alabama and nurtured in his years playing for Memphis State, Andy opened his own barbecue place outside of Baltimore, Andy Nelson's Barbecue. It's now a local legend, thanks to Andy's culinary motto: "Slow cooking, hickory wood, serve no pork before its time."

Artie, having given up his hope of pounding the sidewalks as a Bronx cop, happily became a Baltimorean. He runs a country club in the suburbs of Baltimore, still receiving visitors and reporters in the kitchen. Artie has become nothing less than the comic Homer of that game, that team, that time. He would later write a book that was as hilarious on the page as Artie is in person.

A few months after the touch game, Raymond Berry joined Landry's staff with the Cowboys, as a receiver coach. "I didn't care about coaching—I didn't want to get fired every three or four years—but Tom talked me into it," Ray told me from his home in Murfreesboro, Tennessee.

In 1984, Raymond got the head-coaching job at New England, and enjoyed tremendous success—with a little help, as Ernie Accorsi told me, from Unitas: "Berry called John when he got the job, and said, 'John, can you meet me at the Baltimore airport?' John drives to the airport. Berry's got a legal pad. He says, 'Tell me how you ran the two-minute drill in that game.' John says, 'You were there!' Ray says, "Yeah, but I wasn't paying attention to what you were doing.' "

Raymond began paying attention. The Patriots played in the 1985 Super Bowl, losing out to Mike Ditka and Buddy Ryan's monstrous Bears, and our *Monday Night Football* team had some super games with Berry's Patriots.

Lenny Moore has spent the last several decades giving back to the community that celebrated him on the football field; he works with Baltimore youth, for the Maryland Department of Juvenile Justice.

As time passed, the Colt watering holes moved on from Kusen's and Andy's; soon, Colts from every era were gathering at Johnny's place, the Golden Arm. "On Fridays, after the short practice," Earl Morrall told me, "there was an unwritten rule: If we weren't home by five-thirty, the wives would come down and everyone would have dinner there. They knew where we were. The wives would all be there by six."

Another local saloon drew the Colts as well: Bill Pellington's Iron Horse. And there's a story there. A haunting one.

Like all small-town families, the Colts have suffered their share of setbacks and misfortunes, maybe more than anyone could have anticipated. But even in sadness, they have found a way to come together, as the epilogue of Pellington's life illustrates so well.

Bill died of complications related to Alzheimer's. The disease began showing its effects in 1988.

"My dad would talk about you all the time—he always had a lot of respect for you," his son, Mark Pellington, told me. When I reached him he'd just been looking at a photograph of his dad tackling me in the '58 game. But Mark's favorite photograph depicts his old man going face-to-face with a referee: "He's like a lion, up in the guy's face with his helmet off, laying every f-bomb in the world on the guy. I *love* that photo. It says to me, 'Don't be an asshole, but fight for what you believe in. Be strong.'"

With his winner's share from our game, Bill Pellington built a cottage on the Jersey Shore. Back home, in Maryland, he opened the restaurant, in a shopping center in Lutherville—the archetypal ex-athlete's sports bar: steaks, chops, seafood. It was so dark when you walked in, Mark told me, it took your eyes a minute to adjust before it all came into focus: the painting of Pellington at the entrance, the photographs of the games, the red leather booths, the curved bar: "not the alcoholic's ultrastraight bar—the curved one where you could talk to people," Mark said, and I knew exactly what he was talking about.

Mark played football too, in high school, but he blew out a knee, and became a filmmaker instead. He's directed and produced feature films, television shows, and music videos with the likes of Springsteen and Pearl Jam. But his proudest filmmaking accomplishment garnered little publicity. He called the poignant documentary he made about his father's decline into Alzheimer's *Father's Daze*. The film was first screened at the Senator Theatre in Baltimore in 1993, at a benefit for Alzheimer's research. They were all there—Johnny, Gino, Parker, Mutscheller, Berry. The film's remarkable, heart-wrenching imagery makes it almost too difficult to watch, as it shifts from scenes of Pellington at his maniacal best on the field to sad scenes of Bill near the end, unable to speak, able only to intertwine his fingers with his son's and look out at him from the prison of his sickness.

"My dad commanded respect," Mark told me. "When I hear all these crazy stories about him . . . I didn't really see that. I knew he was a tough sonofabitch. He was very stoic, a good sense of humor. Very tough, but he had a funny side. He was a good dad, When you really fucked up, he never laid into you—when you did something stupid, maybe, but when you really fucked up, he knew you felt bad. He led by example."

On the night of the screening, Mark told me, there wasn't a dry eye in the house—until, following the credits, another film came on the screen—the highlights of the 1958 game. And when that film was over, the Colt band marched down the aisles, playing the Colt fight song. People jumped to their feet.

"You know that community," Mark told me, "and you know how they lament each loss."

The disease's onset, Mark has been told, likely resulted from several factors, including drinking—and the tackling. Mark has no doubt that the football played a part.

• • •

**N**othing shocked the Colts, though, like the death of Big Daddy, on May 10, 1963.

Daddy had continued to live his famously colorful life after our game, and continued to play all-pro football—forcing fumbles, roaming sideline to sideline. He was named to the Pro Bowl in 1958 and 1959. After the '59 season, he took up a new off-season job: pro wrestling, as a way to stay in shape, and get paid for it. And befitting that big heart, Daddy insisted that his character in the ring be a good guy: "Nobody," he said, "is going to say that Big Daddy is a mean man."

But no one doubted that football was his true love, and the stabilizing force of an unstable life. He didn't carry around pictures only of his gruesomely murdered mother; his folder of photographs also included stills from the 1958 game, which he delighted in showing to anyone and everyone. Behind the menacing physique, and the worried face given to mysterious outbursts of tears, Lenny Moore told me, lurked a kind and gentle man: "To go show you what he was about internally—and I found this out later—Big Daddy used to take bags of groceries around to poor families and knock on the door and drop it off to them. Out of his own pocket. Took care of those folks—never told me, never told Parker."

After the 1960 season, the Colts traded him to the Steelers, with Buzz Nutter, for receiver Jimmy Orr. In Pittsburgh, Daddy's off-the-field legend grew: a lot of drinking, and a lot of eating. And a lot of women—sometimes, reportedly, at the same time. But he still had a lot of great football in that big body of his. In 1962, by all accounts, Daddy was getting even better. In his final game, the 1962 Pro Bowl, Daddy was named the lineman of the game.

Eugene Lipscomb was thirty-one when he was found dead on

the floor of his southwestern Baltimore apartment shortly after his final game. "A homemade syringe was found near his unconscious form," reported a Pittsburgh paper. Four fresh needle marks dotted his arm. The only witness to the evening's events was an admitted heroin addict and ex-con who has since passed away. Daddy had supposedly had $700 in his famously fat wallet that night. ("Big Daddy had a bad habit of carrying excess money in his pocket," Lenny told me. "We told him, 'Daddy, don't be flashing your money around.'") The authorities found just $73.

Today, some of his teammates insist that Daddy's death was the result of foul play. Lenny Moore thinks that the man with Lipscomb killed him to take his money.

"There isn't a day that goes by that I don't think of Big Daddy," Moore told me.

"I will never forget that Friday, ever. I was talking to him Thursday. We'd made plans to go up to New York to one of the jazz clubs, to see [organist] Jimmy Smith play. We were going to drive up. Big Daddy said, 'You want to take your car, my car, whatever?' I said it didn't matter. He says, 'We'll go up, maybe stay overnight in a motel, drive back.' After that, he told me, he wanted to go to Pittsburgh to deal with his contract, and see the grandfather who had raised him.

"I wake up seven A.M., hearing the news on the radio: Big Daddy Lipscomb, dead. I said, 'What?' It was all over the news. I called around, and talked to [former Colt running back] Buddy Young, and to Parker, and to Sherm [Plunkett]. We were all real close. I said, 'I talked to him that day. Did you see him?' They said, 'Well, the only thing we know is he went by a club, left the club, ended up down at an apartment.' I said, 'Okay, but who was there?' They said, 'I don't know, other than a couple of guys who did drugs.' I said, 'What was he doing around them guys?' They said,

'We don't know; all we know is he passed out from an overdose, and they waited a long time before they called the ambulance.'

"So I talked to the coroner. I said, 'Do your autopsy checking.' He said, 'Big Daddy was right-handed, wasn't he?' I said, 'Yeah.' He said, 'All the needle marks were in his right arm.' He says, 'The first shot was a heroin shot that was enough to take five people out.'

"Here's the thing: Daddy was scared to death of needles. One time six or seven of us had to hold him down in Los Angeles after he hurt his ankle and they were just going to give him a shot to make it numb. As far as needles, he wouldn't even take the flu shot."

"[Former Colt defensive back] Johnny Sample and I both put up a thousand dollars to have his death investigated," Milt Davis told me. Milt was Daddy's roommate on the road. "We were told to cease and desist, by letter, from lawyers representing Spiro Agnew—'or we're going to take you to jail.' What is that all about? That really happened: Spiro himself. From the governor!

"My roomie," Milt said, "should be in the Hall of Fame. He's not, though, because of the taint of his death."

"He was one of the greatest guys you ever want to meet," Moore added. "All he was doing was trying to fill the void in his life; there was nobody there to fill in the pieces."

Weeb's Colt era came to an end after the 1962 season, after going .500 that year, and 21–19 over his final three years. As Marchetti said, Weeb wore out his welcome, and the old Colts were wearing down. In fact, Gino himself had something to do with Weeb's firing, albeit unwittingly. "We played the Bears on a Saturday night, and they beat us," he told me. "Monday morning I get a call. From Carroll's secretary: 'He wants to see you at ten o'clock at the Sheraton.' I was nervous. I thought I was going to be traded.

"I go in, and Rosenbloom smiles, and says, 'Nothing to worry about.' He said, 'I have my excuse to fire Weeb now.' And I said, 'So what am I doing here?' And he says, 'I want you to recommend someone.' I recommended Don Shula. We'd been roommates when he'd played with the team in the early fifties. So Rosenbloom hired Shula."

So I guess it turns out the Colts owe a whole lot more to Gino Marchetti than just all those years of great play: he gave them a Hall of Fame coach.

Of course, none of it would have been possible without Rosenbloom, the man who oversaw a franchise that after 1956, with Carroll as the owner, never had a losing season—a span that featured three championships and eight division titles.

But Rosenbloom's final act in life was every bit as mysterious—and tragic—as Big Daddy's. The man Bill Curry told me was "the best owner ever"—who could also be "both . . . cruel and loving"—lived his last twenty years embroiled in one controversy after another.

Off the field, player after player told me, Carroll continued to be generous and to take an active interest in their lives. That altruism speaks of a special man; he helped anyone and everyone, long after their own success could have benefited him. He famously helped out on medical bills for anyone who ever needed them.

An Ernie Accorsi anecdote, from the days when Ernie ran the public-relations office of the Colts, sums up this side of the man pretty well: "He called me one Sunday morning, because there was something in the paper he didn't like. My wife was ill; I thought it might be her appendix, and I wanted to take her to the hospital—we didn't have 911 in those days.

"I said, 'Mr. Rosenbloom, I think my wife is having appendicitis.' He said, 'Give me your address, I'll have Dr. Freeman there in thirty minutes.' I said, 'You don't have to do that. I'll drive her to the hospital.'

"He said, 'Don't move.' And a few minutes later, on a Sunday morning, here's the doctor. I said, 'Doctor, you didn't have to come over here.' He said, 'I didn't have to come over here? You should have heard the phone call I had from Carroll Rosenbloom. I had no choice.'"

On the other hand, as the years went on, the relationship between Rosenbloom and the city of Baltimore increasingly unraveled. Faced with waning attendance and a spartan stadium ("Memorial was outdated the day they finished it," says his son Steve), Rosenbloom asked the city for financial help. Not only was he rebuffed, but he soon found himself on the losing end of the pen of famed Baltimore sportswriter John Steadman. According to Steve: "He would go after my father personally about whatever that was happening that he didn't like . . . His attacks would run the gamut on everything." Steadman had been the Colts' assistant general manager before returning to newspapering. Today, Steve Rosenbloom attributes Steadman's attacks on his father in the *Baltimore News-American* to the fact that Rosenbloom didn't hire him when Don Kellett retired as general manager.

According to an old friend of Carroll's who requested anonymity, Rosenbloom, despite all of his achievements, was acutely sensitive to how people treated him, and to how all of his generosity went underappreciated: "He'd always lament about himself, about how no one does enough for 'poor old Carroll.' He was nice to his friends, but he liked to be coddled. Loved people to bow down to him. He was one of the most intelligently manipulative people I ever met. There was nothing he didn't do in the end that wasn't for Carroll."

In the end, the critics beat him down—the newspapers, the

city fathers who wouldn't give him more money. Rosenbloom grew weary of it all. He'd talked of moving the franchise for years, but in the late sixties, no one moved NFL franchises; it just wasn't done. "But he said, 'I'm getting too old for this—all we've done is win, and look what I'm going through,'" Steve recalls. "That's when he first said, 'I gotta do something. I'm not living like this.' That's how this deal was dreamed up."

The "deal" was something that had never before been seen in sports, and never will be again. Rosenbloom traded his team for Robert Irsay's Los Angeles Rams. As soon as the Colts became Robert Irsay's, the team hit a downhill slope, and never recovered, from its first losing season in 1972 to the night in March of 1984 when Irsay packed up the team's equipment into Mayflower moving vans and the team slipped away into the night, to Indianapolis.

In the meantime, says Rosenbloom's friend, Carroll was in heaven out in Los Angeles: "That was the world he wanted. He got Hollywood." Gone were the nagging sportswriters, replaced by a host of luminaries in Carroll's box, from the legit to the not-so-legit. "The visitors to his box in those later years were pretty interesting," says his friend. "Bobby Kennedy, Spiro Agnew, [Maryland governor] Marvin Mandel—with a little Mafioso mixed in. He always mixed with some interesting people. If you didn't know him, maybe you'd say he was part of the underworld.

"He was a combination of tough and spooky. One time, when I had brought a very important guest to his box, who hadn't been there before—he was superstitious about that—we were losing at the half, and he said to my guest, 'We better win this game, or I'll cut your balls off.'"

On April 2, 1979, Rosenbloom drowned in the surf behind his home in Golden Beach, Florida. The circumstances immediately struck anyone who had known him as suspicious: "He was a very good athlete, in good shape," says his friend. "He swam every day."

Four years later, PBS's *Frontline* series debuted with an investigation of the NFL's possible underworld connections, and included interviews with organized-crime types who said Rosenbloom's legs had been held underwater while he drowned. Or, as Artie puts it now, "The Sicilian Frogmen got him."

Rosenbloom's wife, Georgia Frontiere, a former showgirl, inherited the team. She knew nothing about football—"It would be like me telling you that you're taking over the World Bank tomorrow," says his friend. But after she moved the Rams to St. Louis, the team won another Super Bowl. Winning was always, somehow, in the Rosenbloom blood.

At Rosenbloom's funeral, it was fitting that Oakland/Los Angeles Raider owner Al Davis, another maverick who'd been a thorn in the NFL's side forever, gave a eulogy. "Among the great people in my world, Carroll Rosenbloom was the giant," Davis said. "Come autumn, and the roar of the crowd, I'll always think of him."

Why is Carroll's mysterious side at all relevant to this book? Because of the ongoing discussion about that second-down pass to Mutscheller, in overtime, when a chip-shot field goal could have won it. Because of the still-lingering, if ludicrous, suspicion that Rosenbloom, because he had a bet on the game, might have had something to do with Unitas's call. The betting line was 3 ½ points, which meant that a field goal would have won the game, but Carroll would have lost his bet.

Rosenbloom himself later said that he was sitting in the stands for our game, which would have made it impossible for him to have anything to do with the play-calling: "I didn't want to sit in the press box," he said. "I didn't want to be around anyone I knew. I called Timothy Mara and asked him to find me two seats off by myself where I could see the football game and the only ones who would know where I was sitting would be Tim and myself . . . He got me two seats, and Don Kellett went up there with me. They were way up high."

Before he passed away earlier this year, the Colts' center, Buzz Nutter, admitted that the rumor had always been around in Colt circles: "I know that everybody says we went for it because Rosenbloom had a bet, and he'd given four, but I never thought about that."

"I know that he used to bet on college games and stuff like that," Steve Rosenbloom told me. "I'd be at the house. He just liked to do that kind of stuff. Maybe he wanted to distance me from it, but I never knew that he bet on any professional game. People have told me that he did, and that he came clean with them, but I can't say one way or the other. I can tell you this: winning was so important to my father, even if he had bet on games, that became secondary to winning the game. Had he bet on that game? I don't know. After all these years, I think it's irrelevant."

Rosenbloom's friend told me that Carroll did, indeed, have money on the outcome of the 1958 championship game. "I talked to one of his partners, who assured me Carroll bet on that game," said his friend. "He was a betting man, and he was a terrible bettor. He'd lose five of six on any given Sunday. Carroll loved to bet. He would have the day's line; he'd make me go over the day's line every Sunday morning."

But the idea that Rosenbloom could have somehow had something to do with Unitas's passing to Mutscheller, so that the Colts could beat the point spread, is ridiculous. If he did bet, I have no doubt he had some anxious moments down there, but he didn't have anything to do with that call. That call was all Johnny's.

There's one other quote that figures into all of this, though, one made by Johnny Unitas himself. After the game—jokingly, I have to believe—Unitas told some reporters, ' "I went for the touchdown [on the pass to Mutscheller] because I had bet a few thousand on the game and I had given three and a half points."

Later on, Johnny insisted it had been said in jest: "I didn't even know what the points were," he told John Steadman. Bert Bell was apparently not pleased, and "read him the riot act," said Steadman some years later. But it was absurd, as far as I'm concerned. It just sounds like something Johnny would say to get a laugh.

I have weighed all of this, and firmly believe that Johnny Unitas went for that pass because he was Johnny. Period. He knew it would work, and it did. And it was a second-down call. John always made his own calls, even if it wasn't what Weeb wanted. Every call Johnny made was a good one.

What's unfortunate about Unitas's joking quote, and the controversy, is that they planted the idea in people's minds that Johnny Unitas was a gambler. That perception would come to haunt him a few years later.

No one in our game had as bittersweet a life as Johnny—with an emphasis on "sweet," when you take into account his marriage to Sandy Unitas. Johnny married the former stewardess in 1970, and today her fondest memory is of her husband stopping the lawn mower during his yard duties to bring her wildflowers up at their farmhouse. According to Sandy, Johnny liked nothing better than to ride that mower and tend the animals on their Maryland farm. In fact, on the day he'd played his last football game for the Colts, Ernie Accorsi asked him for all of his equipment, to give to the Hall of Fame. Johnny didn't surrender the shoes: "They're good for cutting the grass," he told Ernie.

I finally got to know Johnny some years after our game, in Vietnam. It was the winter of '66. I'd just retired; Johnny had another decade to go in the NFL. Our foursome was Johnny, Willie Davis of the Packers, Sam, and me. We'd gone over there as NFL emissaries to meet our troops, and things got a lot hairier than we'd ever anticipated—or, I'm sure, than Pete Rozelle had anticipated when he asked us to go.

You can learn a lot about a man sitting next to him in a helicopter as it lands in Vietcong-occupied territory, or on the deck of an aircraft carrier in the South China Sea, or when he's talking to hostile Montagnards wearing grenade belts in the jungle. I learned a lot about Johnny. And none of it surprised me.

He was cool under pressure over there, too, when the rest of us were a little less composed. On our first night, we were holed up in a barricaded hotel in Saigon. "You guys better be sure you look under your bed before you go to sleep," our babysitter, a young lieutenant, said. Sam said, "What's that about?" The guy said, "Well, you never know. They may have put an explosive under there. You better take a look." I'm thinking, *Good Lord. What are we into here?* We had some terrifying nights, when we could hear grenades and sirens and gunshots going off—sitting in the hotel, which was guarded, but wondering how long it would be before they got to us.

Johnny never showed the slightest concern. He was there to spread goodwill, and he seemed to enjoy every minute of the trip—especially the very scariest part. There was this one particular South

Vietnamese colonel who was from Baltimore, and he loved the
Colts. This guy was way out in the jungle, right in the middle of it
all, and of course he made a request to meet Johnny. They basically
asked us out to lunch—in the middle of a war zone. On our way
out there, our veteran helicopter pilot said, "I'm going to touch
down and be on the ground for about five seconds. Be ready to get
your asses out. Otherwise they're going to shoot my ass out of the
sky. I'll be back in two hours."

Willie, Sam, and I were ready to go home. "John, this is just
great," said Sam. Johnny just smiled; he didn't seem worried at all.
He'd told us he'd always wanted to be a pilot, but failed the depth-
perception part of the eyesight test, so he was having a ball flying
everywhere in Vietnam.

Johnny was the hero of that lunch, in the colonel's headquar-
ters behind enemy lines, in a shack hidden in the jungle (the pilot
got us back out)—just as he was the focus of attention on our visit
to the aircraft carrier *Kitty Hawk*. In all the places we went, from
the carrier to the outposts in the middle of the jungle, it was almost
as if someone had called timeout on the war to sit down and have
lunch with, to meet, to get a piece of paper signed by Johnny Unitas. A man of few words for the most part, Johnny was amazing
with the soldiers—genuinely glad to be giving them something to
smile about.

Ray Brown told me of the delight John used to take in signing
autographs in the lobbies of their hotels on the road; sometimes Ray
would have to go find him and drag him away from the kids who
were surrounding him, just to get him up to their Saturday night
team dinner. And as Sandy Unitas recalls, Johnny was always a little
uncomfortable about being asked for autographs if there were other
players around—"He'd say, 'This is whoever; wouldn't you like to get

him to sign this?'" she says. "He always would recognize the other players and friends, and not want the attention to go onto him."

In Vietnam, Johnny was the guy, wherever we went.

The first few years after our game, Johnny picked up where he'd left off on the football field. In the '59 title game against the Giants, he opened with a bomb to Lenny Moore, and never looked back. He won two league MVP trophies between '64 and '67. But all the sacks and years of throwing with that overhand snap, that distinctive style that always seemed to produce a perfect pass, finally caught up with him. In the final preseason game in '68 in Dallas, he tore the tendons in his right elbow. He threw only thirty-two passes that year, backing up Earl Morrall. In one game in 1968, when he went one for eleven, the Memorial Stadium crowd booed him.

Don Shula put him in during the third quarter of the 1968 Super Bowl against the Jets, after Morrall had struggled, but it was too little, too late. He led one touchdown drive. He still managed to win a Super Bowl ring, two years later, after the Colts, Steelers, and Browns had moved into the AFC. Sharing duties with Morrall in a sloppy win against the Cowboys, Johnny got his last ring.

The Colts traded him to San Diego in 1973, and it was a bad fit from the start. It pained me to watch Johnny playing—or standing on the sidelines—in one of those flashy pastel Charger uniforms, in that Southern California sunlight, with a bum arm and, by now, two very bad knees.

"When Johnny was traded, he supposedly had right of first refusal," according to Sandy. "But he got a call from a reporter who told him he'd been traded to San Diego. I remember John telling me, 'Honey, I can't afford not to go. It's the largest contract I ever had—$250,000.'"

The Chargers of the early seventies were a notoriously drug-infested team. They were coached by Harland Svare, who had coached the Rams from 1962 to 1965, then taken over the San Diego head spot in 1971. The old farm boy wasn't ready for the pharmaceutical revolution. "What really brought me down was the introduction of not only amphetamines, but marijuana," Harland told me, unable to hide the disappointment in his voice. "We tried to control it. On the Giants, all we had was a few drinks every night, and that was it." (Well, maybe more than a few.)

The drug use, the indifference about staying after practice, the losing attitude, the beach-town mentality—it all turned Johnny off. He'd grown up in a gritty coal town and had his best years in a proud port city, both of them sports-crazy. How could he play for a city full of people whose main sport was worshipping the sun? How could he hit receivers, as he was quoted in Tom Callahan's terrific biography *Johnny U*, who were "smoking that rope"?

Another thing was missing: the camaraderie. In Baltimore, Sandy tells me, Johnny loved to sit around with the guys and talk about games over beers. In San Diego, there was none of that— "they just wanted to grab their surfboards and head for the beach," as Sandy tells it. But win or lose, she says, no matter what team he was playing for, Johnny Unitas always left it at the stadium: "You'd never know if he'd won or lost; he'd just come home, lean down, give me a kiss, and say, 'Let's go to dinner.'"

He retired in July of 1974, not because of his arm, but his knees. He would eventually have both replaced. One year later, Sandy said, the FBI knocked on the door, asking about drug use on the Chargers. She says he wasn't shy about telling them whatever they wanted to know. San Diego had left a bad taste in John's mouth.

For a while, his restaurant, the Golden Arm, enjoyed success, but the place eventually went out of business, and every other business he touched seemed to go bad as well, from a hotel in Florida to an electronics venture that caused him to declare bankruptcy. When Johnny took a job doing TV ads for Bally's Casino, it was a sign of things to come. When he began to pick the point spread in "The Johnny Unitas All-Pro Football Report" ("I have to make a living," he said), Rozelle banned him from appearing at league-sanctioned functions.

Through the years, teammates delighted in seeing him at reunions, at golf tournaments, or at other events, always signing autographs, despite a right hand that had become gnarled from the nerve damage that resulted from the torn elbow. "We had a big reunion in '98," Don Joyce remembers. "We were signing autographs, all lined up in this hall where we were having a big party. Johnny was next to me, and there was a break, and I looked over, and I saw he was holding his pen in a funny way. I said, 'Writer's cramp?' He said, 'No, that's the way I gotta hold it.' He opened up his hand, and there weren't two fingers going the same way. It looked like someone had put his hand under a tire."

In 1993, he had his second knee replacement, and went into cardiac arrest the next night. He succumbed to another, for good, in 2002.

His funeral, in 2002, was held at Cathedral of Mary Our Queen in Baltimore—a soaring cathedral, more than a football field long. The cathedral was packed: men in suits, men in Unitas jerseys. Lines snaked out the door. Overhead, a plane circled, towing a banner: "Unitas We Stand." That day, Lenny Lyles said, "Baltimore became a cathedral."

Berry delivered the eulogy, and I quote from it here, because no one knew him better.

*Thank you, John. You elevated us to unreachable levels. You made the impossible possible . . . You filled our memory bank full. Those im-*

ages of your performances are still there and will never fade. But you did more than perform on the field. Individual achievements and glory didn't have a place on your priority list. All of us knew you were focusing on moving the ball into the end zone and winning the game. You didn't care who did what. Just do our jobs when called on, and we all win together. The Colts were a team, and your example and leadership set the tone.

Of all the Colts I spoke with for this book, maybe no one described Johnny better than the backup receiver and defensive back who only played special teams during the 1958 championship game—Art DeCarlo, a journeyman from Youngstown, Ohio, who retired in 1960. During those glory years, when Johnny was on top of the world, he and Art had a regular Monday golf game, and that sounds like typical Johnny: playing with a backup guy whose name has vanished from the records.

"He was a good golfer, and we'd tease each other about bad shots," Art says now. "But we didn't talk about football. He wasn't a star or anything. Johnny Unitas was just . . . well, he was just a normal guy."

The last time I saw Johnny, my wife, Kathie, was getting an honorary PhD in Washington for her personal fight against the abuse of labor overseas. Johnny was in D.C., too, and he and I grabbed breakfast together. That day, we talked mostly about golf. His right hand and elbow were a real mess, and he showed me the Velcro glove he wore, to fit against the Velcro grips he had on his clubs. It was the only way he could play the game he loved so much. It was a sad moment for me. We didn't talk football. We didn't talk about "the greatest game ever played." We were just old guys who had shared a remarkable moment in time.

To my way of thinking, among all quarterbacks, Johnny Unitas had an unparalleled career. Forty thousand yards passing. A stretch of forty-seven games where he threw at least one TD in each. But the stats aren't as meaningful as what I saw for myself, and what all of his teammates will tell you: this was a man who made everyone around him better. I don't think there's a statistic for that. But ask any football player, and he'll tell you that the ability to inspire your teammates is the trait that matters more than any other.

"The stats? He could have cared less," Berry told me. "All I know is that he changed my whole concept of being a receiver. That he was personable. That he had a great sense of humor. That he was an amazing guy."

For their eighteenth wedding anniversary, Sandy gave Johnny eighteen bantam chickens, to keep their other livestock company: horses, cows, a miniature donkey. The farm, Sandy says, gave him peace—as did watching his children, from the bleachers of some high-school game.

**T**hat is a sentiment I understand. As I've written this book, I've been able to watch Cody and Cassidy play on their respective teams: Cody, playing football through grammar school and high school; and Cassidy, a superb athlete, a few years younger, a standout in both field hockey and lacrosse.

As much as I've enjoyed watching Cody throughout his school years, always just beneath the surface lurked my fear and concern that he'd be injured. His senior year at Greenwich High School in Connecticut, last year, was bittersweet for both of us. His team was within reach of a championship season when Cody suffered a concussion during a scrimmage—his second concussion of the year, and third of his high-school career.

When I received a call telling me that he was just fine, but shouldn't drive, and could I pick him up, my heart nearly stopped.

My first call was to my dear friend Dr. Russell Warren. Fortunately, I caught him during his morning walk. He told me to bring Cody to his house, which was within blocks of our own home. After a lengthy discussion, and an MRI that showed no damage, Russell, who has known Cody all of his life, uttered the toughest words Cody had ever heard: "Your football is over."

For me, it was a relief. For Cody, it was devastating. The pain was eased somewhat when his teammates soared to their conference and state championships, with Cody still a part of the team: holding for field goals and extra points. Later, at his team's award ceremony, I was the proudest dad in the world when Cody received the coveted Coaches' Award for Inspirational Leadership.

As I write this, Cody is on his way to USC for his freshman year. He's just finished a starring season for Greenwich High in volleyball, a sport he hopes to pursue at USC.

I've saved one Giant player for last. His story still tugs at my heart. His memory is with me every day. He didn't star in the 1958 game, and he hasn't gone down in the statistics-heavy history of the NFL as any kind of immortal, mostly because he never drew a single bit of attention to himself. But the players who played with him, and shared that locker room with him, regard him as one of the faces on the game's Mount Rushmore.

It's difficult for me to sum up Kyle Rote with a single sentiment, so I'll leave it to his widow to characterize my beloved teammate. "Kyle was a man's man, and very humble," says Nina Rote today. "And he would want you to leave him out of this book."

That I cannot do. Kyle meant too much to me—too much to all of us. Who else would write a poem for a team meeting, to inspire us in a way only he could? Who else would always listen to every one of us when we had a problem we needed to share? He wasn't just intelligent, talented, and possessed of a great sense of humor and a sense of modesty I've never encountered in anyone else, before or since; he would give you anything and everything he had. He was constantly there for us. For me.

Kyle never bought into the celebrity, the headlines. He never saw himself as a star. And he never saw himself as someone as talented as he really was.

"He didn't put any of his trophies around the apartment," Nina Rote says now. "In fact, when we married, we both had apartments. We chose my apartment. He emptied his apartment and moved to mine. So one day I went through everything in his apartment, and there in a second bedroom, all along the top shelf, were all these plaques.

"I asked him about them. 'Oh, I was just going to leave those,' he said. 'Don't take them.' I packed some anyway, but I didn't put them up. I have some bronzes, and an eagle that's very decorative. The rest of them are under my bed. Isn't that terrible?

"But he never took that kind of thing seriously. He knew that when someone made you 'Man of the Year' or something, they also seemed to be raising money for something—and those causes are important, of course. But with the plaque or trophy you were usually expected to make a speech, or meet and greet a roomful of a thousand or so 'new friends.'

"I don't know how many of the athletes who received those awards ever thought they were actually a 'Man of the Year,'" Nina tells me, "but Kyle never did."

When he retired in 1961, Kyle coached the Giant backfield for a couple of years, then went into broadcasting: radio at first, and then television in the late sixties and early seventies, for NBC. The network phased him out, and he founded an air-freight company. He died in 2002, leaving behind—in addition to his own son, Kyle Rote Jr., a former soccer star—at least ten boys named Kyle, by former teammates and other NFL players, including, as I've said, my own.

One of my favorite Kyle poems, "The Highest Effort," contained in a privately printed collection of his verse, includes a telling stanza that, I think, says a great deal about Kyle's ambivalence about the fame that came his way as a football player. The message of this particular verse, I think, is about keeping perspective: a hard thing to do when people are putting you on a pedestal you never really wanted to climb onto.

> *How high should one reach to acquire accolades,*
> *Or should reaching be part of such human charades?*
> *What height can a person expect to attain*
> *If, in reaching, he's lost more in life than he's gained?*

"Maybe he was *too* humble," Nina says now. "You could walk all over him, and he'd let you. If you wanted to take advantage of him, he'd let you. There was no way he'd flout himself. Quiet as he could be. If you didn't know him, you wouldn't know anything about him. It would never come from him.

"But he was a melancholy man. His mother was killed in a horrible car accident when he was fourteen—a mule, of all things, came in front of the car, at night. Smashed the car; it went into a ravine. His father was badly injured, and Kyle's brother came home from the South Pacific for the funeral. Then his brother went back and was killed at Iwo Jima. Kyle lived with friends to finish high school. So I think his melancholy came from the sadness of being without a family. That melancholy never left him. He wasn't sad . . . if you met him. He was funny. But many people who are funny, underneath it is melancholy." Kyle *was* funny—but so many

times, what you thought was funny when you first heard it, in recollection seemed touching, insightful, and at times, brilliant.

All the things you'd have thought would have happened to
Kyle Rote just didn't happen. From the time he stepped in that hole
in a preseason practice in Jonesboro, Arkansas, everything began
to go a little downhill. At the end, he was a heavy smoker, and he
drank a lot. He was the last guy at Toots when the rest of us had
gone home and Toots had fallen down drunk. He never gave it up.
Eventually, it caught up with him.

God knows what kind of player he could have been. Kyle's
whole career was a one-legged effort. I guess what I remember most
is probably his greatest gift: he made everyone happier just by talking to them.

"Everyone wanted to be his friend," Pat Summerall says now.
Pat has a son named Kyle too. "You were lucky if you were."

That makes me a very lucky man.

I've probably overused the word "family" in this book, but this
will be my last reference to it, because it is the truest: to Wellington Mara, the team was family, and I have been humbled and
honored to have been part of his.

When I was welcomed into that elite fraternity in Canton in
1977, I asked Wellington to be my presenter, and he graciously
agreed. His words are still with me, will always be with me: "For
me, for twenty-five years Frank Gifford has personified the son every father dreams of, the player every coach dreams of, the father
any son would cherish."

And then, the four words that still echo: "I like the man."

It was the highest praise I ever received—until, twenty years
later, in 1997, he asked me to be *his* presenter at the Hall of Fame.

In front of his eleven children, and thirty of his grandchildren, I tried to do him proud. I spoke of his eighteen divisional championships. I spoke of his role in making sure that the blossoming television revenues would be shared with the players, a visionary stance that guaranteed not only the solvency of the league, but its extraordinary growth. I spoke of how "his fingerprints can be found all over just about every successful move the NFL has made over those seventy-plus years."

Wellington's role in this story, of course, is paramount. The New York Giants would be an afterthought in history without him. The modern NFL would not exist. The '58 game would not have happened. Neither would so many of the joys my life has contained.

Wellington Mara scouted me. Wellington Mara signed me, to a generous contract—and each one was more generous. Wellington Mara welcomed me, at every turn, from my first Sunday in a Giant uniform to my last. He was there every step of the way, guiding me, mentoring, but more important, leading by example.

Six years after he was inducted into the Hall of Fame, we had a more intimate gathering to celebrate the man. On the night before the season-opening game in 2003, I threw Well and his wife, Ann, a surprise party at the Tavern on the Green. He didn't want to attend the affair, and never would have showed up if he'd known the night was about him; I had to trick him into coming, with help from Ann, who got him over to the Tavern—where more than eighty-five current and former Giants assembled to honor the man who had welcomed each and every one of them, over seventy-nine years of work for the Giants, into the team's fold.

I've been to a lot of parties over the years—in speakeasy-souled saloons, in Park Avenue living rooms, in small-town bars, in dormitory rooms. None of them were as great as that one.

I said my final good-bye to Wellington in 2005, at his funeral mass at St. Patrick's Cathedral, on a brilliant late-October morning—perfect football weather. As I stood behind the hallowed and legendary altar of St. Patrick's Cathedral, in midtown Manhattan, gazing out at the two thousand mourners packed into the storied cathedral—family, friends, fans—I was struck, once again, and for the last time, by the breadth of the man's influence, the depth of the legacy. He was a man whose faith had always embraced both his religion and his team, and on this day, fittingly, the two came together.

"He was my boss, my father figure, my dearest friend," I said that day. What I didn't say was how much I'd loved him. I can say it now.

I am still lucky to call myself part of the Mara family every Sunday. I watch every home game in the Mara box, sitting next to Ann. (Actually, I sit one seat away from Ann. The seat between us stays empty, to give Ann some space. She can get a little demonstrative during Giant games. She needs her room.)

I was in the Mara box on February 3 of this year, too, in Arizona—and afterward, down on the field, where the celebration, after the Giants' unlikely Super Bowl win over the undefeated Patriots, was joyous and stunning. For me, the thrill created by the Giants' victory extended beyond the Giant family—to my own. I watched Michael Strahan hand the Vince Lombardi Trophy to Cody to hold. That was one moment my son, and I, will never forget.

It was magical down on that field, even for me. The players all came back out. Everyone started milling around, as if they never wanted the moment to end. It was the damnedest thing.

I also wondered, briefly—as the confetti swirled around me, and the waves of Giant emotion filled that field—whether the game I was writing this book about was now the *second* greatest game ever played. The one we'd just watched had been simply astounding, and I couldn't help but see some parallels: Another Southern kid, from

Charlie's alma mater, Ole Miss, had worn the Giant quarterback's uniform—and endured his shares of boos, as had Charlie. And Eli Manning's final drive was certainly a thing that Charlie would have been proud of—and familiar with.

And once again, an enormous national audience had watched that rare championship—a game that transcended the network hype, the histrionics, the fireworks. A game that, despite all the distractions of modern championship games, turned out to be extraordinarily compelling for no other reason than the game itself.

The half-century that has passed since the '58 title game has been full of reunions, celebrations, parties, and gatherings. Sometimes they blur. But for me, none captured the glory of our game like the one in November of 2007, in a suburb of Baltimore. The occasion was a dinner to raise money for the Baltimore chapter of Fourth and Goal, the organization that has taken on the cause of helping older players who need our assistance: the guys who have gotten ill, the guys who have fallen on hard times, the guys who took a lot of shots to the head—a feeling I know as well as anyone.

Everyone in that room that night felt for the old guys who needed help. I wasn't surprised by the incredible turnout, or by the fact that the event raised more than $100,000—give them any occasion to salute their old Colts, and the people of Baltimore will be there. My old nemesis Artie Donovan was the night's honoree, and the evening's hosts had graciously invited me down to attend the dinner. I felt like a king being crowned.

What I hadn't expected was the *feeling* in the room—something I'd never really understood, I guess, until that night. The game that gave birth to the modern NFL had meant as much, if not more, to the Colts: the team in white on the other side of the field. It wasn't really until that night, when I was surrounded by so many of the players from that championship game, that it really hit me: The Colts had been a band of brothers too. And their bond was as strong as ours.

After I had a chance to address the audience, and congratulate all of the Colts who were out there, and tell them how proud the Giants were to have played a part in the drama of that game, Artie took the podium.

"You know what, Frank?" he said. "We'll *give* you that damned first down."

The real highlight of that night, though, didn't come until the end, when Artie capped the evening with, of all things, a song. It was called "I Wish You Love," and Artie sang it beautifully.

Artie told me recently that he'd first heard the song at the funeral of an old friend, some years back. When he first told his wife, Dottie, that he was going to sing it at the end of this amazing evening, this tribute to the warriors we all fought alongside and against, she told Artie that he'd better get ready to cry.

That night was about all of them—not just about the Colts, but about the Giants, too. That night, they brought the game of professional football into full fruition. In one way or another, the game has followed them throughout their lives, as it's followed me. And the thing that has been most gratifying for me is that, in following the path of that game for this book, it's led me back to all of them.

I think the final words should be Kyle's. The poem is called "To My Teammates."

So many things I've wished I'd said
And wished much more I'd done
Back when we functioned as a team
Back when the game was fun.

So many times—I now recall
Those humid summer days
When we could barely practice through
Our list of basic plays

But then—someone among our group—
Would walk that extra mile
And lead us to complete the task
To exit with some style

The mind grows dim as years move on—
And details fade away
But essence of that band of boys
Is with me ev'ry day.

I've often thought that if we've learned
Some lessons during life,
The best of them at least were learned
Back then—on fields of strife.

I also feel the bonds we made
Did bind—solidify—
Those careful, precious memories
Until the day we die.